CHASE

ANTONIO F. VIANNA

authorHOUSE®

AuthorHouse™
1663 Liberty Drive
Bloomington, IN 47403
www.authorhouse.com
Phone: 1-800-839-8640

This book is a work of fiction. People, places, events, and situations are the product of the author's imagination. Any resemblance to actual persons, living or dead, or historical events, is purely coincidental.

Published by AuthorHouse 11/18/2013

ISBN: 978-1-4918-3575-3 (sc)
ISBN: 978-1-4918-3574-6 (e)

Library of Congress Control Number: 2013920958

Any people depicted in stock imagery provided by Thinkstock are models, and such images are being used for illustrative purposes only. Certain stock imagery © Thinkstock.

This book is printed on acid-free paper.

CHAPTER 1

"Agent Noble, are you sure you want to go through with this?" Area Director Jackson Law stares unblinkingly. His dark brown eyes show the weightiness of the matter. Although sitting in a chair, his belly still hangs over his pants. He squirms in the seat, uncomfortable with the tightness of his belt. Flecks of dandruff are noticeable on the dark blue button-down dress shirt. He is fifty-one years old but looks older.

Sarah Noble is just slightly over one year as an F. B. I. Agent. She does not waiver before answering, feeling comfortable with her decision at the moment. At five feet one inch tall, most people underestimate her physical strength and agility. Her feet are her greatest weapons; she is quick and accurate with each kick easily subduing an opponent at close range. Her mental toughness is not as equally rugged; she has compromised her core values one too many times and as a result she grapples with a sense of self-identity. "I'm completely confident with the assignment." Her eyes are green and sparkling, her white skin is like natural looking cream, and her hair is glossy black. She is twenty-six years old.

"Your parent's victimization isn't an issue in this matter?"

"I've put that aside. Doc Shure says I'm good to go. You've read the psychological report." Her voice is now tight and her stomach begins to growl. She hasn't fully recovered from the ordeal, yet she is not willing to admit it.

"Yes I have. I know all of it. But I'm asking you, point blank, are you sure about being able to control yourself? I don't want you to get into another compromised situation where you'll explode. I've used up a hell of a lot of favors to get you back into the Bureau. I've got to be convinced, totally convinced, that you're one hundred percent fit for duty."

"Like I said, I'm ready. You've got nothing to worry about."

Law presses further. "For your sake, I hope so." He pauses for a split second as he quickly glances away and then he returns to look at her. "Seniors are the easiest targets, the textbook target of scammers. Many are sitting on a wad of money, honestly saved over the years for their retirement. They are not looking to harm anyone or be harmed themselves. They want to live out the rest of their lives in peace. But, in too many cases, with no trouble, they become victims. They openly talk about their lives, their families, their careers, their kids and grandkids. They even open up to strangers to talk about their financials. Many of them are lonely, and when they get a call from someone who seems to be OK, they become trouble-free prey. And . . ."

"Excuse me, sir; I know where you're headed with this. Yes, my parents got duped. They lost almost every penny they saved. And yes, I got intimately involved in finding the bastards who did this to them. And, finally, another yes, I lost it. I viciously kicked the crap out of the master closer who did it to my parents, who crushed them. I did it, I'm not sorry, but I'll not do it again. I settled the score."

"In all honesty, I'm not convinced. However, you are otherwise a good Agent, and I suspect can become a very good one over time. I'd hate to lose you. But, you're still relatively young, and every time you're considered to be on a case that resembles the troubles your parents experienced, you're going to be evaluated over and over again. You do understand what I'm saying."

"I understand that I'm under the microscope. I also realize that you'll probably not waste any time yanking me from any case if you even remotely think I'm about to go ballistic. I know it, and I accept those conditions."

"Your background before you came to the Bureau wasn't exactly stellar, was it."

She twists her nose, wondering why he's bringing up her earlier rebellion years into this conversation. "I thought I already passed the interview a while back. Why are you bringing that up now?"

"Because it keeps cropping up every time you're confronted with a personal dilemma."

She hears her own rapid breathing so she tries to settle down. Sarah remains quiet for a short time. She has no immediate answer that would satisfy the Area Director.

He keeps a long stare at her waiting for a response.

She takes a big risk by making the conversation personal for both of them. She figures there is nothing to lose. "I suppose you never went through a difficult time in your life where you were trying to figure out who you were and what you wanted to do."

"Is that a question or a statement?"

"Both."

"I don't know why I'm allowing this conversation to continue. If it were any other Agent I'd tell them to shape up or get out. I'm more tolerant with you for some reason."

"Maybe it's because we've both gone through similar experiences, you more successfully than me."

"That could be. How do you know I'm still not going through some difficulties?"

"I don't, but if you are, you're sure covering them up quite well."

"That's something you're going to have to do yourself. I don't want your personal life to interfere with the Bureau's business. It's a load of crap when the Human Resources Department gives a spiel about having a balanced work-personal life, it can't happen. What do they know about what we do? They've never been in the field. Sometimes I think they're all idiots."

A round of stillness interrupts their conversation.

Sarah returns to the original topic, eager to put to rest one way or another, her status with the Bureau. "Sir, I want you to believe me when I say I'm fit for work. I want to continue with the Bureau as an Agent."

His deep swallow goes unnoticed by her. "OK, then it's settled for now." He pauses to find the right words, "I'm keeping you on the case."

She feels a sigh of relief. She tries to hold back her joy but a slight smile appears on her face. "Thanks for your support. I won't let you or the Bureau down."

"Fine," he nods his head only slightly before continuing. "What have you found out so far?"

She puffs another sigh of relief. "You know that I've been in training, to learn the ropes, so to speak. The real closer is Jim Ranger. It seems the big leads are passed onto him. The Bureau knows him by other names, but he runs this particular operation using the name of Jim Ranger. Every trainee has to observe him in action, to see how he does it. I think it's an ego thing with him, but again, these crooks have big egos."

"Enormous is more like it, but go on."

"My cover is secure. No one suspects who I am."

Law interrupts again. "A few more favors were called in."

Sarah hesitates to figure out whether he has more to say. When he remains silent, she continues. "Tomorrow I'm scheduled to meet Ranger, to watch him, and I suspect for him to test me. I've got my story faultlessly prepared."

Law butts in. "He's going to make a play for you. You're attractive and he'll want to exercise his prowess. Be careful. I don't want you to get sexually intimate with him."

"Don't worry about that, it's not going to happen."

"Just the same, be very careful. He might use force and you have to resist."

Sarah grins. "Well, I'm pretty good with my feet."

Law lets out a laugh. He replies, "Touché." He pauses and then continues. "Is there anyone you've met or suspect who might turn on him?"

"Not so far."

"I don't need to warn you again to be careful, but there's nothing like a snitch or two to help us shut him down."

"I understand. Is there anything else?"

"Not for now. Just be careful."

««»»

Jim Ranger sits in his large office, his body comfortably resting in a phony French upholstered chair. He smacks his lips and then swallows a small red pill. His eyes quickly get wider than normal. He looks at a portrait of himself, an attractive woman, and a young boy and girl, all fictitiously representing his family. He places his hands flat on top of an imitation mahogany desk, and then lets out a sinister sounding laugh. To his back, on top of a credenza, are fake awards and two manipulated photos of himself smiling with famous actors. He rehearses his line aloud one more time before making a phone call. "Get your credit card and let's start making you some money." He wears a charcoal grey pin-striped suit, white shirt, and yellow silk tie. At forty-seven years old he is fit, with broad shoulders and a square jaw. His blue eyes are enhanced through contact lenses, and his even teeth are bright white.

Sitting a few feet away from Jim is Sarah Noble, a newly hired employee who is almost finished with her training. She wiggles her eyebrows enough to join in on pent up enthusiasm from watching the boss do his magic. She's practiced her part well enough to be convincing.

Jim glances at a three-by-five card that contains the name and phone number of the person interested in learning more about investing in precious metals. Jim nods his head once to give himself the go-ahead to dial a phone number. His confidence is about to peak so that when he asks for the money there will be no wavering or uncertainty. Externally he is pleasant with a likable personality, but internally he is a predator without a conscience.

"Hello. This is Jim Ranger. I'm calling for Adam Weber." He listens for the woman's response.

"Yes, I'll get him. Just give me a second." Her voice is soft and friendly sounding.

Jim grins with an evil looking smile, anticipating the crush, the moment when he closes the deal. He hears a man now talking.

"Hello, this is Adam Weber."

The man's voice quivers a bit signaling to Jim that his emotional needs are close to the surface.

Jim puts on his false social mask to make it easier to pull off the scam. He's ready to put the victim under the ether, a bleary emotional state when Adam won't be able to intellectually argue. Emotions will clinch the deal, much to the victim's chagrin.

"Good morning Adam. This is Jim Ranger. You asked me to call you about investing in precious metals." Jim listens for Adam's next response to find out his emotional state.

"Oh, yes, I remember. It was that television commercial, you know, the one with the actor. I've already forgotten his name, but I've admired him as an actor. Oh, what's his name?"

"Well, Adam, we have so many famous people who've invested with us, it's hard to pinpoint the one celebrity you're referring to. But, let's be honest, if these trustworthy people are willing to tell the world how much they believe in us, it must be a good. What's the amount you want to invest?"

"Uhm."

"Let me help you decide. Go get a pencil and paper right now. I'll wait. I want you to write down my name on it, and then we'll figure out the best investment amount."

"OK, I'll be right back." The tone of his voice is high-pitched, almost meek and obedient sounding.

"I'll stay put." Jim is in control. He waits only a few seconds before Adam is back on the phone.

"OK, I'm back."

"Alright, now write my name on the paper. It's Jim Ranger and it is spelled just like it sounds."

"OK, I've done it. Huh."

"What?"

"Your last name is the same as the masked man, you know who I mean."

"Yes, and you can always trust the Lone Ranger. Next to my name, write your name. Do that now."

"OK."

"Next to your name write five thousand dollars."

"Wow, really? That's a big number."

"Adam, I'm going to show you how you can double that number in three months. Go ahead. Write five thousand dollars next to your name."

"Really, do you really mean it? I can make five thousand dollars in three months."

"I wouldn't say it if the Lone Ranger and me didn't believe it."

"OK, I did it."

"Look at it, the five thousand dollars written on the paper. It looks good, doesn't it?"

"It sure does, real good."

"OK, get your credit card and let's start making you some money."

««»»

In less than three minutes later Jim hangs up the phone and gives a big grin towards Sarah. "It's over, and that's how it's done."

"Impressive. You made it appear so easy."

"It's all about creating the right personality, about playing a role like an actor. You have to appear confident. Otherwise, everything will fall apart. You've got to picture yourself as successful and as wanting to help your client realize his financial dream. You've got to believe in yourself in order for your client to believe in you."

"I see. But it's tougher to do than it looks."

"If it were easy, then everyone would do it. I don't want to hear you start doubting yourself. It'll be all over for you, you'll be worthless. Think about them, those people with emotional needs and how you can help them solve their emotional problems."

"I don't understand. How am I solving their emotional problems?"

"Everyone has emotional needs, you and me included. The difference between them and us is they don't know how to solve their own problems."

"We do?"

"Damn right we do. It has little to do with logic or intelligence, more about emotions and how well you control your emotions. They can't control their emotions, and that's why they need us, to help them. We're in a way counselors to them. This means you have to help them open up to us. Even before they've called in for information, they're in turmoil. They're looking for help, someone to guide them to solve their financial problem. And it's you and me, only you and me, who can help them. And there are only two emotions powerful enough to do that . . . need and greed."

"How do you figure that out?"

"Easy. Ask a bunch of personal questions to get them to open up to you. They will eventually tell you more than you want to know, and definitely more than they intended to. And it doesn't matter what they tell you as long as it is personal . . . recently divorced, kid in college, lost a job. I don't really care and neither should you. While you want to help them, you can't get too attached to them because you'll get lost in their emotional turmoil and not be as helpful to them as you otherwise could be. They're looking for someone who will listen to them without criticizing them. We need to sympathize with them, to emotionally connect with them. Then we guide them through figuring out how much will be invested, and how they want to pay for it. You've got to be firm. Ask them for their credit card number, or ATM card number and PIN. Avoid accepting checks because they will have time to back out of the investment. When they're in pain, that's when you need to give the solution. Are you following me?"

"Is this legal? I mean, aren't we tricking people?"

"Legal, of course it is. Otherwise, I wouldn't be doing it, I'd be shut down. Tricking people? Come on. Are you threatening anyone, do you have a gun to their head? Are you lying to them? Hell no. These are people who want to invest and what we're doing is facilitating that action. That's what this is about, just facilitating what they down deep inside want to do." He looks intently at Sarah, eyes a bit closed, calculating whether she has what it takes to do it.

"That makes sense."

"Of course it does. Anything else you want to ask me?" He is a little suspicious.

"I understand the emotional need. What about the emotional greed? How does that work?"

"That's easy; just tell them that they can possibly earn a huge return on their investment, just like I did with Weber. Double your money in three months! You're not guaranteeing anything. There is a risk in all investments. Deep inside, everyone is a little greedy. That includes you and me. They want us to give them permission, to tell them they can make money. They want us to make them feel good."

"This doesn't sound very ethical."

"What has ethics to do with it? As I just said, you're not guaranteeing them anything. You're giving them an opportunistic point of view. There is risk, of course, in everything we do. But without risk there is no reward."

She keeps quiet, eyes unblinking.

He returns to his original suspicion. "Tell me, honestly, do you really want to do this?"

"What do you mean?"

"I mean what I asked, do you want to do this, really do this?"

"Don't you have confidence in me?"

"I did before now, but I'm wondering."

"Let me put your mind at ease. I'm ready, willing, able, and eager to start." Her eyes open wide with enthusiasm.

He stares at her face, appraising whether she has what it takes, making an effort to uncover any sign of weakness. "I'll take your word on it. Your results will tell us for sure."

She realizes she's under the microscope so she decides to shift the conversation away from herself. "How long have you been doing this?"

"Ask me what you really want to ask me. You really want to know why I'm doing this."

"I thought I was clear, I guess not."

"No you weren't." His expression quickly turns to a glare and then back to an expression without emotion. "I've probably been doing this one way or another all of my life. It's in my DNA. I've got an innate ability to help people do things that they otherwise might be hesitant in doing. I'm the coach, the one who motives people."

"So, you like what you're doing."

"Without passion there is boredom."

"Do you think you'll ever quit?"

"Why would I want to quit something I'm very good at? I'm helping people realize their financial goals and I'm paid very well to do that. It's a win-win situation."

"That's how you see it, huh, a win-win situation."

"What else is there? If you're looking for something else to do then you should quit now. You'll only get frustrated yourself, and worse, you might not offer the best advice to your clients. If you don't want to help people in this way, then you should go right now to do something else. Your trainer thinks you've got what it takes, but if it's not in your blood, then switch to something else."

"No, it's what I want to do."

"Tell me about yourself, why do you want to do this?"

"This?"

"That's right. What's your motive?"

"You probably know more about me than I'd ever admit willingly."

"Pretend I don't."

"This is a test, isn't it."

"I've got to protect my assets. One pathetic loser hurts my business worse than one winner helps. It's your turn. I'm listening."

She concocts a story that's already been prepared ahead of time for this exact moment. "My parents argued all the time. I thought I was going out of my mind so I started with pot to get away from them. That led to heroin when I was 18. I got instantly addicted. I got kicked out of the house and lived on the streets, moving from place to place, and then in and out of rehab centers. The drug habit forced me to develop two survival skills, selfishness and greed. When you're strung out and need a fix, you'll do anything . . . I mean anything . . . to feed the addiction. I hustled for money and drugs."

"Are you still an addict?"

"Proud to say, that's gone forever, the drug addict part."

"What part can't you shake?"

"A little self-confidence, sometimes I don't believe in myself."

"You're going to have to kick it. This is all about self-confidence. But there's something else you're not telling me, isn't there?"

"Honestly, you really want to know?"

"Sure, tell me."

"A lot, I've got it all locked up in a safe place where only I have the key. Sorry, it's just not going to happen."

"I've told you everything about me."

She smiles. "That's unlikely. Let's keep our personal lives separate from one another."

"I'm a persistent son of a bitch. I'm eventually going to find out what you're hiding, so make it easier on both of us."

"I'll get right to the point." She pauses and then resumes. "I don't pop open for just anyone."

««»»

Later the same day, at noon, Sarah walks towards the fifth floor elevator. She presses the **Down** button. She watches the elevator light above the doors adjust as it makes its way to her location. Then she hears the elevator chime as the doors open.

A man about her age is inside. He steps to the corner, nods his head without saying a word. He appears nervous. She stays quiet. The elevator's descent is slow as it stops at each of the remaining floors before arriving at ground level. Sarah exits first before the man steps out of the compartment.

Then she slowly walks outside the building only to notice the man from the elevator run ahead. She hears a rumble of thunder echoing off the buildings and down the street. The air is muggy. She smells rain in the air so she hurries to a nearby cafe for lunch, a favorite place for many employees. She walks to the corner of the street, looks both ways, and then crosses against the traffic light. A few drivers honk their car horns to sound their disapproval. She visualizes giving them her middle finger in return but only grins.

Once she reaches the cafe, she steps inside. The place is like any other ordinary work day filled with the typical lunch crowd. Yet, each time she has lunch in the place she feels an eeriness that she is not able to explain, as if hidden eyes are watching her trespass on sacred grounds. She looks around for an open spot. She is out of luck, all places are occupied. Sarah lets out a disappointing oomph sound.

At the corner of her eye she spots the same young man from the elevator exchange something with another man of similar age. Their hand movements are quick and on the sly. No words are spoken as each of the two men puts something into their pockets. Then they walk away from one another, outside into the open air.

All of a sudden Sarah hears someone call out, "Hey you, over here, here's a spot."

She looks around, at first not able to match the sound with a person. Then she notices a waving hand from someone she recognizes from work. Sarah tilts her head upward, smiles, and nods. She moves forward.

"I saw you looking around for an open seat. This place gets crowded very quickly. We work at the same place, I've seen you around. I'm Betty."

"Thanks Betty. I'm Sarah." She sits down, putting the mysterious exchange between the two men aside for now. "Feels like rain outside."

"It's that time of the year," Betty smiles. "What do you do at the company?"

"I'm in training. How about you? What do you do?"

"Part-time payroll and part-time receptionist, I'm the payroll specialist who is responsible for reviewing all non-exempt pay sheets to make sure employees get paid properly. I only do non-exempts. Someone else covers the exempts. I cover the receptionist spot when Kristy, she's the regular full time person, is absent for any reason or is given other tasks to do. What are you being trained to do?"

"Sales."

"That's tough, I could never do that. I'd rather have a regular paycheck coming in twice a month. It makes my life less stressful." A tranquil look touches her eyes.

Sarah shakes her head. "I agree that selling isn't for everyone, but I'm going to give it a try."

"What did you do before?"

"Nothing much of importance, lots of odd jobs to pay the rent." She quickly changes the topic. "How long have you been working at the company?"

"Only about six months, the former payroll specialist left. I think there's a lot of employee turnover for some reason. I've heard that many employees are relatively new."

"I haven't met anyone to talk with other than the other sales trainees. The sales training is pretty intense. So, I don't know anything about employee turnover. Everyone seems to be nice, though."

"Me too, I don't know many employees either. I kind of stick to my work and don't socialize much. Do you know what you want to eat? I only have a half-hour for lunch, so I've got to order."

««»»

The conference room at first appears to be from the movie palace era of theater construction. The walls are decorated with expensive looking Art Deco works that emphasize classic geometric forms, and the colors highly contrast with one another, brilliant to the extent of being gaudy. However, they are all phony. Tables and chairs easily pass for authentic French imports as they too are imitations. Yet, the authentic smell of newly picked flowers fills the air, one of the few seemingly real items around. On an imitation mahogany credenza is a generous supply of liquor, mixers, ice, and crystal glasses. There is a variety of cold sandwiches, salads, and deserts. A warming tray contains hot-from-the-oven pepper seasoned chicken, artichokes, and asparagus.

Seated in separate chairs are Jim Ranger and his executive team; Vince Allen, Reggie Ward, Teddy Deaton, Marshall Crum, and David Shea.

Jim is the first to speak. "How are the trainees progressing?"

Vince swallows the last of his scotch. "I suspect we'll have the same retention rate as previous; eighty percent won't make it while twenty percent will."

"Tell me about Sarah Noble. What's your prediction?"

"She's at the top of the class, a real winner. She's got all the goods."

"You don't have any reservations about her, none whatsoever?"

"Not at the moment, but you do."

"Instincts, just instincts, that's all it is." Jim turns to Reggie. "What's our financial position?"

Reggie takes hold of the tumbler with both hands. "Solid. Costs are down and revenue is up. Our close rate is at ninety-seven percent. If we keep that up for the rest of the year, we'll surpass our target revenue by at least fifteen percent."

Jim asks Teddy, "How is marketing? Any need to change our course?"

Teddy lays down a half eaten ham and cheese sandwich on his plate. "I don't see any need to change. The first month we ran the television ad, we generated over twenty-five thousand phone calls. The celebrities really legitimize our operation."

Jim turns to Marshall, "Any legal issues?"

Marshall smacks his lips before answering. "The celebrities' contracts state they are not held responsible for the accuracy of their endorsements in the script. All they do is read what we tell them, they get paid for one day of work, and leave. Any complaints we receive, we promise to refund their investment and have them sign a release. But we delay it for months until we close the shop. Everything is neat and tidy."

"And security?"

David nods, his deadpan face is expressionless. "Fully functioning. No intruders what-so-ever."

Jim grins and then slaps the sides of his chair. "Fucking fantastic! I love you guys!" He stands to head for the table of liquor and pours himself two full shots of whiskey. "We'll ride this one out until the end of the year before we close shop. I don't want to overplay our stay."

"Amen," says Marshall. He hoists his glass in the air.

Jim turns to face the team. "Any of you ever get busted?"

Marshall replies, "Twice, I don't want it to happen again."

Teddy says, "Close once. I got out in the nick of time, but not as fortunate later on."

Reggie answers, "Once, back in the day. I want to forget it."

Vince says, "You and me boss. It's wasn't pleasant."

Jim nods his head. "It's inevitable. It's going to happen. It's just a matter of time if you stay in it long enough. Vince, you want to describe to the guys what happened to us."

"Sure boss." Vince clears his throat. "I just need a refill." He moves to the table of drinks to pour another scotch. Then he turns to face the men. Jim moves off to the side. "We didn't think it was going to happen to us. But it did five years ago when over thirty F. B. I. Agents came into the office, unwelcomed I might add." He takes a sip of scotch. "Jim had one full floor in a plain looking office building. I remember exactly what the Lead Agent yelled when he burst in. Do you remember Jim?"

"Fucking right I do. No one move, it's all over. I had over fifty people working for me at the time of the raid, clerical staff included. Most of them had no idea what the business was. They were paid very well so even if they had suspicions they kept it quiet. Some of the others, of course, knew exactly what was going on but not everyone. Those who knew and those who didn't know didn't care because they were making a ton of money. The Lead Agent knew who I was. I think somebody snitched but I can't be sure. The son-of-a-bitch came directly to me, handcuffed me, read me my rights, and gave me a search warrant. The rest of the Agents had boxes in their hands and immediately began to load them up with everything that wasn't tied down. There was no time to clean the computers or to shred the documents. The Agents got to it first. I was taken away quickly. In the end I did twenty-five months, more than the rest of the guys. How much time did you do, Vince?"

Vince says, "Six months. I got off easy."

Jim continues, "You'd think that would have cured us, Vince and me. You'd think that, wouldn't you? But no, it didn't. We're at it again, although in a different State, but at it again. I was born to do this. I love the crush. It's in my blood. And I'm not alone, am I?" He grins at the men before him. "No remorse."

««»»

Tony's Jackal is one of those run down old places that has been scheduled for demolition for several years. Yet, insufficient city funds keep the wrecker's ball away. For the regular trade, it is the only place for chili relleno and chimichanga.

A man and woman sit in wooden stools in the middle of the long bar. He drinks a draft beer while she sips a margarita. A heavy set man sits alone at the end stool sipping a whiskey. He glances at the mirror behind the bar when Sarah walks in. He waves her over.

"What'll you have?" Area Director Law takes another sip of whiskey.

"Diet Coke, I've got to stay away from liquor. I go crazy. But you know my resume."

"I appreciate you coming on short call." He waves to the bartender to serve up Sarah's order.

"No trouble. What's happening?"

"There's someone who is worried about you."

"That's nice to know. Who's got my back?" She takes a sip of the soft drink.

"You don't want this type of guy to be worried."

"So, come on, tell me, who is it?"

"Jim Ranger. He suspects you are not who you claim to be."

"How do you know, who's told you?"

Law curls his forehead and puckers his lips. "I can't tell you who it is. Sorry. But the information is true. At least I can guarantee that much."

"Then why are you telling me this if you won't tell me the source?"

"That's just how it is. The least you know about who's our insider the better off you are. You're less prone to show your hand."

19

"I don't like this arrangement one bit!"

"Pipe down, you're talking too loud. You've got to stay in control."

Sarah turns away from Law. She finds herself staring in the back bar mirror. "OK, but I still don't like it." The skin on her face is taut. She almost does not recognize the woman gawking at her.

"Listen Sarah, you've got to be more than OK with it. You've got to be absolutely satisfied with it or else you're going to have problems."

"I know." She continues looking in the mirror, but her eyes shift from her reflection to Law. Her eyes relax. "Sometimes I think I care more than I should."

"That usually leads to many disappointments, both in you and in others. I advise against it."

She acknowledges with a nod of her head.

Law finishes his drink in one quick swallow and then rolls the empty glass in his fingers for a short time. "It's the best way to protect you."

She softly repeats, "I know."

"If you want out of the case, it's not too late to tell me. Don't let your emotions rule. The stakes are too high for you and everyone else associated with bringing Ranger down."

Sarah continues to look at Law in the mirror, not saying a word.

"Talk to me, say something so I know I can count on you."

"You've got a great reputation, you know that. People respect you. You've made your way up to the top."

Law frowns, "So?"

"You probably have your fingers everywhere, all the time. You most likely know the good guys and the bad guys. In all probability nobody likes to mess with you."

Law repeats the single word, "So?" He turns to face Sarah.

"Sir, the way I see, if I can be frank, is that you're concerned more about the case than about me. I'm in only until you say I'm out. It's your decision, not mine."

"Sarah, you're absolutely right on every account. I care about the Bureau more than anything else. I've devoted my entire adult life to it, and I am not interested in any person, unless they fuck it up. Then I'm very interested. I'm willing to trade you for someone else if it advances the case. I'm even willing to give you up for important information. I'll do whatever it takes to put Ranger away for a very long time. This means I need your complete loyalty to the Bureau and to me, and I need you completely fit to perform your tasks. If for one moment I think you're not up to it, I'll yank you out faster than a speeding bullet. I thought we had finished this discussion, but maybe I'm mistaken. Are you in or are you out?"

She feels her lips pulling back in controlled anger. She turns to look directly into his eyes that seem full of exasperation. She takes in a deep breath and grins. "I'm going to ask Ranger out to dinner. I'm sure he wants to fuck me. The best way to find out about what a man is thinking is after you've fucked him silly."

CHAPTER 2

Law drives to **Sunbeam Senior Living**, a home-like, resident-centered alternative to seniors who require special personal care.

His father has been a resident for the past four years. After several failed attempts to move him out of his home after his wife died, Law's father reluctantly agreed to make the move. He's become irritable and testy ever since he arrived.

This trip is Law's obligatory weekly visit to be with his father, something he's become to dread more and more each time. Arguments have taken over their conversation.

After parking his car in **Visitors Parking**, he unenthusiastically walks into a large building with white stucco exterior. The room is ample common space for sitting, reading, and talking. There is an inside waterfall. Off to the left is a library and chapel. Down the hallway is a barber shop, beauty salon, and movie room. To the right is a **Welcome** reception area where visitors check in, as well as those inquiring about its services can ask questions.

Law is known by most of the employees and residents by now.

"Good afternoon Jackson."

He turns to his left to spot Martha Reeves, a lovable, down to earth woman with a heart of gold. She has been a widow for nearly twelve years but still shows off a warm smile.

"Hello, Mrs. Reeves. How are you today?"

She flirts with him. "I'd be better if you'd come sit with me for a while."

He is unable to resist her charm. "How far have you gotten on your memoir?"

She gently touches his face with her wrinkled hands, deciding not to answer the question, "You are a handsome man. If you were only a few years older I'd show you a few things." She giggles out loud. "Imagine me showing you anything." She continues to laugh.

"You're very sweet to say that."

She finishes off teasing with him. Her face is serious looking as she candidly speaks. "Your father is not getting any better. No one wants any part of him."

He pinches his lips together.

She continues, "But I understand the role of the son. You have a duty to your father."

He lets out a puff of air in frustration.

"You're a good son. He might not say it to you, but you are. Take my word."

"Thank you. It means a lot coming from you."

She nods her head to the side. "You'd better visit him. He's expecting you. Try not to quarrel with him. It's not good for the soul."

He leans over to kiss her on the cheek, and then leaves her sitting alone.

ANTONIO F. VIANNA

Law walks down the hallway past the barber shop, beauty salon, and movie room. He looks through the windows of the barber shop and beauty salon to see if he spots anyone he knows. He waves as he passes by. The end of the hallway leads to a circular atrium with three corridors that in turn become the passageway for reaching each resident's room. He takes the middle corridor to room thirty-two. He knocks on the door. "Pop, are you in?"

"Where the hell would I be?"

Law opens the door to see his father sitting in a rocking chair reading a printed local newspaper. Metal framed eyeglasses rest crookedly on his face. "You're late!" He keeps his eyes focused on the paper.

"I was talking with Mrs. Reeves. She's a nice person."

"She's an idiot!"

Law tells himself to settle down, and then he walks towards a chair nearby his father. He leans over to kiss him on the cheek.

His father pushes him away. "Don't do that! We're men, we don't do that!"

Law keeps his thoughts to himself, and takes a seat. He remains quiet, waiting for his father to start the conversation.

His father keeps his eyes on the paper for another few seconds, and then tosses it in the corner. "That was a waste of my time."

Law decides he needs to make the conversation positive. "Have you joined the dance classes?"

His father takes off his eyeglasses and squarely looks at his son in the eyes. "What do you think I've become, a dancer all of a sudden?"

"I thought you said last week that you were going to give it a try. Don't you remember?"

"I never said it."

"I must have misunderstood."

"That's what you do best."

"Can't we just have a conversation with no arguments, just for once?"

"Who's arguing? I'm telling the truth."

"Then what have you been up to?"

His father tilts his head to side. "Up to? What the hell can I be up to in this place? There's nothing to do here, and everybody is an idiot."

"Have you tried meeting them? They may be different than who you think they are."

"So now my son is giving me advice. When did you become such a know-it-all?"

"I'm just saying . . ."

His father interrupts him. "You always had your own ideas. You never listened to me. It was always you, you, you. Not once was it me, never!"

Law is not able to hold back any longer. "All you wanted to do was control me, to tell me what to do and how to do it. You never cared about what I wanted to do, who I was, and what my dreams were, not once, never!"

"You were a selfish boy and you still are."

"Did you ever love me, I mean really love me?"

"What the crap does that mean?"

"Just what I said, did you ever love me?"

"Love! Your mother and . . ."

"Don't bring my mother into it! It's you I'm talking about!"

"Don't raise your voice to me! Remember who I am!"

"I know who you are and I've about had it with you!"

"What is that supposed to mean!"

"You never loved me, you never cared. All you did was to tell me what to do. You were and still are a control freak!"

"Love! I spent my entire life caring for you! I worked two jobs to put food on the table and pay the bills! Not once did I ever miss a payment! I didn't want you to be like me! I wanted you to be better than me! Love, what's love got to do with it? I was trying to survive!"

Tears appear at the corner of Law's eyes.

His father dismisses the watery face. "You have no idea what sacrifices I made for you! And now you disapprove of how I brought you up! Get the hell out of this room! Don't ever come back to see me again, never! I don't want to know where you are or what you do! Get out!" He points to the door.

"Pop!"

"Get out!"

CHAPTER 3

"You asked to see me?"

"Yes, come in, please. I've got something to talk with you about." Ranger steps around his desk, a big smile on his face. "Here, sit here." He points to a spot on a long couch.

Sarah looks around his office. It seems different to her, the second time around. "I'm flattered you want to see me. Are you going to let me peak into your special world." She gives him her best smile.

"Only if you're a good girl." His face now appears more like a creepy grin than a sincere smile of just moments ago. He sits on the couch. "Come, sit by me." He pats a spot close by.

"You know my profile. The odds are against it." She sits close to him. A ginger aroma from his body flows through the air toward her.

"Vince tells me you're at the top of your class. He's impressed. And when he's impressed so am I."

"I guess I should say that I'm also impressed." Sarah crosses her legs slowly enough for him to get a peak at her upper thighs.

"I need people like you, a person who will do whatever is necessary."

"I'm all yours. What do you have in mind?"

"I'd like to see your house."

"You mean where I live?"

"No, no, what you're made of."

"I'm sorry, I'm not following you."

"I want to see how you respond to me, to figure out everything about your emotional make up."

Sarah frowns but then realizes his meaning. "Oh, I understand." She reaches towards him to run her fingers down his arm. "Is this what you mean?" She gives him an inquiring look.

"I'm curious."

"No, I think you're clever." She smiles at him, a damp coy smile that is a ripe invitation.

He reaches over towards the three buttons keeping her white silk blouse closed. With one finger he flips each one lose, one at a time, until her breasts pop out, high and firm not needing a bra. Her nipples look playful and alive to him.

She puts her arms around his neck. Her eyes are full of pleasure and adventure in spite of her true feelings.

He cups each breast with his hands. They feel warm to his touch.

She touches his face with her hand, knowing what he is feeling and what he is craving. She doesn't stop him when she feels one of his hands touch between her legs. She lets out a sensual moan and spreads her legs just a little wider to invite him deeper.

She manages to loosen his zipper and then reaches in to find him hardened. She gently squeezes until he groans. She blows in his ear and then whispers, "Do you like my house?"

"You're bad, very bad."

"What you see in me, I see in you."

A partially muted sound hums from atop his desk. "Mr. Ranger, you have a call from Mr. Allen. He says it is urgent."

Sarah holds her breath.

Ranger's eyes show disappointment and anger. "Yes, I'll take his call in a minute."

She feels his hands lift off her body, relieved for now, but convinced there will be another time.

"You need to go." He zips his pants and moves to the desk. "Vince, I'm just finishing up here, so hang on for a second until I'm alone." He nods towards Sarah to get a move on.

««»»

Tong Liu is his given name, but he is called Midnight because if you haven't paid him or if you try to take off without paying him, you'll either be dead or seriously injured before midnight. He works for a loan shark, Mr. Xia. Midnight prides himself in completing all jobs assigned to him. The only weapon he carries, beyond his fists, is a metal baseball bat. He is athletic with quick moves.

Midnight waits in the underground garage, near the same elevator he suspects Ranger to use. It is seven in the evening, and Midnight begins to visualize his next move.

The elevator door opens. Midnight steps back into the shadows. He watches Ranger move to his Mercedes C 63 AMG, and then follows close behind. "Evening. Lovely isn't it." He clenches the baseball bat in his hand.

Ranger stops in his tracks. He does not recognize the sound of the man's voice. Slowly he turns around. Immediately he sees the bat. "Listen, I don't want any trouble. What do you want, money?" He puts his hand into his pants pocket. "Here, take this. It's all I've got." He extends his arm to hand over a wad of bills.

"You're Jim Ranger, huh?"

Ranger pauses, thinks that he might be able to deny the truth and get away safely. "I'm . . ."

"Sure you are. I've seen you before."

"Then what do you want? Who are you?"

"I work for Mr. Xia. You're past due."

"I - I just need one more day. I'll have everything then. I promise."

As Midnight swings the bat he realizes he is about to miss. He almost stumbles to the concrete floor.

Ranger ducks so quickly that the air above his head where the bat swiped is pushed downward. He hears a whiffing sound. Then he charges Midnight, low and hard. His shoulder digs into the opponent that drives him back against a wall. In spite of his physical conditioning, he feels the wind knocked out of him.

Midnight, a younger man with greater agility and skill in street fighting, slams the bat on Ranger's head. Then he pushes him back to prepare for another full swing of the bat.

Ranger sees stars, feels his strength quickly dissipate, so he drops to a partial crouch. He raises both hands to protect the ensuing attack. He feels dizzy.

Midnight's next swing is not as potent as he wants but good enough to put Ranger to one knee. He readies for another slam as he swiftly lifts the bat above his head. However, an unexpected noise throws him off.

The tires of an oncoming car squeal on the concrete floor. A late model orange colored Ford Mustang makes its way from three parking floors above closer to the two men.

Ranger takes advantage of the interruption to grab the bat with both hands. He pulls the weapon away from

Midnight, stands, and takes a wild swing that misses by a wide margin.

With a straight punch from his right hand, Midnight hits Ranger squarely in the nose.

Ranger is thrown back on his heels. Blood gushes out of both nostrils. He tries to regain his balance but Midnight quickly hits him again, this time in the mouth that splits his lip. Ranger drops the bat. It begins to roll away from both men.

Midnight curses himself, figures his only chance is to dive for the bat. Without delay, he leaps towards the metal weapon.

At this moment, a woman exits the elevator. She sees the two men fighting, but for a brief moment is frozen in place.

Ranger spots the woman, yells out, "Call the cops! Call the cops!"

With the bat in both hands, Midnight looks back and forth between the woman and Ranger. He immediately decides the job is blown and he has to get out as quickly as possible. "Fuck it," he yells. "You owe Mr. Xia and you haven't seen the last of me!" He spins and runs away.

A man in the late model Ford Mustang nods towards Ranger as he drives past, unaware of what's just happened.

Ranger spits blood from his mouth, looks at the spot where the woman with the phone was standing, but sees no one. He looks up and closes his eyes. Then he takes in a deep breath of air. With his eyes now wide open he spots the chunk of bills on the floor. He leans over to pick up the money and then stares at it for a second. "I've got a problem. I don't have enough money to pay Xia."

«‹»›»

Ranger walks to his car, gets inside, and the pulls out of the garage. He heads for the highway that he hopes will take him safely home. He drives slowly as if he is afraid to be behind the wheel. He checks his watch and then tightens his grip on the steering wheel. Several minutes pass before he is out of the city and driving on an open stretch of highway. He accelerates. The road contains a few turns, and the traffic is minimal due to most commuters already at their final destination for the evening. He tells himself to relax, that he'll figure out how to get Xia the money soon, very soon.

Behind Ranger is a Nissan Pathfinder that Ranger gives no special recognition. It's just another driver making his way home after a day of work, or so it seems. On this stretch of highway Midnight sees for at least a quarter of a mile ahead. He tightens his grip on the steering wheel and decides now is the time to make his move. He pushes the accelerator to the floor to get even with the Mercedes, and then steadies the Pathfinder to stay parallel for a short time.

Ranger takes a quick look to his left, surprised the Pathfinder hasn't pulled ahead. He doesn't fully recognize the driver at this moment.

Before Ranger can react, Midnight yanks his wheel to the right, crashes into the Mercedes. The vehicles trade paint and the tires screech.

Ranger sees who is behind the wheel of the Pathfinder, realizes he is in danger. His eyes open wide. He is not able to keep the Mercedes on the road. It swerves off to the right, skids a few yards, and then comes to a complete stop.

Midnight stops the Pathfinder immediately behind the Mercedes. He jumps out of the vehicle with the metal baseball bat in his hand. "Get out," he yells. "Get out of the car!"

Ranger is not able to move, frightened more than he's ever been. Through the rear view mirror he sees Midnight get closer. His adrenaline is pumping and he assumes his death is near. He figures the only way to avoid a direct confrontation with Midnight is to outsmart him somehow. He finds the willpower to move to the passenger seat and then to quickly open the passenger door. Ranger is out of the car standing on the ground. The only thing between him and his attacker is the disabled Mercedes. He hesitates, not sure if he should make a run for it or deal with Midnight face to face.

"Come on, come to me!" Midnight screams at the top of his lungs. He is wound up tighter than a drum.

"Let's talk this out." Ranger feels his body go weak.

"What're you gonna say?" Midnight is still keyed up.

"I'm going to get the money. I've already told you that." His voice sounds pathetic and limp.

Midnight picks up on the feeble sound. He believes Ranger is powerless to do anything. He enjoys the odds in his favor. "We're gonna skip the talk, asshole."

Ranger now feels numb all over his body. He feels his legs about to buckle. Then he spots another vehicle stopped about thirty yards behind Midnight. He sees a man carefully step out of the vehicle. From his angle the car looks simple and plain, but the man appears to wear some sort of dark blue uniform.

"Stop or else I'll shoot!"

Midnight shifts his head to the side but is not able to get a look see. "This is none of your business. Go away."

"This is the police. I said stop or else I'll shoot."

Ranger's feelings begin to slowly return. He can't believe what he hears. "Yes, he wants to kill me! You've got to stop him!"

Midnight knows he's cornered but he is not about to be taken in alive. He's got an image to uphold. He steps to his right and starts to make a run for it.

"Stop, or else I'll shoot!"

Midnight is now about ten yards further away. He thinks he has a decent chance to escape.

The first sound is that of a single bullet being discharged. It hits Midnight in the calf of his right leg causing him to spin around and land on his side in a pile of leaves. The baseball bat falls away. Then in a second, Midnight gets to his feet to restart his getaway. Another gunshot is heard. This time, the bullet hits his skull, between his right ear and nape of his neck. Midnight flops to the ground, blood splattering on the ground. His head is blown up.

Ranger stands still, numbness returns to his body and mind.

The police officer still holds the gun with both hands. He walks towards Midnight as he talks to Ranger. "I'm Holmes. Are you OK?"

Ranger blinks his eyes, and then he answers. "You saved my life."

Holmes stands a few inches from Midnight, gives him a good look over. "He's dead for sure."

Ranger says, "You sure came in the nick of time."

"Somebody called in to say there was some kind of argument in a parking garage. I was the closest. When I arrived I saw him run away. I recognized Midnight so I figured I'd follow him because the guy he was arguing with seemed unharmed at the time. You're lucky I was around when I was."

"Yeah, I guess so."

"Were you arguing or fighting with anyone in a parking garage?"

"Not me, no sir."

Holmes walks towards Ranger. "But you're OK?"

"Yeah, I'm just fine."

"I'm going to call this in, but after I do I think maybe you've got some information to tell me."

"Like what?"

"Midnight was a collector. He was only interested in convincing gamblers who were past due to pay up."

"That's not me. I have no idea why he was interested in me. That's the truth, honest."

"Have it your way, but I still need to write a report. You're going to have to come down to the precinct anyway. It's up to you what you say. Do you want some advice?"

"Sure."

"There're probably several more guys like Midnight who are in line to collect the money you owe the boss-man once he realizes Midnight's dead. These people don't like it when they don't get their money. I'd be careful, very careful."

"But I don't owe anybody anything."

"Yeah, have it your way."

««»»

The interview room at the police precinct is square and just about fits a six foot long table with four metal chairs. Jim Ranger sits in one chair as Detective Deleon sits in one across the table.

"Thanks for coming," Deleon says. His eyes survey the man sitting across the table looking for any signs of unusual nervousness.

"I don't think I had a choice." Ranger forces a smile.

"Yeah, that's how it is with police work." Deleon keeps a solid stare towards Ranger.

"What do you want to know?"

"What do you know about the man who was trying to kill you?"

"Nothing, just like I told Officer Holmes who shot him."

"So you're saying you don't know anything about the man who was out to kill you? Is that what you're saying?"

"Yeah, that's right. I have no idea who he is, I mean was, and why he was after me."

"OK, let's agree that's your story. Do you want to know who the man was?"

"Officer Holmes told me he was somebody who finds people who owe other people money. I think that's what I remember he said."

"And you don't know the man, never saw him before, never did business with him before, nothing. Right?"

"Yeah, that sums it up."

"But Officer Holmes said he got a call to look into an argument that was taking place in a parking garage. The caller said she was concerned that somebody was in trouble. Holmes arrived at the garage just when Midnight, that's the dead man's street name, was leaving. He realized who he was so he decided to follow him. You know, to see where he was going."

"I see. That's interesting."

"What were you and Midnight arguing about?"

"Like I said, I never met the man before. I wasn't arguing with anyone. I don't know why he was following me. Maybe because I drive a Mercedes he thought I was an easy target for something. I don't know. Honest."

"I see. OK, let's put that to rest. Can I ask what you do?"

"Excuse me?"

"You know, how you make a living, your occupation."

Ranger hesitates before answering. "I know you're going to find this out sooner or later, so I'll tell you."

"Great, it's best to get everything out in the open. What do you have to say?"

"I have record and spent some time in jail. I'm clean now and have no interest to return to prison."

"That's interesting. What were you convicted of?"

"I ripped people off. I'm sorry I did it, and will never do it again."

"A con artist, is that what you were?"

"Yeah."

"And I bet you made a lot of money."

"Yeah, a real lot. I went to prison for it. I had all the time in the world to think about what I did."

"You're clean now, huh, is that it?"

"Cleaner than a whistle. I promised myself I'd never go back to my old ways."

"Thanks for being upfront, but you still haven't answered my question."

"What's that?"

"What do you do now?"

"I'm actually in between opportunities."

"So you're looking for work."

"Honest work, that's what I want."

"I see. Is there anything else you want to tell me, or is there anything I should know?"

"Other than it hasn't been easy for me, but I try each day to make it right."

"And you have no idea why Midnight was interested in you?"

"No idea what so ever. I'm just happy your officer was at the right place at the right time. He saved my life."

"Indeed he did."

ANTONIO F. VIANNA

"Is that it?"

"I've got to tell you I'm still a little confused. There is something that is still bothering me."

"What's that, what's bothering you?"

"You're driving a Mercedes C 63 AMG but don't have a job. See, that's what's bothering me."

"Oh, is that it? I can explain."

"Really, go on."

"I'm fortunate to have someone who thinks the world of me. She'll do anything for me. She believes in me."

"No kidding? She's loves you so much and believes in you that she keeps you in a fancy car, and maybe buys your clothes and gives you a few bucks. She does all of that because she loves you and believes in you, is that what you're telling me?"

"Yeah, that's the truth, no kidding."

He looks at Ranger's fake driver's license and then grins. "Well, Mr. Franklin, you are one lucky guy." He slides the fake plastic coated license across the table toward Ranger.

"I sure am. Is that it, can I go?"

Deleon grins, "No, just one more question."

"Yeah, and what's that?"

"Above your right eye, you've got a recent bruise. And you lip is swelling, looks like a cut. Care to tell me what happened?"

Ranger touches a spot just above his right eye. "Ouch!" He then gently smacks his lips together.

"Yeah, that's the spot."

"I must have hit my head someplace and fell over. I don't remember. Maybe it came from him ramming my car."

"You're going to have a real good shiner and that lip could use a stitch or two."

"I guess so. Is that it?"

"You can go now, but I'll want a residence address or a phone number to contact you if I need to."

«‹•›»

Her cell phone rings at 5:27 AM. She rolls over, looks at the alarm clock and lets out a grunt. "This better be important." There is one more ring before she picks up.

"Naomi, I need your help." The voice is frantic sounding.

She blinks her eyes and frowns before answering. "Who's asking?"

"This is me, Jim, Jim Ranger."

"Jim! Hell, do you know what time it is?"

"I know it's early, but I'm in trouble."

Naomi sits up in bed, rolls her shoulders to loosen up a bit. "What's wrong now?" With a free hand she reaches over to grab a cigarette.

"I've got to see you as soon as possible."

She cradles the cell phone between her shoulder and cheek. She grabs a lighter, puts the cigarette in her mouth and lights up. She takes one long puff, lets the smoke settle inside her mouth and then exhales.

Jim asks, "Are you there?"

"Of course, I'm here. Settle down. Give me a little space. I'm not used to getting up this early in the morning."

"That's a luxury I don't currently have."

"Are you in jail?"

"No, but I'd be safer if I was."

"I haven't heard from you for a while. I was beginning to think you had forgotten all about me."

"Can we talk about that some other time?"

"I had high hopes we would see each other on a regular basis."

"Naomi, please, some other time."

"Whatever." She takes another drag from the cigarette. "What's on your mind?"

"I need some money."

Naomi suddenly tightens her face, a bit angry. She takes another puff from the cigarette.

"Are you there?"

She replies, her voice now sounding curt and frosty. "How much is it this time?"

"Thirty thousand dollars." His voice is weak.

"Jim!"

"Sorry, I know it's a lot of money, but I'll pay it back. I promise."

Naomi now sounds concerned. "Jim, what's wrong? Who do you owe?"

"I don't want to get you involved. Can you help me?"

"I guess you zigged when you should have zagged."

"Yeah, something like that."

"I don't know. That's a lot of money."

Jim sounds desperate. "Naomi, please."

She puffs the last on the cigarette, stuffs it out in a nearby ashtray, and reaches for another.

Jim continues, "If you have any money, I could use it. I could write you a check to cover it but not to be cashed for a month or so."

A clicking sound is heard on the phone.

Naomi lights the second cigarette, and takes a quick puff. "Did you hear that?"

"What?"

"I just heard a clicking sound. Do you have an incoming call?"

"No incoming call to me. I didn't hear anything."

"Well, maybe it was nothing."

"Naomi, how about it, any amount? I'll dig up the rest somehow."

"When do you need it?"

"Right now is ideal. I can be at your place within the hour."

"I'll check my account to see how much is in it. I'll write you a check."

"Oh, it can't be a check. It's got to be cash. A check could be dangerous for you."

"Dangerous, why dangerous? Who do you owe?"

"Like I said before, I don't want to get you involved. Let's keep it at that."

"Jim, if I give you money, I am involved."

"Not the way I mean. I don't want them to know. I need to protect you."

"I'm flattered, but I'm a big girl. Who are they?"

"Naomi, not with these people. Please, listen to me. No check, only cash."

"Have it your way. Get over here. I'll have something for you." She disconnects the phone and slowly gets out of bed. She reaches for a nearby sweatpants and a cotton sweater to put on. Then she heads for the bathroom to wash her face and comb her hair.

««»»

Jim makes the trip in forty minutes, not much traffic this time of the morning. He pulls into the driveway and quickly gets out of a rental car. His Mercedes is still in the body shop. He heads for the front door, rings the bell, and hears a muffled voice telling him to enter. He steps inside without questioning the hoarseness of the sound.

The living room is dark, curtains pulled closed. "Naomi, where are you?" He takes another two steps forward, looks up a circular stairway that leads to a master bedroom and den. "Are you upstairs?" He proceeds to take one step at a time. "I'm coming up."

"That's not the right way."

Jim turns around to spot a man holding a gun.

"That way." The man with the gun points his revolver towards the kitchen. He wears a ski-like cap, black clothes. A thin mustache barely shows above his upper lip.

Jim walks first, followed by the man with the gun.

Naomi sits on a kitchen chair. Her hands are tied behind her back. Her eyes are abnormally widened. Fear covers her face. A dish towel is jammed into her mouth and her jaws are taped shut. There are dry spots of tears still visible on her checks.

"What is this?" Jim turns to the man with the gun.

"Settle down, all I want is the money you own Mr. Xia."

Jim is terrified but decides the only chance of survival is to keep his wits, stay calm, and hope to get the man with the gun the money he owes Mr. Xia. He looks at a terrified Naomi and then back to the man with the gun. "Untie her and take off that gag."

"First the money."

"She's got it, not me. Like I said, untie her and take off the gag."

The man with the gun hesitates. Then he shrugs his shoulders, leans down towards Naomi to pull off the tape across her jaws and yank out the dish towel.

"Ouch," she yells.

He says to her, "Shut up or you're dead." Then he faces Jim, "You move and you'll get shot. Where's the money?"

Jim stares at the man. He is bold. "Now untie her." Then he looks at Naomi. Further words are not necessary.

Icy fear consumes her to the point of fainting. She resists but her mind does not hold still, racing but not settling on anything specific.

The man with the gun says, "I'm losing my patience. I'll untie her when I get the money. Where's the money?"

Naomi finds the strength to say to the man with the gun, "I don't have much cash in the house." She then faces Jim, "I told you that. I told you I don't have thirty thousand dollars in cash."

"Lady, say that number again?"

Naomi frowns, "Thirty thousand."

The man with the gun smirks, "Lady, he owes fifteen thousand, not thirty. He's trying to con you." He lets out a vile laugh.

Naomi turns to Jim, "You're despicable!"

"Listen to me. I . . ."

Naomi interrupts, "You're disgusting! You're not getting one dollar from me! Handle your own affairs or find another sucker."

"But Naomi . . ."

"OK, stop it. I don't give a fuck about your relationship. All I want is fifteen thousand dollars in cash, or else both of you are dead. Is that clear?"

Naomi says to Jim, "You're a real prick!"

The man with the gun says, "I said, no more. Just give me the money."

Naomi says, "I don't have that amount of money in cash in my house. You'll have to wait until the bank opens later on today."

The man with the gun says, "How much do you have?"

ANTONIO F. VIANNA

She replies, "Probably, no more than one thousand. I'm not sure. I don't count it on a regular basis."

"Don't be a smart ass with me. It's a good start. Let's get it now. Now go get it." He waves the gun in her face. "I said get it!"

She nods towards her still tied hands. "Have you forgotten something?"

He looks at Jim, "Untie her but be careful. Don't do anything crazy."

Jim steps forward to free Naomi's hands.

Naomi stands but her legs feel wobbly. She reaches out to touch the nearby kitchen counter.

Jim glances her way, to reach out to help, but she manages to steady herself.

"I'm OK, just a little shaky."

The man with the gun quietly looks on.

Jim spots a set of carving knives neatly inserted into individual slots within a wooded knife holder. Without hesitation he grabs a large knife, quickly turns, and shoves it into the gut of the man with the gun.

"Ahh." The man with gun lets out a horrific scream as the hand holding the revolver loosens. The gun drops to the floor, followed by the man. He lays motionless on the floor, atop the gun.

"Is he dead?" Naomi stares at the body on the floor.

"I don't know," answers Jim as he too looks at the body.

"Go see, go on, go see."

Jim nudges the man on the floor with his foot. "He's not moving. I think he's dead."

"What do we do now? I don't want a dead body in my home."

"After I leave, wait about ten minutes. Then call 911 to report it."

She switches her stare towards Jim. "Report what, that you stabbed him?"

He continues to stare at the body. "Be serious, Naomi."

"Oh, excuse me, but I've never seen a dead man before, especially in my home. And further, I've never seen someone kill another person." She remains looking at Jim.

Jim takes his eyes off the man to look at her. "Listen to me." He grabs her by the shoulders. "Wait ten minutes after I leave. Then, call 911 to say that a man was trying to rob you, but you were able to defend yourself. Say you stabbed him and that you think he is dead. That's it, no more."

"Oh really, that's it?"

"Naomi, don't give me an attitude. We're in this together."

"Attitude? You killed him, not me. You owe him money, not me."

"Please, just do as I say. I'll take the rope, tape, and dish towel. You don't want to have to explain that."

She puffs out a breath of air. "OK, OK, go. Get out of here."

He hesitates, "One other thing."

"And what's that?" Her head is erect and her eyes stare angrily.

"How about the money, you know, the thousand that you have? I still could use the cash."

She waves her figure and then points to the front door. "Get out! You're lucky I don't shoot you."

««»»

She stands inside the walk-in shower stall, streams of cold water dings on her head. Her thick hair softens the blow. Sarah's eyes are closed as she enjoys the shiver she gets from the icy liquid running down her entire body, across her breasts, between her legs, and onto the emerald colored tile floor. A soft groan makes its way out of her mouth, her lips parted sufficiently as she licks them with her tongue. She moves her hands to the V of her body. She squirms a little in anticipation. She knows what is going to happen next. Then, at will, she lets her fingers encourage her legs to part a little. Her skin vibrates and her heart beat picks up as she pleasures herself. The euphoria thrills her for the moment. She tries to keep it up for as long as she can, but reality settles in too soon. Lack of sexual intimacy with someone special remains her arch-rival. It explains a lot about who she is, the need to push herself, the competitiveness, and the risks she brings to her life. Sarah recognizes now, but not then, the early symptoms and what they meant to her problems. She feels empty inside despite her accumulated knowledge, skills, and abilities. Even her achievements cannot match how lonely she feels.

Buzz, buzz.

She hears the sound from her cell phone resting on the nearby counter top. "Shit." She is out of the self imposed fantasy.

Buzz, buzz.

"Fuck you, I'm coming!" This time she yells as she reaches to shut off the flow of water. Then she steps outside the shower, grabs an extra-large white cotton towel to pat down her body. Finally, she puts the cell to her ear. "Noble here."

"Just a heads up before you get to work."

She recognizes Area Director Law's voice. "What do I need to know?"

"Ranger was almost killed. He owes money to a loan shark, a guy named Xia. That's his last name. To make a long story short, he got hold of someone named Naomi Lebaz to give him the money, but he eventually pissed her off to the point where she refused to help him. Ranger got beat up a little to reinforce the message not to mess with Xia. When you see Ranger today or in the next few days, if you do, just be attentive that he narrowly escaped getting killed. He might be somewhat edgy for the next couple of days."

"Thanks. Anything else I need to know?"

"Not at the moment, but be careful."

To Sarah, the gesture of kindness is what she needs at the moment. She smiles at its importance. "I will."

It takes Sarah less than twenty minutes to get dressed and leave her apartment.

««◊»»

Vince Allen looks around the room, quickly calculating the number of empty seats to the number of occupied seats. "Good morning everyone. As you can see around you, there are more empty seats today than last week." He scans their faces to pick up anyone's apprehensions. He sees none. "You may remember what I said the first day we met." He waits for someone to acknowledge.

Dick answers, "Yes, you told us the eighty-twenty rule that eighty percent would not finish for one reason or another."

"Correct. And as I count the occupied seats, I figure you are the twenty percent. This is the final week of your training, and I do not imagine anyone not making it to the end. So let me preliminarily congratulate each of you." Vince applauds.

All three men and two women join in the applause.

"Please understand that you still have to successfully finish this week. I don't want any of you to interpret my comments as a guarantee. Understood?" He sees everyone nod in the affirmative. "OK, let's continue with your studies." He clears his throat, and then asks a question. "Sarah, we've talked about the importance of perception in the selling process, that of vision, hearing, touch, taste, smell, and the kinesthetic and vestibular senses. Put it all together for us."

She twists a little in her seat before speaking. "Moving sensory information from our sensory receptors to the brain is not enough. Just as important is how one selects, organizes, and interprets the information. If we do our selling jobs right, we can help the client properly make an appropriate buying decision by how we present the information over the phone. We don't have the luxury of using all the senses, mostly just the hearing one. But we can speak in ways that help the client see and feel what it would be like to double or even triple their investment. You told us earlier that everyone is choosy about what information is used to make decisions. So it seems to me that we have to highlight the positive and more persuasive information without lying or defrauding the client. Otherwise, we would be violating the law, and according to our Code of Conduct, that is impermissible."

Vince smiles, "Excellent Sarah. Anyone else want to add anything?" He looks around the room.

Karen lifts his head upward. "I agree, Sarah's explained it simply."

Vince continues. "You've all heard sounds that either pleasured you or frightened you. Perhaps, you've heard sounds that seem to have no effect on you, although that is unlikely. All sounds affect us one way or another. Someone give an example of a sound that has a positive effect on you."

Tommie grins. "When I'm with a woman, the way she moans when I touch her."

Slight laughter is heard.

Matt says, "That's not a moan, it's a gripe. She's complaining!"

Louder laugher is heard.

Vince raises both hands and then grins, "OK, that's enough."

The room silences for a few moments.

Vince asks, "Any more positive sounds?"

Sarah says, "The melody of a beautiful song, the crunching of autumn's leaves beneath my shoes when I step on them. I love those sounds."

Karen adds, "I love the sound of a violin."

Matt says, "I like the tenor sax."

Dick chimes in, "The drums."

Tommie finishes, "I don't like music. It reminds me of thunder. The sound of thunder scares the hell out of me. I know that lightening comes first and is followed by thunder but I've never liked the sound of thunder, even as a kid. During combat all noises sounded like thunder to me. I hated it!"

Another round of silence lasts for a few moments.

Vince continues, "What we're saying is that certain sounds please us while others do not. The quality of the sound is called timbre, and it results from the sound waves moving from the source to our ears. Then there is the pitch of the sound, high or low. I don't want to get too technical with you, but the idea is for you to make the sound of your voice work for you. Avoid monotone, too fast or too slow, too loud or too soft. Speak clearly, use words that your client will understand. Avoid slang and terminology that the client is not familiar with. If you plan and organize what you're going to say, you'll be better prepared to deliver your message. You should practice aloud some of your main points not just to remember what you want to say, but as importantly to hear the sound of your own voice." He pauses, and then resumes, "Does this make sense?" He sees everyone nod affirmatively. "Any questions?"

Karen asks, "Go over one more time the five steps of a convincing pitch."

Vince turns the question to the class, "Who knows the first step?"

Dick says, "Gain attention. You said the goal in this step is to get the client to get into the conversation quickly."

Vince asks, "How can you do that?"

Dick replies, "Say something like, how would you like to double your money in one year or less?"

Vince continues, "Excellent. What's the next step?"

Matt offers a reply, "Establish a need. In other words, get the client to identify a problem that he needs solved. For example, ask him if he has a kid in college but is struggling with how to pay for the student loan. Tell him that I sympathize with his problem, show empathy."

Vince goes on, "Yes, great example. What's next?"

Tommie says, "Relevant information. I give the client just enough information for him to understand that I'm the guy to help him solve his problem. I can give him an example like Matt did to show him I understand his problem. I can tell him how I solved my problem."

Vince takes up again, "Next?"

Sarah reacts, "Mental picture. My goal here is to help the investor see how his problem can get solved. For example, I tell him that he has the opportunity to earn thirty thousand dollars within one year with a thirty thousand dollar investment."

Vince looks at Karen, "What is the final step?"

"Agreement. Ask him for a check or his savings or checking account number to withdraw the money."

Vince smiles, "Yes, this is the moment of truth. You have to ask for the money. In other words, if you don't ask, you'll probably not get it." He looks around and then picks up again. "You're going to get resistance from some clients who may not be emotionally prepared, although they are the ones who've called us, not the other way around. The key is to find out at what stage, the first, second, third, fourth, or fifth, that you lost him. Don't move onto the next stage before you have his agreement. Always emphasize how much you understand his situation by offering one of your own. Stay focused on your end game which is for him to invest. But don't, I repeat, do not lie to him. Some clients take longer to act than others. If the client backs away, ask if you can follow up in a few days. Be polite." Vince takes a sip of water before he comes to the end of his talk. "In ten days you all will be prepared to take the final examination that will allow us to register you with the Securities and Exchange Commission. You'll have a few days to review the material before you take the exam. I'll be available during that time to answer any questions, but once the exam begins, you'll be on your own. We'll have someone from the office to proctor it, not me. Are there any questions?"

Sarah mumbles softy to herself, "Vince, you are smooth, real smooth."

Vince asks, "I'm sorry Sarah, I didn't hear you."

"I was only giving myself a pep talk, that's it, nothing else."

««»»

Later that night Sarah meets up with her sister at **Sparkles**, a club that is crowded on the weekend but mostly empty on Monday evenings. They each sip a drink at a table, silent, as their thoughts stray through their minds. Songs of the '90s play through several loud speakers just gentle enough to enable conversations to be heard.

Andrea is the first to speak after the wait. "You don't really want to settle down, do you?" Her face is calm and considerate looking.

"I don't know. I really don't know."

"What do you mean? It's quite simple." Andrea watches her sister for a while.

"Maybe it's easy for you, but I haven't figured it out. It's complex to me." Sarah frowns.

"It usually means one thing."

Sarah lifts her chin slightly, "And what's that?"

"For starters, marriage, usually with kids."

A shadow comes across Sarah's face. "You're in a better position to know that, you've figured out what you want."

"If you're saying that it only takes worldly experience, then I disagree. I'd say that marriage is an experience all by itself. You really don't know what you're getting yourself into until you experience it."

"There's got to be some way to figure it out before you commit." Sarah takes a sip of a diet soft drink.

"Not really, more likely like I said, it is the experience itself."

Sarah sits still for a few moments.

Andrea continues. "Are you telling me you wouldn't consider a proposal from the right guy?"

Sarah shrugs her shoulders and remains quiet.

"So, no one worthwhile has come forward, is that what you mean?"

Sarah looks away for a split second and then looks squarely at her sister. "A few times I've been tempted, but too afraid. I pulled away."

"What are you afraid of?"

"Haven't you been afraid of something at least once in your life?"

"Don't put it on me. We're talking about you, not me." Andrea narrows her eyes a bit before continuing. "Of course I've been afraid. Do you remember our ninth grade English teacher, Miss Little?"

Sarah's eyes widen. "Oh yeah, I was petrified of her, especially when she reminded me that you were her best student a year before. The implication was that I better measure up to your performance. But, I never knew you were afraid of her. Didn't you ace her course?"

"I did but I was still terrified. I mean, she never physically harmed anyone, but she was ruthless with grading book reports. Everything had to be perfect."

There is a long pause. The sisters' recollection of similar high school experiences temporarily shifts the attention away from Sarah. Then they both laugh aloud, looking at each other.

While one year younger than Andrea, Sarah has similar physical characteristics to her sister. Each has bright green eyes, blemish free cream looking skin, and smooth black hair. Andrea is two inches taller than Sarah and her hair is much longer. Strangers easily identify their relationship to each other.

"I was hoping you'd find a man to be with." Andrea quickly bites her lip, and makes a grimace.

"Are you afraid I'll get old alone?"

"I just want you to be happy, that's really all there is."

Sarah smiles, gently covers her sister's hand with her hand, "I know, but maybe I'm not built to be married. My job is stressful and I could be transferred anyplace at any time. That wouldn't be fair to any family."

"But what do you want? I think that's the million dollar question."

There is a blank stare from Sarah, followed by a reply. "It's impossible now to consider settling down. I'm on a very important case that's draining me of every bit of energy inside me. It's just not the right time."

"Can you talk about the case?"

"Actually I can't. You understand."

"Anything like with what happened to Mom and Dad?"

Sarah puckers her lips. "Why are you bringing that up?"

"Seriously, Sarah, it almost got you kicked out of the Bureau, or have you forgotten?"

Sarcasm seeps into her voice. "No, I haven't forgotten, but thanks for reminding me."

"So you are on the same type of case."

Sarah glances away from her sister, swipes her tongue over her lips, and then looks back. "Maybe we should trade places."

"Huh?"

"You seem to be able to figure things out quickly."

"I just don't want you to get hurt, that's all. You know I love you and that you can tell me anything. And I do mean anything. You know that, don't you?"

Sarah's eyes moisten up a bit. "Yeah, I know, I really do."

The two sisters gaze at each other in silence for a moment.

Andrea twists her nose and then breaks the stillness. "I know I can be a pain in the ass especially when I ask personal questions."

Sarah keeps quiet, but gives a slight nod of the head to agree to more talk.

"But if you want kids, I mean if you really want children, you can't wait forever. Biologically speaking, it isn't in a woman's favor if she waits too long."

"To be honest, sis, I don't get any strong feeling one way or the other from the notion of having children. That's the truth."

Andrea hesitates before answering, "Really?"

"I'm being frank."

"I'm surprised. I never knew that about you."

"Don't get me wrong. I love your children, and I'm proud to be their aunt, but having kids of my own is something else."

Andrea sips her wine while Sarah remains silent.

Sarah picks up on the conversation. "Don't get me wrong, I enjoy sex. I find myself completely involved when it happens."

"How often does that happen?"

"Not often enough." Sarah laughs out loud.

Andrea grins, "It's not restricted to single women."

"It's comforting to know I'm not alone."

"At least, I've got Jeremy to prod to do it, who do you have?"

"You've made your point." Sarah looks fondly at her sister and then takes another sip of the soft drink. Then she continues. "You are one of the most remarkable people I know."

Andrea turns her head to the side. "Really, why do you say that?"

"You know I've always looked up to you, your intelligence and self-assuredness. It seemed that you always knew what you wanted and then went after it. I found that to be amazing then, and I find it amazing now. You knew you wanted to be a wife and mother even though you could have successfully done a million other things. You are so passionate about it, and that carries over to how you care about me. I'm not like you, although I wish I was in a way. I'm obviously trying to come to grips with who I've become, who I am."

Andrea keeps quiet, not sure what to say, if anything, so she leans forward to listen.

"You're a wife and mother. You work at home helping startup companies promote and market themselves. You've figured out the social media thing and kept yourself current with technology. You're amazing. I'm nothing like you."

Andrea keeps silent.

"All my life I sought to make myself look indestructible, invincible. I didn't take crap from anyone, girl or boy. And I got into my fair share of trouble, maybe more than my fair share. I wasn't a good listener and felt beyond the reach of anyone's judgment, including Mom and Dad, you, teachers, you name them, anyone. And yet, down deep inside, I always felt exposed knowing perfectly well that I was incomplete and imperfect. I knew there was a clink in my armor. When someone wanted to get close to me, I shut them down. I chose to go it alone. I'm sure that's why marriage and kids are so far removed from my thinking today."

««»»

Two weeks pass by quickly. All five remaining trainees pass their tests and prepare to get on the phones, oblivious of the real intent to deceive unwitting investors, except for Sarah and one other person.

Vince addresses the bunch. "Do you remember the first time you fell in love?" He looks around, smiles, and continues. "Sure you do. I do. We all do. To me it was the most amazing feeling, and in a way it's hard to put into words today. But I do remember the feeling right now. I knew we belonged with each other, and today, after twenty years we're still together, happy as ever, in love with each other even more than when we first met." His eyes widen as he forces a few tears to show themselves on his face. "Sorry, I get choked up when I talk about my love." He looks away from the group who continues to stare at him. He takes in a planned deep breath, refocuses on them, and continues. "I remember telling Joan that I'd love her forever, that I'd do anything she wanted me to do. I'd put my life at risk to save hers." Vince takes another pause for emphasis and then resumes. "That's how I want you to feel when you talk with them. I want you to love each and every one of them, to care for them, to help them make the right financial decision that's in their best interest, because what ever goes around comes around. In other words, if you help them, you will help yourself. I'm very proud of each and every one of you. You've been my best pupils ever, and I really mean that, the best ever. Now, go to your desks and make those calls."

The group gives him a loud applause. Then, one by one, Sarah, Tommie, Matt, Karen, and Dick take their places at various desks.

Sarah takes a deep breath before she flips through a neat pile of cards arranged on top of the desk in front of her. "I don't think I can go through with this," she whispers to herself. She feels the palms of her hands sweat. She looks around to see the other four already on the telephone. She feels the presence of someone watching her, yet she does not have the guts to look around. She takes the top card in one hand, reads the information, and makes the call. A few seconds pass until she hears an outgoing voice message. She gives a sigh of relief, waits for the message to end, and provides a short message herself. "Hello, Mrs. Vons, I'm responding to your inquiry about investing in precious metals. We all deserve more than a simple cup of sugar, and as your friend, I can help you achieve a good return on your financial investment. I'll call again within the next two days. Thanks, and have a wonderful day." Temporarily relieved the first call is finished, she takes in another deep breath of air.

Vince stands nearby, gazing over the five people, watching their motions, taking mental notes, and arriving at preliminary decisions. He walks towards Sarah.

"Not as easy as it looks."

At the sound of Vince's voice, Sarah jumps, taken by surprise. She looks up. "Y - yes, I thought I'd nail it the first time, but I got a voice message."

"I've been there, although awhile back. It's a long swim, and I know how you're feeling, but you'll do just fine. I have all the confidence in you."

She feels as if she is slowly drowning, as if her head is beginning to go under the water's surface.

"Your voice sounded a little weak, not as convincing as it should be. So, I want you to visualize the face of the person you're talking with, the gratitude he or she is feeling, how thankful you're offering more than a cup of sugar. Can you do that?"

"Of course, that's a great idea. Visualize, yes, I'll do it."

"Alright, try another call now as I watch and listen."

The sinking feeling returns, yet the only thing she can possibly do is make another call. She looks at the next card, reads the information once, and starts to phone up.

Vince stands motionless as he gazes over her face. Then, he suddenly turns away when he hears his name. He nods towards Tommie, and then faces Sarah again. "Excuse me, Sarah. I need to see what Tommie wants. Remember to visualize the expression, grateful and appreciative. OK?"

"Definitely, thanks for the tip."

Vince walks away.

Sarah feels rescued, now above the water line, swimming steadily away.

CHAPTER 4

Vince Allen walks into the men's room, heads for the back where the stalls are located. He opens each stall door to check inside. Satisfied he is alone he moves inside the stall reserved for the disabled, flips down the seat cover, and sits. He makes a call on his cell. "Let's meet at our normal place, say ten tonight, I've got something important to talk about."

"Are you going to give me a hint?"

Vince hears a sound from within the men's room. He pauses before continuing. In a lowered voice he says, "Let's just say it's something you need to know about her. I don't think she'll keep her cover."

"You better be positive about that."

"I wouldn't have called you if I wasn't."

"OK, see you at ten tonight."

Area Director Law folds his cell phone. He clenches it for a long moment. His facial expression is taut. He mumbles softly to himself, "I hope nothing has gone wrong."

Vince continues to sit on the toilet seat. He flips closed his cell phone with one hand, and then tosses it between his right and left hands, nodding his head along the way.

Finally he folds his right hand around the cell phone to stop the drill, and then pockets it inside the breast pocket of his suit coat. He continues to quietly sit on the toilet seat for another few moments. Finally he stands to return to the main office. As he walks towards the door to leave the men's room, he bumps into Jim Ranger. "Oops, sorry, didn't see you coming."

Jim's face is straight forward with a splash of annoyance creasing his forehead. "No problem."

Vince gets a glance at Jim's bruised forehead and cut lip. "What happened to you?"

"Oh, this?" He points at the red discoloration.

"Yeah, it looks nasty."

"Somebody hit my car while I was parked, and my face hit the dashboard. Bastard! I'm driving a rental, a black Impala." He huffs an annoying sounding noise.

"Lucky you weren't injured. Sometimes all it takes is a little jolt."

"The guy said it was my fault!"

"Everyone wants to shove the blame on someone else."

Jim smirks, "Yeah, who can you trust these days?"

Vince stares quietly at Jim and then takes a deep swallow.

Jim shrugs his shoulders and continues. "My insurance should cover everything, but it's a pain in the ass just the same."

Vince clears his throat, "Let me know if I can do anything for you?"

"Sure." His voice is not persuasive. Then he asks, "How're the new sales people?"

"They're all settling in. They'll work out fine." Vince forces a grin, "No one suspects what's really going on."

Jim smirks back, "That's how it's supposed to be. Good work. They'll be a sizeable bonus for you when we close this shop and leave the State."

"Thanks."

Jim asks, "Hey, want to get something to eat later on tonight, say around nine or ten?"

"Sorry, Jim, I've got plans tonight. Another time, OK?"

"Sure, no problem." Jim pauses and then resumes. "I almost forgot why I came in here. I've got to take a piss."

"A man's got to do what a man's got to do."

Jim walks away from Vince towards a nearby urinal. "He sure does, and sometimes it hurts."

«‹›»

At night, later the same day, Vince Allen drives a gray colored Nissan Maxima. It is drizzling rain that switches between soft and hard. He keeps his eyes mostly glued straight ahead with an occasional glance in the rearview mirror to make out if he is being followed. It takes about fifteen minutes to leave the city's noisy sounds into the rural area where it is peaceful and quiet. He glances at his watch to check the time. Ahead of schedule, he assumes, with about ten minutes to spare. He compliments himself with a smile for being in good time.

The paved road narrows to one lane each way. The turns and twists of the road make certain he stays focused. The further away from the city, the more desolate it is. A broken down vehicle or accident would certainly not be noticed by many others, only a strong cell phone connection would get him help if needed.

He takes another look see into the rear view mirror. Far away headlights appear and quickly they get larger. He pays no attention at first, resets his eyes to look straight ahead.

The headlights from the oncoming vehicle intensify. As he looks into the mirror he squints, "What the hell!" He only recognizes the vehicle as dark colored.

Suddenly, he feels his Nissan lunge forward. "What the fuck!" He looks again into the rearview mirror. He experiences another whack from the dark colored vehicle behind, this time with more force.

He tightens his hands around the steering wheel as another forceful bump from the rear is felt. He screams, "Who the hell are you?" His grip makes his knuckles turn white. His eyes are wider than normal.

Vince tries to keep the Nissan on the road as another attack occurs from behind. This time the Nissan swerves off the paved road. He manages to stay in control for a short time, but the momentum plunges the Nissan into a muddy ditch. The abrupt end of the Nissan's forward movement propels his face against the steering wheel. Quickly, his nose begins to bleed. He passes out for just about one minute.

The dark colored vehicle stops at the edge of the road, on the side dirt. A man gets out of the vehicle, now recognized as an Impala. Jim stares at the disabled Nissan below. There is a revolver firmly held in his right hand. Slowly, he makes his way towards the Nissan. The hand holding the revolver is pointed straight ahead. He slips, almost loses his balance on the wet ground, but reaches out with his left hand to touch the earth just in time to prevent him from falling over. He slowly continues walking forward.

Now, alongside the Nissan, he sees Vince, slumped over the steering wheel, motionless. Little remains of the driver side door window. "Hey, are you alive?" Jim waits for any sign of life.

Vince's body moves slightly along with a faint grunt, "Ah."

Jim puckers his lips, disappointed the man isn't already dead. It would make it a whole lot easier than having to kill him with a gun. He lowers the hand holding the revolver, and waits for more movement from Vince.

"Ah," Vince repeats. Slowly he straightens his torso. He notices red smudges on the steering wheel, and then with equal hesitancy touches the smear. "Blood, my blood?" He takes in a long deep breath to settle himself down.

"That's right, it's your blood."

Vince looks to his left to spot Jim. "What are you doing here?"

Jim gives him an evil looking smirk. His voice is calm. "How could you do this to me? We've been together for a long time, covered each other's back, and made a ton of money. Tell me, how could you have done this to me?"

"What are you talking about?" Vince remains poised.

Jim sounds perturbed. "You're a snitch. I would never had believed it if I hadn't heard you myself on the phone, in the bathroom."

"Jim, I still don't know what you're talking about." His voice is now slightly agitated.

"Tell me where you were headed tonight, for your appointment at ten, tell me!" Jim is very angry. He points the revolver towards Vince.

Vince takes a deep swallow. He sounds worried. "I want you to settle down. Don't do anything foolish. Just help me get out of here and we can talk this out."

Jim stands motionless gazing at Vince, the man he's teamed up with for a very long time. He waves the gun from left to right. He is mostly calm. "I'm going to kill you right now. That's just how it has to be."

"What?" Vince exclaims in surprise. "No, let's talk this out!"

Jim shrugs his shoulders, "That's just how it's going to be, there's nothing to talk about. A man's got to do what he's got to do even if it is unpleasant."

"You know I've always had your back, from the early days. Come on, you know that. We've been through a lot together. Just give me a chance to tell you."

"And that's what's so disappointing. We have been through a lot in life, fortune and hardship. I'd die for you, you're like the brother I never had."

"And me too, that's how I feel about you. Come on, Jim, help me out of the car, and then we'll talk."

"Who were you talking to earlier today in the men's room?"

"It's complicated."

"Try me, make it simple."

"You know the girl, Sarah Noble, don't you?"

"What about her, I'm listening."

"I'm embarrassed to say this, but, well, we're seeing each other."

"No shit, you and her? She's probably mid to late twenties, and you're my age. I suspect what you see in her, but what on earth does she see in you?"

"Actually, that's what the meeting is about."

"I'm listening."

"I'm going to tell her it's off, that we can't see each other anymore."

"No shit, really?"

"That's the truth, honest Jim, that's the truth."

Jim's voice turns cold and angry. "One damn thing is for sure."

"Yeah, what's that?"

"You're fucking lying to me." Jim lowers the gun and then quickly returns it to point directly at Vince.

Vince's voice cracks, "No, I'd never lie to you."

"That's not how I see it." He pulls the trigger two times, lowers the gun, and stares a Vince. "A man's got to do what a man's got to do."

««»»

Early in the morning at 7 AM three days later, Sarah and Law meet at a diner for a breakfast meeting.

"He hasn't been at work for a few days. It's not like Vince to be gone. Something is up."

Area Director Law takes a sip of coffee. "I know."

She tilts her head to the side, holding the cup of coffee halfway between the table counter and her face. "What?"

"I said I know." He takes another sip of coffee and then sets the cup on the table top.

Her face looks confused, indistinguishable crisscrosses line her face.

He says, "You look baffled."

"Baffled, mystified, perplexed, whatever, yes I am. How do you know?"

His voice is calm and reassuring. "He was working for us, the good guys."

"For us?" Her eyes widen more than usual.

"Settle down, not so loud."

She holds back a choke. "Go on, what else should I know?"

"This is obviously hard for you to accept, but there are things you'll not be told. It's just better that way."

The sound of her voice and her poise are visibly upset, "Better for who?"

"For everyone and for everything. You have to accept that you won't be told everything, only what you have a need to know."

"And who makes that decision to tell me what I need to know?"

"Isn't it obvious?" He points to himself. "I'm the Area Director and you're not. I treat all the Agents and I mean all of them, in the same way. If you can't accept this arrangement, then maybe it's time for you to leave the Bureau." He settles back in the chair. His eyes narrowed, fixated on her.

She tries to hold her stare for a time, but the intent look lasts for only a short while. She keeps quiet despite the fact that her insides are churning.

"You're a good Agent, and you have the potential to be great, but your attitude has to change. At times you seem to be an injustice collector, amassing all your experiences of perceived unfairness and inequality, and then all at once cashing them in, paying no attention to logic." He waits for a response that does not come. He keeps looking at her but all he sees are her eyes starring right through him. He decides to continue. "Vince Allen is dead."

She looks right at Law, no longer disregarding his comments. "My God, what happened?"

Figuring her comment as a sign of connection, he continues. "He was working with us, undercover, just like you, to take out Ranger once and for all. Vince was his most trusted ally over the years and we knew if we could get to Vince Allen we could get to Jim Ranger. We did."

"Did he know about me?"

He lies, "No."

"Back to the need to know, right?"

"Yes." He continues to lie, "He had no need to know who you were and vice versa." His thoughts drift off and then quickly return. "It all was working out very well until he called me for an urgent meeting recently."

"What happened?"

"He never showed. I knew something went wrong, so I had a few Agents search the roadways he probably took to make contact with me. They found his dead body slumped inside his car, two bullets in his head at close range. The car seemed to have spun off the highway and it also appeared it was bumped from behind by another vehicle. We're looking for any evidence of who the killer was, but it was a rainy night and I don't have high hopes of finding anything of value."

"I actually thought he was a nice guy, the way he treated me and the others. I'm sorry about him."

"That's how it goes."

"But you think it was Ranger who did it, don't you?"

"Either he did it himself, or he had someone else do it. It's my guess he did it. Two bullets close up are indicative of personal revenge. Yeah, it's my guess Ranger did it, himself."

"I haven't heard anyone ask about his absence from work." She shrugs her shoulders, "But I guess, why would any of the employees wonder about him? He trained us and let us loose."

"But I wonder if any of the executive group has been asking Ranger where Vince is?"

"Hmm, yeah, me too."

"Do you want to find out?" Law leans forward towards Sarah.

"Of course, what do you have in mind?" She bends over to get closer to Law.

"You have to place recording devices throughout the office."

She grins, "Oh, is that all?"

"That's all. We already have all phones monitored, but we don't have the main conference room, the training room, and each of the executive's offices wired. That's where you come in."

"Do you have the devices?"

"We're all ready." He halts briefly and then continues, "Oh, one more thing."

"What's that?"

"Inside each of the restrooms, the women's and men's."

Her voice is enthusiastic, "When do I begin?"

"Today, I'd like to have them all functioning within two days. Can you do it?"

"Yes, you can count on me."

He leans back in the chair, convinced the job will get done right. His facial muscles slacken, and his face looks less severe. "Are we good?"

She nods her head, "Yes, we're good."

«»«»

Later the same day, after everyone has left to go home, Sarah leaves her work cubicle. First, she heads to the women's room, looks around to make sure the cleaning crew has finished their jobs. She spots no one so she proceeds to mount a small recording device below the middle sink. She feels her heart pound a little, stands and stares. She grins proudly, showing a sense of accomplishment.

Next, she moves to the men's room to find it empty as well. She looks around for the best place to insert the device, and then decides to replicate the same action as previously done. She finishes this part of the assignment more quickly than the first.

She picks up her pace to set in motion the installations for the conference and training rooms, as well as the executives' offices. It is all done with the same precision as before. She checks her watch. There is one more device to set up, Jim Ranger's office. She purposely planned this fitting to be the last as a way of showing distain towards him.

She stops at the closed office door with unexpected agitation that it might be locked, something she had heretofore given no thought. She presses down on the door's lever hoping it will easily respond. It does. She feels a sigh of relief. Without delay she pushes open the door to enter his office.

As she steps inside, her body stiffens and her eyelids partially close as she recollects the two times she had been here, alone with him. She gently slides her hand over her breasts as if to protect them from his touch. Her heart starts to pound again, this time more assuredly than before, as if it is intent of breaking out of her body. She looks around to think of the best place to mount the tiny piece of equipment. She heads towards his mahogany desk, ignoring the French chairs, awards and photos along the way, all fake. She pushes the chair away and then crawls underneath the desk to finish the job. Satisfied the mechanism is properly in place, she crawls out from underneath the desk and stands. Then, she hears a voice on the other side of the door.

The office door slowly opens as a cleaning lady pulls a large sized trash can. She is followed by another crew member with a vacuum cleaner. They both stop in their tracks after they spot Sarah.

Sarah stands motionless for a brief moment with her eyebrows raised and mouth open wide. She is about to say something. However, the woman pulling the trash can speaks first.

"Oh, excuse me. I thought everyone had left the building." She turns to the other woman, "We will come back when the office is empty."

"Oh no, please come in. I was just leaving. I left Mr. Ranger some documents I was working on." She perspires a little and worries if her voice is convincing. She'd like to have a retake.

The woman pulling the trash can asks for clarification, "Yes?"

"Yes," Sarah confirms, "please, you have work to do and I have finished mine." She quickly steps in front of the desk, smiles at the two women, and leaves the office. Her muscles tremble a bit with purposeless movements as she takes in a deep breath of air to settle down. She feels like jumping up and down to mark her narrow escape.

«‹›»

Early the next morning while Jim gets ready for work, his cell phone buzzes. He stares briefly at it from a distance, curious why he's being called at this time. He finishes tying his shoes and then looks at the phone number. He recognizes it and immediately connects. His voice is aggressive, "Yeah, what's up?"

David Shea, Chief of Security carefully states the problem. "There was a mild breach in our security system last night. I got the call about 8 PM, so I put a team together to get to the bottom of it. I don't have details yet, but I suggest you convene a meeting with your executive team in the safe room to discuss this."

"What the fuck!"

David remains quiet.

"What the fuck!" Jim's angry voice is both angry and hostile sounding. His chest expands and nostrils flare. "Alright then, call the other guys. Don't bother with Vince. We'll all meet pronto in the safe room."

David keeps silent for another second and then recommends, "You might want me to tell the guys not to go to their offices, but directly to the safe room. We don't yet know the extent of the breach."

"OK, do it." Jim's eyes look ablaze with anger. "Fuck this!" He disconnects the phone.

««»»

The safe room is a twelve feet by twelve feet square room accessed from Jim's office. Only Jim has the combination to the lock that allows for entrance. He is the first to arrive. One by one, his executive team settles in.

Jim is the first to speak. His fists are clenched tightly while his nostrils widen and narrow every other second. He is peeved. "David told me earlier this morning of a breach of our security. He's on top of it but we need to talk this through. I'm angry as hell." He faces David, "Tell us what happened."

Unblinkingly, David updates the team. In a calm voice he says, "All of you know I carry a device that is linked to our main security computer. I'm always in contact with it, so I'm updated on a regular basis. Last night, around 8 PM, I got a message that something alien was interfering with our security system. I put a team together to investigate. Since I didn't have anything to report earlier, I didn't contact Jim until this morning. Our financial and marketing data is still protected. That's good. I should have an updated report shortly. My guys are both checking the technology and doing a sweep of the entire floor. I don't think it is wise to go to your offices right now until I get a preliminary report. At minimal your phones could be tapped."

"Crap," snarls Marshall.

"I'm relieved our financials are secure," Reggie says. He sounds calm.

Teddy asks, "Where's Vince?"

All eyes shift toward Jim.

With a tinge of anger that is noticeable to him but not the others, Jim says, "I put him on a special assignment to look at other locations to operate from after we close this one down. I'm not sure how much we'll see of him."

"Excuse me, I just got an update." David looks at his cell phone to read a text message. "It seems that all the executive offices have a recording device underneath their desks."

"Holy crap," shouts Marshall.

"I'm going to have them removed and brought to me to inspect. Maybe I'll figure out something about who manufactured the devices and who are the most likely buyers." He types a text message.

"Fuck!" yells Jim. "What else can go wrong?"

"Wait, there's more," David holds up a hand and then continues. "The training and conference rooms as well as the men's and women's restrooms also have the same devices."

"Fucking crap!" Jim screams.

David finishes, "After my guys remove those devices, they'll conduct a further search of the floor."

"Who the hell did this?" Reggie asks. His voice is petulant.

David answers, "We'll probably not know."

"Could be an employee or the authorities?" says Reggie.

"Or both," Jim adds. "One of our employees could be a snitch."

Teddy adds, "Come on Jim, that's highly unlikely. Vince did a thorough job in checking every one of them out."

Jim clears his throat, displeased at the comment. "Yeah, I'll talk to him about it."

David carries on in a deadpan voice. "I'll have my guys check the video tape of who was the last to leave last night. Maybe that will give us a clue."

"I want whoever it was questioned, grilled, and cross-examined! I want to know who did this!" Jim's eyes are wide open and his voice is glowering.

There are a few moments of silence until Jim ends the meeting. "OK, everybody back to work. Don't say anything to anyone about this." He turns to David, "Let me know what else you find out as soon as you find out. Understood?"

"Yes boss," David nods his head.

Jim feels a shortness of breath and the beginning of a headache. He heads to his office to grab a pink colored pill to relieve the anxiety.

《《》》

The next day Sarah enters the office building at her regular time. About to head for the elevators she is stopped by a uniformed guard. "Pardon me, miss, but I need to see your identification."

Her eyebrows rise so they become curved and high. "Huh?"

"We're inspecting everyone who enters the office today. Sorry, I'm just doing my job." His face does not take sides.

"Why, what happened?" She wrinkles her forehead.

"I don't know, but everyone is being checked. Please, can I see your identification?"

"Sure, I'm not trying to be difficult, I'm just curious." She reaches inside her wallet to retrieve a plastic card with her photo. "Here it is." She hands the ID over to the guard.

The man takes a peek at the photo and then at Sarah. "Yes, that's you." He returns the ID. "Sorry to cause any inconvenience."

She feels the perspiration on her skin dry quickly. Then she forces a weak smile. "No problem. I've got to say you are very polite. I appreciate that."

"Yes, thank you." He nods his head to acknowledge the compliment. "You can go now. Have a good day."

As Sarah walks away she notices others behind her getting the same treatment. She hears her stomach growl and then a voice call her name.

"Sarah, wait up."

Sarah turns. "Hi Betty."

Betty quickens her pace. "What's going on with the security?"

"Your guess is as good as mine?"

"Do you think they're checking all the offices, or just ours?"

Sarah's jaw drops ever so slightly. "What makes you ask that?"

"Oh, I don't know, I was just wondering."

Bing.

Betty walks into the elevator first, followed by Sarah, and presses 5. "So, how is everything?" Betty sounds happy, already forgetting the security check.

Sarah does her best to cope with the surprised security check. Her mouth slightly draws back at the corners to smile, "So far, so good." She tilts her head down to avoid direct face to face contact.

Betty asks, "What's wrong?" The lightheartedness in her voice is replaced with curiosity.

Sarah's pupils quickly dilate and then contract just as fast. "Wrong?" She hesitates. "There's nothing wrong." Her voice sounds tight.

"It's none of my business. I'm sorry. Sometimes I get too nosy." She remains cheery.

There is silence for a few seconds, and then the sound of the elevator reaching its destination. Bing. The elevator door opens.

Sarah exits first with Betty close behind.

"Have a good day." Betty walks away.

"Yeah," Sarah manages to say. Then she heads to the women's rest room figuring to make a call to Area Director Law.

««»»

Inside the women's rest room, Sarah heads to the furthest stall at the back of the room. She enters it and closes the door. Then she pulls out her cell to make a call. She speaks rapidly, but quietly. "This is Sarah. Something is going on here."

"Slow down. Where are you, and can you speak louder?"

"I can't afford to be overheard. I'm at the office, actually in the women's rest room. I just arrived."

"I understand. State the problem."

"There are security guards in the lobby verifying employees' identities."

"All employees for all companies in the building, or just yours?"

"I don't know. When I asked the guard he only said everyone was being checked. I assumed he meant everyone who enters the building, but I really don't know."

"Check the spot where you placed the recording device. Do that now."

Sarah leaves the stall to walk to the wash basins. She kneels underneath the middle one. "It's gone." She feels her body tense.

"That means they've figured it out, and probably have removed all the devices. Shit!"

"Not necessarily," Sarah tries to argue. Her voice is louder than before.

"I'm playing the odds."

"What do you want me to do?" She rolls her tongue over her lips.

"They might start questioning people, so you need to come up with a convincing story about your whereabouts last night."

"That's easy." She sounds mildly relieved.

"Not if there is a video tape that recorded who left the building and in what sequence. I suspect there is one."

"Oh, I see." She swallows, feeling trapped with no way out. Her external calmness doesn't last very long.

"Did anyone see you or did you see anyone last night?"

"Only two cleaning women. They came into Ranger's office as I finished placing the device underneath his desk."

"Shit, that's not good." His voice is judgmental. "What happened?"

"I told them I was dropping off work for Ranger."

"Do you think they believed you?"

"I think so, but I can't be certain." She feels a little dizzy trying to defend her actions. "Maybe I should leave."

"No, that's too revealing. You've got to stay there. You're my only hope of getting this guy. You can't leave."

"What do I do?" She feels a little nausea.

"Let's assume the worse. Let's assume you are visible on the tape as the last one or one of the last ones to leave the office. Further, let's assume the two cleaning ladies say they saw you inside Ranger's office that night. Here is what you say. You tell them you were indeed working late because you were trying to figure out persuasive selling approaches and practicing out loud, but that you did not go into his office. It's going to be their word against yours, so you have to be very persuasive. Don't let any other thought enter your mind when you're questioned. My hunch is that all the employees will be questioned, but especially you since they'll see you leaving the office late at night. Is this clear?"

"Yes it is." She feels the need to head for a toilet.

"Can you do it? Be honest."

"I have to do it. You can count on me."

"OK. Give me an update later today. Do you need anything from me?"

"No, I'll call you later on."

The cell phones disconnect.

Sarah runs to the nearest toilet to vomit.

««»»

By late morning, all executives are busy at work in their offices as the sales team makes phone calls to potential investors. Nothing is mentioned to the staff about the morning's new security process. However, Matt is interested. "Hey, Sarah, got a minute?"

She turns to Matt, sitting a few feet away. "Yeah, sure, what's on your mind?"

He moves his chair closer to hers. In almost a whisper he asks, "What do you make of the security check this morning?"

She shrugs her shoulders. "A little strange but I haven't really given it much thought."

"I've got a theory. Want to hear it?" He wiggles his eyebrows.

"Sure, tell me." She feels her stomach begin to churn.

He looks around and then leans over to get closer to her. "I think it was a bomb scare drill to prepare the security personnel for the real thing."

Sarah feels her jumpiness fade away. "Hmm, that's interesting."

"I've heard of companies training their security force without the employees knowing what's going on so the employees don't freak out." He smiles; fully confident he's onto knowing the truth.

"That could be. It makes a lot of sense."

"You want to get together tonight, you and me?"

The unexpected change of topic triggers a change in her mood. She feels anxious, "Umm."

"I know it seems out of the blue, me wanting to get together with you, but you know, I've been thinking about asking you for a while."

She breathes comfortably, tries to get her body to settle down. "I hesitated not because of you, but, well, I recently split up with a guy and I'm just getting over him."

"So you need some time to be alone, is that it?"

"Yes, exactly, I'm glad you understand." Her eyelids open wider.

"Actually, me too, but it wasn't me who split up with her. She left me for a woman!"

Sarah tries to hold back responding to the unexpected information, but is unable. "Oh!" Her jaw drops.

"So was I surprised, really surprised. I had no idea."

Sarah manages to regain her composure. "How long were you two together?"

"Over a year." He shrugs his shoulders.

"And you had no idea?"

"None whatsoever, zilch."

"Surprises happen when predictions fail."

Matt cocks his head to the side. Then he narrows his eyes. "Sounds like reality construction."

"I don't know what that means."

"Oh, I thought you knew. The phrase you just used is the essence of reality construction."

"I still don't understand."

"When our expectations don't match reality, we get surprised."

"How do you know this?"

"I've got a Ph. D. in Cognitive Behavior."

She curves her lips so they face away from her eyes.

"Don't look so confused. There aren't many jobs that care about a Ph. D. in Cognitive Behavior, maybe teaching and research."

"So, why aren't you teaching or conducting research?"

"Neither pay much and there aren't many job opportunities."

"But why here?"

"To make money." He looks into her eyes for a while. "Do you have any idea how much a doctorate degree costs?"

"No, I don't have a clue."

"I owe seventy thousand dollars."

"No?"

He tightens his lips, "Yes."

"I had no idea."

"And you, who are you and why are you here?"

She clears her throat. "This seems like a job interview."

"Sorry, that's what a degree in psychology does to people. It causes you to appear nosy."

Her frame of mind changes to a more sociable point of view. She feels less threatened by his questions. "Let's talk about this tonight, after work."

His eyebrows rise. "Great, that's wonderful."

««»»

"Sarah, we need to talk."

She turns her head away from Matt, towards the call out where she spots David Shea. She hears her stomach churn. "Me?" She points a finger at herself.

"Yes, this is important." He waves her to come closer to him.

Sarah turns to Matt. "I've got to go." She stands, albeit wobbly at first, to walk towards the Chief of Security.

"Follow me." He moves quickly towards Jim Ranger's office.

Inside Ranger's office she looks around to see the boss sitting behind his desk. His nose is wrinkled and his lips are turned down. "Close the door," he barks at Shea. "You," he points his finger at Sarah, "sit down." He stares intently at her.

Sarah feels a layer of perspiration coat her skin. She remains quiet.

He gets right to the point. "Where were you this past Tuesday night?"

She hears herself clear her throat and then she swallows. "I worked late, here, at the office. I wanted to perfect my pitch. I haven't been as successful as I've wanted."

Ranger turns to Shea. He snorts. Then he stands behind his desk. "Deceit is not an admirable quality. It can become a deadly game."

She refuses to be intimidated. "I don't understand why you're saying this to me."

"Dishonesty is, well, like fraud. It creates an atmosphere of mistrust that creates greater problems for everyone." He steps around his desk and then takes a seat across the room.

"Are you accusing me of something?"

"Those who cheat, lie, steal, and misrepresent are desperate people." He pauses for a short time and then continues. "What were you doing in my office that night, alone?"

She straightens her back. "I wasn't in your office that night, alone."

Ranger turns to Shea who picks up on the conversation.

"The cleaning crew told us that they saw you inside Jim's office, behind his desk. They said you looked surprised to be spotted."

"I disagree. Whoever was in this office that night wasn't me."

Shea continues, "Why would they lie?"

"I'm not saying they lied, I'm saying I wasn't in this office that night, alone."

"So you think they're mistaken?" He looks at Ranger.

"That's obvious, isn't it?"

"Is it?" Shea asks.

"Does this have something to do with the security checks in the lobby?"

Ranger rejoins the conversation. "What makes you ask that?"

"Something must have happened that night, although I have no idea what that might have been. Now, you're checking out the employees." Her self-confidence starts to rise, and her voice sounds stronger and more convincing than just before.

Shea takes over. "We have a tape of you leaving the building that night, alone, after everyone left."

"That makes sense. I just told you I worked late that night to perfect my pitch." She glances back and forth between the two men. "Your worry about me is baseless."

Shea continues, "I don't believe you. You're holding back something, I just know it."

"If you think I'm not frank, then fire me. That would solve it once and for all." She jets her jaw slightly for emphasis.

Ranger says, "Alright, I've heard enough. You can stay."

She hears air gush out through her nose, and then stands. "So, I passed your test, is that it?"

"Yes, at least for now. Go back to work." He turns to Shea, "We've got others to talk to."

She walks away from the two men.

"Shut the door on your way out," directs Ranger.

««»»

Alone with Ranger, Shea asks, "You really believe her?"

"Hell no, but she does."

"What's next?"

"We should talk with all the other newly trained sales people to make it appear authentic. Then, we'll fire someone to send a message."

"Do you want me to keep an eye on her?"

"No, I'll take care of her in my own way. Get Matt in here. Let's see what he knows."

««»»

Later that night, mid-week, Sarah and Matt set out for **Sparkles**, the same club she and her sister, Andrea, met just a short time ago. The same songs of the '90s play through several loud speakers just gentle enough to enable conversations to be heard, just as before. Sarah feels at ease with the familiar surroundings. She stares briefly at Matt as if curious about something, yet evasive at the same time.

Unabashed, he says what's on his mind. "Are you satisfied with what you see?"

Wide eyed and opened mouth, yet no words escape. She appears taken by surprise.

"You were staring at me but then quickly looked away when you saw me catch your glance." At first he is expressionless, but then he grins. "I like what I see."

Sarah feels her body heat up, and if she could see her own face she'd know the reason. "Really, I didn't realize it."

He keeps his grin, knows he's right and happy for it. He decides to move to another topic, safer for her, less personal. "Sure was a strange day. What did they ask you?"

Glad the subject has shifted to another topic, Sarah answers. "Probably the same questions you and all the other sales people got."

"You tell me what they asked you and I'll tell you what they asked me?" Matt enjoys the cat and mouse game.

Now expressionless to conceal emotion she answers. "They wanted to know why I was working late that night as if I was up to no good."

"What did you tell them?"

"The truth, that's what I did. I told them the truth." She begins to feel a bit cocky.

"And what was that?" His face is now deadpan.

Feeling a little resentful that she's the one answering questions rather than asking them, Sarah tries to cover up but her sulkiness is evident. "I told them to fuck off."

"Whoa! I just was asking a question." He puts both hands up in the air over his head.

"I'm a little cranky right now! I worked hard to make it through the program and then they accused me of being deceitful as if I was covering up something! I'm about to quit!"

"Hey, calm down. They obviously believed you or else they would have fired you on the spot." He puts his hand over hers. "It's going to be alright."

"Where the hell are our drinks?" Sarah looks around to find the waitress who took their order.

"Just chill." He squeezes her hand. "Look at me, hey, look at me."

Sarah's obstinate look simmers. "I'm OK, really I am. But I'm just really angry with them, I mean very angry." She turns to face Matt's sympathetic look.

"That's better." He turns his face away from her to look for the waitress. "Hey there," he waves towards a woman a few feet away. "You haven't forgotten our drinks?"

The waitress shakes her head, "No, coming right up. Sorry."

Sarah lets out a breath of air and lets her shoulders slump a bit. Then her expression becomes less severe. "What did they ask you?"

Matt has already prepared his response. With only a slight but noticeable trace of injustice he answers. "I think they were looking for someone to fire to send a message. I don't think anything happened that night. If you ask me, it was another test."

Sarah's mouth opens wide. Then she says, "Really?"

"That's what I think."

"Why would they do that?"

"They want to show who's in control. I'll bet you someone is going to get fired in the next day or two."

"Come on, really?"

"It's textbook. They're following the standard model of intimidation."

"And how do you know?"

"Sarah, remember? I've got a Ph. D. in Cognitive Behavior."

Out of breath and looking harried with eyes that come across as wild and unruly, a waitress appears. "Sorry about the delay. Here are your drinks, one soft drink and a PBR." She sets them on the table avoiding eye contact with Matt and Sarah, "Anything else?"

"No, that'll be all. Thanks." Sarah searches for something comforting to say, but fails to find the right words.

The waitress quickly turns away to serve another party.

"You don't know what you're missing. PBR tastes real good." Matt picks up the bottle of beer.

"Oh I do know what I'm missing." She takes a sip from her glass. "I don't handle alcohol very well."

"No problem, you're with me. I'll take care of you."

Sarah grins but remains quiet.

He nods towards the waitress. "I guess we're not the only ones feeling a little anxious." Matt tries to brighten the situation with humor that falls short of its intention.

Sarah shrugs her shoulders, and then takes another sip of the soft drink. "Whatever."

Silence cuts through the conversation as Matt takes a sip of his drink as well.

She takes up on a previous topic. "Who do you think they'll fire?"

"Good question, it could be anyone."

She is persistent, not willing to let him get off the hook so easily. "I know, but you don't have any idea of who is on the chopping block?" Her eyes search his for an answer.

He slowly sets the beer on the table, eyes looking downward. "My guess is Tommie."

"Really, why him?"

"Do you remember how much he hates the sound of thunder?"

"What does thunder have to do with it?"

"It's not thunder per se, it's how he reacted to Vince's question about sounds we enjoy and those we don't."

"So, this is more of academic gobble-gook."

His nose wrinkles and then snorts, "Say it anyway you want, but it's all been proven. Do you want me to explain?"

She raises her hand, palm towards him, "No thanks, I'll take your word on it." She takes another sip of the soft drink.

"Who do you think will be axed?"

"I actually thought it was going to be me, in fact, it still could. I don't think they trust me." She wiggles her eyebrows a few times.

"Can you be trusted, I mean, really trusted?"

She leans back into the chair, mouth partially open for a short time, and then sarcastically says, "What's that suppose to mean?"

"Don't be so touchy. I only asked a simple question." He pauses. "I'm not accusing you of anything or blaming you. I'm just asking a simple question."

"It doesn't sound that way to me." She moves on to another topic. "Let's change the subject."

Matt's eyebrows rise to become curved and high. "Fine with me."

There is another temporary halt in the conversation. Background music from the loudspeakers continues to be heard but now they take center stage.

Sarah twists her upper body in the chair from left to right a few times, just enough to loosen her back muscles. She spots someone in the corner, frowns for a second and then turns to Matt. "Isn't that Betty from the office sitting by herself in the corner, over there?"

Matt turns in the direction. "Yeah, sure looks like her. Want to invite her over to join us?"

"Yeah, I'll do it. Wait here." Sarah leaves Matt alone for a few seconds, and then returns with Betty close behind.

"Here Betty, sit here," Matt says. He pulls out a chair for her to sit. His voice is upbeat.

Quietly she sits down, a half empty drink in her hand.

"What's up?" Matt continues.

Betty's eyes focus on the table top. Then she bites her fingernails.

"What's the matter?" Sarah asks. Her voice is sympathetic sounding.

Tears form at the corners of Betty's eyes. She rubs her nose and then starts to cry.

Sarah continues, "What's happened?" Her eyes open wider than normal. "What's happened," she repeats.

"I - I can't talk about it." Betty's lips begin to quiver.

Sarah and Matt simultaneously look at one another with mouths partially open, and eyebrows momentarily lifted.

"Why, what happened?" Matt enters into the conversation.

Betty sniffles and then carries on. "I agreed not to talk about it."

Sarah presses on, "Are you still working with the company?"

Betty looks at Sarah. She kneads one hand with the other. Her voice trembles, "No, no longer."

Sarah questions, "Why did you leave?"

Betty swallows, drops her eyes, and quietly says, "I can't talk about it."

Matt joins in. "I'm guessing you signed an agreement with them that prevents you from saying anything. Is that it?"

Sarah presses, "Come on Betty, you can tell us. It'll just between us, no one else."

Betty continues to knead one hand with the other, and then shakes her head to the side. "No, I promised."

Sarah looks at Matt for encouragement.

Matt adds, "She might have received a severance of some sort to keep her quiet, regardless of whether she did anything wrong. That's how it's done these days. Some people call it guilt money. I call it a payoff."

Sarah carries on, "Is that it, is that why you left?"

Betty repeats, "I can't talk about it. Please, don't keep asking me anymore."

Sarah continues, "Do you have another job lined up?"

Betty answers, "I'm going to take a little time off, relax a bit, and then I'll get back into the job market. I feel I need a rest." She takes in a deep breath to settle down.

Matt advances an idea. "If you want to know my opinion, I think they wanted to send a message to all of us that they're the ones in charge; that they can do anything they want to do, I mean anything at all. I think that's the reason for the security check in the lobby and for all of the one-on-ones today. That's just my opinion." He takes a swallow of beer.

Sarah looks concerned. A frown on her face illustrates the worry. "Listen to me Betty. Call me anytime if you want to talk." She grabs a pen from her pocket to scribble her phone number on a napkin. "Here, take this. It's my cell number. Call me if you want to talk." She folds the napkin in two, and then she pushes it towards Betty.

Betty looks at the once-folded over napkin on top of the table without blinking, as if she is preoccupied with another thought at the moment.

"Please, take it. Call whenever." A sliver of a smile makes its way to Sarah's face.

Without comment, Betty takes the napkin.

CHAPTER 5

The vacated building, in need of repair, is only identified from the outside by a stenciled sign in faded black paint that identifies the name of the former company, **Books4U**.

Inside the structure are odds and ends of printing presses, collating machines, copiers, and miscellaneous equipment that clutter the space. Oil and grease stains mark the cemented floor that resembles an auto mechanic's messy repair shop. Smell of paper, ink and dye still stench the air. Inside the building, just above the main entrance a sign hangs, **Quality Is Our Middle Name**.

Mr. Xia, a small man in stature, sits prominently. To his sides stand two much larger and bulkier men who watch his every move, to protect him from those who might want harm done to their boss.

Seated in front of their boss is another man who looks nervous and anxious, appropriate for someone who perceives peril is up ahead. Zhi Yan feels weak, out of breath, and jumpy. He'd prefer to be someplace else.

Mr. Xia speaks with passion and vigor. "Some things are worth the effort, while other things are not. We must all learn what is important and what wastes one's energy. Do you understand?"

Yan nods his head affirmatively. He knows better than to speak unless specifically asked.

"Liu was one of my best warriors, but he failed me. He is no longer one of my warriors. I wish I could have seen his demise personally." He pauses. "I consider you to be one of my best warriors; one who would not only fight any battle but who would be victorious. I pay you well, very well."

Yan forces to keep his mouth closed and his eyes normally wide, yet he feels his muscles shiver a bit.

Xia continues. "I do not employ warriors to do marginal battles. I respect all warriors too much to squander their time and my money. Warrior work must be effective and efficient, not just some of the time, but all of the time. I do not enjoy failure."

Yan squirms in his chair, feeling the need to pee.

Xia resumes. "Self-inflicted mistakes should not be confused with unexpected obstacles. There are always unintentional things that come along, but they should not be misinterpreted for errors of poor planning, faculty reasoning or inept execution."

As Xia stands, the two body guards get ready for a command.

Xia waves them off. "No, I am counting on Zhi Yan." His grin is grotesque looking.

Yan takes in a deep breath.

"Liu has failed me but you must not. You have another opportunity to confirm to me who you are. In twenty-four hours you must put an end to Ranger's life, or else, in exchange, it will be your life."

«‹»»

CHASE

Yan enters the house easily, the small metal device working efficiently in his hands to unlock the back door. He looks around quickly to get a sense of the interior's layout. He promptly moves to the kitchen where he spots the gas stove.

Out of his jacket pocket he removes a wad of putty, squeezes it a few times to soften the texture. He lifts open the stove's top cover that reveals four burners that are separately joined by a small tube that feeds the gas supply. He divides the putty into four equal sections. Then he sets one section of putty on top of one of the tubes, pressing it firmly with his hand to secure its place. Then he reaches for a small bottle from his other jacket pocket that contains igniting liquid. He uncaps the bottle and slowly pours enough liquid on top of the putty to properly saturate the material.

His grin is distorted and bizarre as he continues.

With equal patience, he repeats the process three more times until all four sections of putty are set in place and properly dosed with igniting fluid.

He covers the stove top to its original condition.

Yan looks around the kitchen, his eyes taking the place of a camera lens snapping pictures of everything in view. He catches sight of what he's looking for. He walks to a set of cook books on a shelf only a few feet from the gas stove. He reaches for the larger of the two, opens the cover and sneers. He removes from his jacket pocket the last component of the plan, a green gooey substance wrapped in a clear plastic bag. After making a tiny whole at the edge of the bag, he squeezes the mushy substance inside the cover, closes the book, and firmly presses against the cover to make a good seal. Then, he carefully replaces the cook book to its original position.

Satisfied he's done everything as perfectly as planned, he leaves Jim Ranger's house to head to a nearby location to watch the explosion.

«‹›»

One hour later, sitting in his car, Yan checks his watch. He cracks his knuckles and twists his jaw, anxious that Ranger has not returned home for the night. Then he sees headlights from an approaching car. His mouth draws back at the corners in a smile. He pulls out a pair of binoculars to watch.

A car pulls into the driveway, idles for a few seconds, and then the engine stops. The headlights remain on.

Yan focuses the binoculars to see through the rear window. He sees two people embraced, kissing each other. He raises his voice, "Get over it! Do it inside!"

As if on cue, both front car doors open. A man exits the driver's side and a woman exits the passenger's side. They join together, holding hands as they walk towards the front door. "That's better," Yan says aloud. "Now, go inside."

The man takes out a key to open the front door, steps aside to allow the woman to enter first. "That's kind," Yan says.

For the next few minutes Yan only sees the outside of the house, so he puts the binoculars on his lap. He checks his watch. "Go into the kitchen and either ignite the stove or open the book!" His voice sounds fiery and impatient.

Another few minutes pass by without any noticeable activity.

Then Yan sees the front door light turn on, followed by the front door opening wide. He puts the binoculars to his eyes to make out Ranger stepping outside, moving to the parked car. "What the fuck?"

All of a sudden the house explodes, flames roar out and pieces of wreckage fly everywhere.

The energy from the blast throws Jim Ranger off balance and away from being harmed.

Yan quickly drives away, determined to vanish forever.

««»»

His head is still as it rests against the bed's pillow. There is a pleasant looking smile across his face, handsome in the way of encouraging further interest from the woman next to him. His wide open eyes shine brightly. He keeps quiet for a while.

She too is silent, but unlike the guy along her side, she is distracted with another thought. She worries about what might come next and no longer feels playful.

Matt says, "This is how it starts." His voice is soft and pleasant sounding. He keeps looking up towards the ceiling. He feels the bed's mattress move a bit that tells him she has shifted her body. He waits for her to respond.

Sarah takes in a deep breath, trying to shake off the distraction. Her eyes, as well, look to the ceiling but unlike Matt's they appear gloomy. Her head shakes sideways a bit. "What's that supposed to mean?"

Matt shifts his body a little and then curls his shoulders to loosen up his neck muscles. He hears a clicking sound coming from his neck. He keeps grinning. "It only takes once." He starts to chuckle to himself but the quiet laughter turns into a giggle that Sarah hears.

ANTONIO F. VIANNA

She lifts her head to face him, and then props her arm beneath her body to make it easier to look his way. "What's so funny?"

He keeps the same position, yet out of the corner of his eye he clearly sees her face. "Someone as wonderful as me to come along to make someone like you feel fantastic." He pauses to notice her face grimace. "Don't get me wrong, you too were wonderful, and you made me feel fantastic as well. Yeah, just one time, that's all it took."

"I don't think this was a good idea. I don't know what got into me. I should have never come here." She sounds sorry, in a way apologetic, for having agreed to have sex with him.

"Let's face it; it was good for both of us. You can't deny that." He mirrors her position in bed. "I'd like to make this regular."

Matt is good-looking to her, she admits to herself, in the sense of arousing sexual desires, but she figures she shouldn't get too close to anyone at the office. She has a job to do and does not want anyone or anything romantic to interfere. "I don't think that's a good idea." Her voice is matter of fact sounding.

"Really, I don't believe you. You're just like everyone else, female or male, who is interested in having an admirer, a lover, who wants to make you feel like you're on top of the world. I do, I admit, and you do that to me."

"It's not that simple. Guys make it seem so black and white. It's more complicated than that, much more complicated."

"If you're so sure, then explain it to me. I'm a good listener and I catch on quickly."

She feels as if her face has been permanently etched in a crooked facial expression. "It's not that easy to explain."

"Oh, I see, so it's like if you don't get it by yourself then I can't explain it." His voice sounds sarcastic and displeased.

"Listen Matt, I agree this was good, you and me, I'll grant you that. But there's no future here, at least for me. I'm sorry, but that's just how it is."

"So, it's over, never again?"

"Yeah, it should have never started. I've got to go." She flips off the covers on the bed and steps one foot on the bedroom carpet. "I'll find my own way out."

"You are serious."

"That's the problem, I am and you're not." She walks a few feet away to put on her clothes.

Matt is relentless and unremitting. He is not about to easily give up. "OK, can we start from the beginning, without any sex? Let's have a cup of coffee as if we were meeting for the first time and see where it takes us. What do you say, huh?"

She finishes putting on her clothes and finally her shoes. Then she turns to face Matt. "Good try, I've got to give it to you, but no cigar, pardon the pun." She stares briefly at him as if she is curious about something or waiting for a response. The truth is she is pleased with her decision and is fascinated at his surprised look.

He puts his hands on top of his head, eyes and mouth now wide open.

She waves him goodbye saying, "I'm going for a run" as she leaves the bedroom to exit his apartment.

««»»

Matt stretches his body on the bed. He smirks, unperturbed of Sarah's departure. "She's sure ruthless when it comes to saying good-bye. She'll be harder to crack than I thought." He yawns as he extends both arms above his head. "But I do like a challenge." He lays still and in silence for a short time. Slowly he closes his eyes and within minutes falls back to sleep.

««»»

Sarah steps outside into the cool night. There is a half moon staring down on her. She looks intently at the earth's only known natural satellite. "What's your problem?" She shouts out. "I know what I'm doing. I'm not yet ready for a commitment." She hurries to get inside her car to take off.

She drives to her apartment in silence, only thoughts swirling around insider her head. Then she breaks her own stillness. "What a bizarre night. First, Betty's firing and then his absurd offer. I've got to focus on putting Ranger away for a long time, not these other silly matters." She hesitates and then resumes. "Although I might get Betty to open up to me, woman to woman, there's obviously more to it than what she's already said." She nods her head approvingly of the notion. "I'll call her in a few days, say that I'm concerned that bottling things up inside isn't healthy, that I'm always available to listen."

She stops the car for a red light. "Yeah, that makes sense. I'll call her."

««»»

"I'll not be in today. Something unexpected happened that I've got to attend to. What's been the reaction about Betty's termination?"

David Shea listens intently to his boss. He picks up anger and strain in Jim's voice. "It's quiet so far, but I suspect once people notice she's not working today a few questions will be asked." He then looks down at his cognac colored dimple-styled Alfani dress shoes.

Jim Ranger asks, "Do you remember the plan?"

David rejects the notion of asking him how he's doing, but rather he sticks to the question. "Yes. Without making a fuss, say she had something personal to take care of. That we offered her a personal leave of absence; that she thought she needed more time to take care of the situation so she resigned."

"Perfect. Make sure the rest of the guys understand that to be the message; no deviation."

"I've got it covered."

"I'm counting on you. You're my number two man."

"I won't let you down." He waits to hear more, but when he doesn't, caution is replaced with empathy, "Anything I can do to help you out with whatever you're dealing with?"

Ranger reacts in a brusque sounding tone, "No."

David's eyes widen with surprise, now thinking twice before asking another sympathetic question. "When will you be back to work?"

Ranger is not in the mood to talk any further. "I'll be in touch."

David hears the phones disconnect. What is normally only a fraction of a second facial response becomes longer. Horizontal wrinkles remain on his forehead for a few more seconds.

««»»

Ranger turns to Naomi. Emotional residue from the telephone exchange linger. His eyes remain narrowed and the skin alongside his eyes is wrinkled.

ANTONIO F. VIANNA

"Jim, what kind of new trouble have you gotten yourself into this time?" Her voice is mixed with pity and ridicule.

"You're not my mother! Don't mock me!"

"Remember who's come to see whom?" She curls her lip.

He tries to soften his voice, but back peddling has never been his strength. "I'm not in the mood to be scolded. I'm here because I need a place to stay for a while, just a short time. Then, I'll be out of your hair."

"What's happened to your place, have you sold it or rented it out?"

He wrinkles his nose, "I only wish."

"I've never seen it or been there."

"Can we forget about that for now, they'll be another time?"

She is surprised, eyebrows are raised. "Then what, tell me?"

"The house is gone, it was blown up." He sounds calm and settled all of a sudden.

"What?"

He lifts his shoulders. His face is expressionless.

"Why are you so unruffled and composed?"

"I got out alive."

"But, there's more, isn't there? Who were you with and what happened?"

"I was alone, really."

She twists her face in disbelief.

"Honest, I'm telling you the truth, I was alone."

"Whatever." She raises her eyebrows, "Have it your way. What else happened?"

"I stepped out to get something from my car. Then, the house exploded."

Naomi puts her hands to her mouth, "Oh no!"

He lifts his shoulders again without saying a word.

"You were lucky."

"It's the mirror of all success."

"I think you're in shock. That's why you're so calm. Have you seen a doctor?"

He shakes his head sideways. "I'm actually alright. I just need a place to stay for a short time. That's why I'm here."

"I can get you an appointment with my doctor. She'll see you immediately if I ask."

"Let it go, I'm alright."

Naomi extends her arms towards him, "Come here."

Reluctantly, he slowly steps forward. His hands remain at his sides.

She holds him close to her body. "Everything will be alright."

His arms continue to dangle and his face remains detached looking. His mind is off to other more important thoughts.

««»»

After changing into her running clothes, Sarah leaves her apartment. It is early morning, the time of the day when she feels refreshed from a night's sleep. However, this morning, she feels tired after spending time with Matt. She begins stretching her legs, arms, and neck to loosen up for a three mile run. Then she twists her body at the waist to complete the warm up exercises. Finally, she gives herself a send off message, "This is my time," before taking the first step.

After fifteen minutes running smoothly and evenly, she decides to pick up the pace. She moves her legs faster until she figures she's close to an eight minute clip. A grin covers her face, happy with how free she feels. She tells herself, "This is how it's done."

Sarah decides to extend her normal three mile run into a longer work out so she takes a new and unfamiliar route all the while taking mental notes of the surroundings not to get lost. Up ahead she spots another runner coming her way.

As she gets closer to the jogger she nods her head once without saying a word. It's the runner's protocol. The man responds with a single nod himself. Wordlessly they pass one another, each in their own world, privately thinking. Sarah checks her sports watch to notice her pace has slowed down. She ramps it up again.

Another ten minutes pass. She continues to be within herself, feeling in total control, and more pleased about her life at the moment. Then she smells something in the air, not the usual morning freshness, but something grimy and polluted. She slows her pace enough to look around, to see if she can catch sight of the source of the odor.

Then suddenly, up ahead, she recognizes a marked police car, an ambulance, and a fire truck. "What's going on?" she asks herself aloud. Without giving herself an answer, she heads directly for the location.

There are several people talking to each other as they look at a structure that has been blown up. They stand behind a line of hanging yellow tape intertwined among trees and a street sign. Sarah taps a person on the shoulder. "What happened?"

A woman about Sarah's age turns around. "Don't know for sure, but it seems this house exploded. The firefighters came quickly followed by the paramedics and cops. I live a few blocks away, but the sound was loud enough for me to hear the boom."

"Anybody injured?" Sarah asks as she glances back and forth between the woman and the building debris.

The woman shrugs her shoulders, "Don't know."

A man standing close by joins into the conversation. "I live a few doors down the street. I think there was a guy who was renting the place, but I'm not sure. I never introduced myself, maybe I should have."

A uniformed police officer walks by. "Please, go home, there's nothing you can do."

"Excuse me," Sarah calls out. She heads toward the police officer.

He stops, glances at her trim body in an approving way. "Yes, can I help you?" He gives Sarah a big smile.

She ignores his gaze. "I was wondering if you could tell me about what happened." Sarah puts on her official serious looking face.

"We're investigating it now, nothing much to say other than what you see here, a house is blown up."

Sarah knows better than to reveal her identify at this time, under these conditions, even if it is to someone in law enforcement, yet she is curious about the situation. She is about to explain to him that she is F. B. I., but before she can say another word the officer is called away.

"Gabnowski, get over here."

The police officer walks away from Sarah. "Gotta go."

Sarah follows close enough behind to overhear a conversation between Gabnowski and the other police officer, Sabatini.

"We cordoned off the area outside, but now we've got to make sure no one goes inside. The forensics team is looking for clues."

Gabnowski says, "If anybody was inside the place before it blew up, they're toasted."

"Yeah, I know, but just the same we've got to make sure no one goes beyond the tape."

For an instant, Sarah contemplates asking Gabnowski for more information, but despite her curiosity she stays put. Then, little by little she feels her leg muscles tighten. Realizing there's no point of staying around, she turns to jog away.

A few minutes later, a two-person forensics team appears from the debris.

The Deputy County Medical Examiner, an attractive black-haired woman in her late forties carrying a black bag, says to Sabatini, "There is a dead body, we think a woman, but it's hard to tell right now. We'll need time to sift through the building rubble and inspect the body for clues that might tell us what happened and who she is. No one can set foot anywhere near this area. It's going to take a while to inspect everything. Let's hope for cool weather with no rain, or else important evidence could be washed away."

The man accompanying the Deputy County M.E. keeps quiet.

Gabnowski says, "I'll tell the Chief he needs back-ups. He's not going to like it."

Indifferently, Sabatini says, "Just do it, let him worry about overtime pay."

《《》》

By the time Sarah finishes her run, showers and gets ready for work she feels renewed. Her face looks radiant and content. She swallows a packet of seven vitamin pills, one at a time with orange juice. She leaves her apartment to head for her car that is parked nearby. After about ten steps outside, her cell rings. She reaches for the device, thinking it is probably her boss. She checks the caller ID but does not recognize the number. Sarah hesitates, wondering whether to answer or let it go to voice message. She decides to connect. "Hello."

"Sarah?"

She recognizes the voice but is not certain who the caller might be. "Yes, who's this?"

"It's Betty. Can we talk?"

Sarah stops walking, her lips slightly jut outward. "Of course, what is it?"

"I'd rather we talk in person."

"No problem, name the place and time."

"Have you had your morning coffee? I'll buy." The tone of her voice resonates with uneasiness.

"How about the Coffee Roasting Company?"

"Yes, that's fine. I can be there in a half hour."

"OK, Betty, a half hour." Sarah hears the phones disconnect.

««»»

Betty's face looks worried and anxious, the kind of outer shell that signals distress. She makes an effort to smile, but her emotions snag the attempt to cover up her feelings. "Maybe this isn't a good idea. Everyone has their own problems to deal with."

"No, no, Betty. I'm here to listen. That's what friends do." Sarah struggles to stay in control of her own feelings.

"I wanted to be a professional writer when I was younger."

Sarah is not sure the relevance of the statement but lets her continue just the same.

Betty picks up again. "Maybe even a best-seller author, have a movie made from my book, go on interviews. You know, everything."

Sarah nods for support.

Betty resumes. "I was even the editor of my high school newspaper. I thought that I'd enroll in college with a major in journalism. I was very optimistic and self-confident then. I'm less so now." She looks away for a second, and then continues. "One day during high school I stayed late to edit an article I was writing for the school paper. It wasn't anything inflammatory that would have offended anyone. It's strange though, that I don't remember the topic today. Well, anyway, I was close to finishing it when two boys from school came into the room." She swallows and then takes a sip of coffee before continuing. "I was surprised to see them since they weren't the type of boys who were interested in writing or even reading. They were, well, sort of the rough crowd that I didn't have a lot to do with. Anyway, I remember asking them what they wanted, how I could help them." She hesitates. Her eyes tear up and then open wide as she stares at Sarah. "Why am I telling you this?" She covers her face with both hands and begins to cry.

Sarah's heretofore quizzical demeanor turns sympathetic. "You don't have to go on."

"I've never told anyone this, not even my parents, no one, up until now."

Sarah feels her body tense, a sense of apprehension for what Betty might say next.

Betty takes in a deep breath before resuming. "They just grinned at me, the scary kind of grin that makes your skin crawl. I was scared at that exact moment but I didn't know why, I just was." She swallows again. "Then they both came at me. I won't go into the details, but they dragged me into the boy's room and . . ." She doesn't finish the sentence. She only stares at Sarah.

Sarah feels anger and rage build up inside her, emotions that could cause her to inflict bodily harm on the two boys, yet she is without words to comfort Betty.

"I don't know what I did to deserve it. I mean, I never did anything to the two boys to cause them to act that way. Why did they do it to me?"

Sarah's smile is intended to be sincere but it feels fake to her. She finds a few words to say. "There's nothing you did to warrant that action." She searches for more to say but finds nothing further to express herself.

However, Betty has more to say. "I continue to write, I love it. It's very therapeutic." She clears her throat. "But that incident with the two boys has other importance. What I really want to talk with you is about someone else."

Sarah's eyebrows rise in surprise. "Yes, who is it?"

"I don't trust many people, mostly men. I've tried to stay away from them as much as possible, in an intimate way I mean." She breathes out through her nose. "It's about Matt."

"What about him?"

"I don't trust him."

"Why?"

"There's something about him that makes me nervous. I don't know what it is, but he's up to some evil."

"Why do you want me to know about this? I'm not his boss."

"Yes I know that, but you work with him at the same company. He said it himself when the three of us talked."

"I guess I don't remember what that was.

"I don't remember the exact words he used, but at the end of the conversation he said he thought the executives of the company wanted to send a message to all of us that they're the ones in charge. Don't you find that interesting that he would say something like that? I mean, why would the executives need to do that?" She pauses. "Why would Matt even think of saying that?"

"I guess he told me before the three of us were together. He told me he has a doctorate degree in psychology."

"What does that mean?"

"In my opinion it means he over-thinks things. I wouldn't put much weight on what he said about sending the employees a message. I think he's got too much time on his hands."

Betty shakes her head to the sides. "I think he provokes people to get them riled and then belittles them afterwards. I saw the way he looked at you. I'd be careful around him. He is not who he claims to be."

The grim assertions from Betty about Matt do not sit well with Sarah. She doesn't know if she should pass them off as credible or simply dismiss them as coming from someone who has not emotionally healed from when she was in high school.

"I can tell you don't believe me." Betty is even tempered.

"I don't doubt for one second that you believe Matt can't be trusted, that's clear to me. Remembering your teenage experience from the past certainly brings up hurtful memories. However, I'm not sure it applies to Matt."

"I'll never be able to forget what they did to me, that I'm sure. And I will never forgive them. But I'm not labeling all men. I'm not making general accusations. That's illogical. I'm smart enough to know that. But I do know threatening people when I meet them, both men and women. I know a phony when I meet one."

Sarah scans Betty's face. It is deadpan and expressionless with no sign to cue her as to how Betty might be feeling.

"You look puzzled," Betty says.

"There's a lot to process."

"More coffee?" A young man stands nearby with a coffee pot in hand. He smiles at the two women.

"No thanks, I've had enough." Betty places her palm over the top of the cup in front of her.

Sarah looks at her watch. "Oh, I need to get to work." She glances at the man, "No more for me."

The man walks away, towards another table.

"I'm sorry I kept you here so long." Betty sounds a bit apologetic.

"No, no, don't worry. You've given me something to think about." Sarah stands and then reaches to hug Betty.

The two women walk away from each other in opposite directions.

CHAPTER 6

The Chief of Police, Max Monaco, stops by Area Director Jackson Law's office.

Law moves around his desk to sit in a chair across from Chief Monaco. "I take it this isn't a personal visit."

Chief Monaco looks tired, eyes puffy from overwork. "I could use a cup of coffee."

Law gets up from his chair and opens the office door. "Debbie, will you get the Chief and me each a cup of coffee, black?" After closing the door he returns to his former chair.

"You're a good man."

"We've known each other for awhile. How's the family?"

The Chief grins, "You mean the current wife, not numbers one and two?" He chuckles and then continues. "Kids from my first two marriages are all grown up and have their own lives. I rarely see them."

"Who's counting? How are you doing?"

"Should never have remarried after Evelyn died. She was the life of my life."

"We all make mistakes. It's important to get over them, to learn from them."

The office door opens. "Here are your coffees. Anything else I can do?"

"No thanks. Please hold all calls unless it is urgent. The Chief and I have something important to discuss."

Debbie closes the door.

"Salute my friend." Law holds up in the air his cup of coffee.

"Yes." Monaco mirrors the hand movement and then takes a sip. "The Bureau sure knows how to make a good cup of coffee."

"We've got more money to spend than you do," Law smiles. "What's on your mind?"

"We're investigating what seems to be an intentional bombing of a residence in the area. The remains of a woman's body were found inside. We've identified her as a highly paid prostitute, a local girl." He takes another sip of coffee. "Someone had money to pay for fun." He wiggles his eyebrows. "So we can rule out anyone in law enforcement." He grins.

"So far it seems this is your jurisdiction, why tell me?"

"The house was rented to Mr. Jim Ranger. His body was not inside."

"Oh, now you've got my attention."

"There were several devices used. It looks sophisticated. I can turn the case over to you, or I can keep it myself and advise you along the way. It's your call. I'll do whatever you want."

"Not enough money in your budget, is that part of it?"

"Could be, but again, this is your call. I've got other cases waiting in line."

"How far have you investigated the case?"

"Just in the preliminary stage. I've got a forensic team of two on it now. You know Madeline Courier; she's my Deputy County M.E. She's leading the team."

Law smiles, his mouth draws back at the corners. "She's come a long way in a short time."

"That's another story. Let's not get into that right now. Do you want the case or not?"

"I might have to talk with her directly to get up to speed."

"Put away your fantasies. You had your chances with her a while back and it all backfired. Let it go."

"I'm all business these days. I've learned."

"You're one of the few men who have." He grins.

Law keeps silent as he mentally rewinds memoires with Madeline Courier.

"Let's get back to my question. Is your answer yes or no?"

"Is it your best estimate now that the job was professionally done?"

"There's no question about it, yes."

"And nothing was taken from the house, like from a robbery?"

"Not likely. But the recent rains have now washed everything away, so we can't be certain."

"But it is your best guess that the house was purposely blown up by a professional. Do you suspect Ranger was the target and that the pro was in the wrong place at the wrong time?"

"I'd say so."

The Chief and Area Director exchange glances in between sips of coffee.

Law shakes his head, "OK, we'll take it."

"I thought you'd agree." He pulls out of his coat pocket a document. "I've done my part of transferring evidence to the Bureau. You know where to sign and I'll complete the process today."

Law smiles, "Well, that was easy." He leans over to grab the document. Then he stands to head for his desk, takes a pen in hand, and signs in the right place.

The Chief stands and takes the document from the Area Director. "I'll personally see to completing the handoff today."

"Say hi to Madeline for me."

"I don't think so. Facts are stubborn things. What's over is over."

««»»

The next day, early, Area Director Law takes a ride by himself to the County Morgue. He pulls into the parking lot, spots a few reserved spaces. One in particular he notices is set aside for Madeline Courier, Deputy County Medical Examiner. His face shows a slight surprise of the unexpected situation. He parks alongside her silver metallic Audi A6 Sedan and then gets out. His look turns serious as he heads for the entrance.

"Hello, I'm Jackson Law, Area Director of the F. B. I." He pulls out an official badge to prove his identify. "Is the Deputy County Medical Examiner in?"

The receptionist takes a close look at the photo on the badge and then his face. Her lips quiver slightly. "Oh, yes you are. I'm sorry sir that I didn't recognize you."

"There's no reason for you to have known. Don't let it bother you." He clips the badge on the lapel of his suit coat.

"I'll call her now. Please have a seat." She nods to two mismatched chairs a few feet away.

Law nods his head, moves a few feet away but continues to stand.

The receptionist says in an upbeat voice, "Ms. Courier is just finishing up with something. She said to bring you back to her office." She stands. "Please follow me."

He isn't sure what to expect when he and Madeline meet after all these years. He closely follows the receptionist.

"Well, here we are. I guess she's still finishing up. Do you want me to wait until she comes?"

"No, that won't be necessary. I'll just find a place to sit and wait. Thanks for your help."

The receptionist walks away.

Law looks around at the messy office, papers in almost every conceivable place along with boxes both empty and still unopened filling space on the floor. "Not one feminine touch anyplace," he mumbles to himself, "not what I remember her to be." On the coat stand is a large-sized plain-looking jacket, and two pairs of women's shoes are on the floor nearby. He gives away his inner thoughts with a single word, "Hmm."

"I'm not who I used to be, but I'm still very particular."

Law turns to see Madeline. He is unable to hold back a big smile. "It's been a while."

She returns a smile with one of her own, but much less intense. "Yes it has, and much has changed." She extends her hand to shake to keep a safe distance from him. "The Chief told me what's happened. I'll have everything to you in the next few days, no more than three at the most."

"Right." It's the only word he can come up with at the moment.

"Do you want a tour of the place? You know, where we do our work, where the locker rooms are, where we put on the scrubs and shields, where we shower to clean up. Do you?" Her voice is matter of fact.

"Actually, no thanks, but it's great to know there are dedicated people working in the County." He feels miffed with her attitude.

"Was there anything specific you wanted to talk with me about?" She stares at him without a single blink.

"Of course there was but I've changed my mind."

Staring at him she says, "You were never able to figure that out then, and it seems you still can't."

"What's that supposed to mean?"

She twists her face, "Really, you don't know?"

"Are you seeing anybody?"

"That's none of your business."

He tilts his head downward, "I know."

"Listen, Jackson, it was a long time ago when we were together, or tried to be together. It didn't work out then and it seems you haven't changed much. So why bother trying to get us back together after all these years. I'm sure it is painful for you."

"And you, how do you feel?"

"I followed your career since we split. I was very proud to see you get to where you are now. I too had career aspirations, but when we were together it seemed yours were more important than mine. I didn't particularly care for that arrangement. We needed to get away from each other to do whatever it was we wanted to do. I'm very happy for you. Just be happy for me."

"So you're saying there're no feelings on your part towards me?"

She closes her office door. "I didn't say that or mean that!" Her voice raises a notch. "Don't put words into my mouth! You did it then and now you're doing it again!"

"I'm sorry, but that's how you sound."

"Then listen more closely! If you don't have any official business with me, then please leave! I'll have everything to you in the next few days!" She opens her office door, extends her hand and says, "Good day sir. Thanks for stopping by."

《《》》

He answers the door bell. He is a tall man, over six feet three inches, yet weighs only one hundred forty-five pounds, mostly bone and skin. His dark brown hair is cut short, ragged and unkempt, and his brown eyes are markedly flat. His facial features are pale, thin lips and a small nose. He needs a shave. There is nothing stern or hardened about his appearance. He appears at first to be aloof and distant. "Yes?" His voice is faint.

Agent Le Boeuf shows her badge. "I'm investigating the explosion that took place two days ago, just a few houses away. Can I come in?"

He leans over to take a look at the emblem, and then glances back and forth between her face the badge to assure himself she is who she claims to be. "Sure, come in." He steps aside to let Le Boeuf inside his house.

She steps inside and quickly makes a quick visual assessment of the place. Nothing concerns her at the moment. She notices his worn slippers as footwear.

"I was wondering when someone would come around to talk with the neighbors. It's unusual for something like that to happen, a house getting blown up."

"Can I sit here?" She points to a nearby chair.

"Sure, sit anyplace you want. I don't get much company." He watches her take a seat. "Sorry if the place looks in a mess. It's only me and my dog, Patches. He's out back in the yard."

"Can you tell me your name?"

"Sure. It's Joe Messerle."

"Did you hear the sound of the blast?"

"Sure did, and so did Patches. We nearly jumped a full foot in the air. Very loud."

"What did you do next, after you heard the sound?"

"Do next? What do you mean?"

"After you heard the sound, what did you do?"

"Nothing, absolutely nothing. Patches and me stayed tightly together, to comfort each other. None of my business what happens. No, none of my business."

"Did you know who owned the house that blew up?"

"No, and don't care to. It's none of my business. I stay mostly inside this house. I like it inside."

"So, you don't go out much. Is that what you're saying?"

"Right, I stay inside. Just me and Patches."

"Did you notice anything unusual the day of the explosion?"

"Like what?"

"Oh, I don't know, like unfamiliar vehicles parked on the street, people you haven't seen before wandering around, things like that."

Joe pauses to think for a second. "Yes I did. I even told Patches."

She prevents showing surprise in her face. "What was it that you saw?"

"I'd say about an hour and a half before the explosion, maybe it was longer, I really don't know, a dark colored van parked a few houses down the street. I saw a man wearing a wool hat walk past my house towards the one that blew up. I couldn't see exactly what happened next but twenty minutes later the same man walked past my house, obviously in the reverse direction, back to his van. Then he sat inside until it was dark." He stares at Le Boeuf.

"Is that it?"

"Well yeah, that's it. It was time for me to go to bed, ten-thirty, right after the news. I always go to bed at ten-thirty after the news."

"But you heard the explosion."

"Of course, it woke me up and startled Patches."

"About what time was that?"

"Ah, good question. I don't think I looked at the clock. If I did I don't remember."

"Is there anything else you can tell me about that night?"

"Like what?"

"That's why I'm asking."

He pauses for a second. "No, I can't think of anything."

"Would you come to my office to describe the person you saw to one of our sketch artists? It could be very helpful to us."

"Like I told you, it wasn't much that I saw."

"I understand, but what we've found over time is that once the sketch artist begins drawing, the witness, in this case that means you, begins to remember more."

"OK, if it would help."

"I'll call you tomorrow to set up an appointment. You've been very helpful. Here, take my card. Give me a call if you remember anything else in the meantime. Will you do that?"

"Of course I will, why wouldn't I?"

"Mr. Messerle, I hope you don't mind me asking you this, but what do you do for a living?"

He clears his throat. "I'm the only child of wealthy parents who are long gone. They willed everything to me. I don't have to work, so I don't. I live in this modest house because I want to. I read, watch movies on television, and have a good time with Patches. That may not sound like a good life, but I enjoy it. I stay out of other people's business and they stay out of mine. I'll probably die right here in this house."

Le Boeuf smiles at him thoughtfully. "I see what you mean. There aren't many people who are happy at what they do." There is a pause before she continues. "You're a lucky man in many respects."

Joe's face brightens. "Each man's belief is right in his own eye."

«»

Jim Ranger wakes up early. He stretches his arms above his head, and then glances towards Naomi who contently sleeps by his side. He rubs his eyes, and then grudgingly gets out bed. He goes to the nearby bathroom to empty his bladder. He takes a good look at himself in the mirror, surprised he looks as weary as he does, resentful it isn't a dream. He takes a quick glance to see that Naomi has turned in bed, she now occupies the middle making it problematical for him to rejoin her at the time without waking her. He decides to shave and dress. Later he figures he'll call her to give her an update. There is someone else he needs to see. He tiptoes past Naomi hoping not to awaken her.

"Are you going to be OK?"

He turns to glance at Naomi whose hands reach to the back of her head. "I didn't want to wake you."

"Of course, that was sweet of you."

He takes in a deep breath. "I've got to see someone. It's important."

"Yes, I understand."

"I'll be back later today."

"I know you will."

"I'll call you before I return."

"I know you won't."

"It's complicated."

"Don't let whatever you're about to do and whomever you are about to meet dissuade you from doing what you want to do."

He nods his head, grins and leaves her alone.

《《》》

Minutes later, he is in his car headed north to 69 Conte Way West. As he pulls into the parking lot, he spots several empty spaces including the ones reserved for top officials. He notices one in particular, so he decides to park at the far end of the lot. He checks his watch, half-past seven in the morning. He figures he'll have to wait a while until she arrives. He slouches back in the seat, closes his eyes, and breathes comfortably, all the while listening to approaching vehicles.

Fifteen minutes later he hears the sound of a car's engine. His eyes open wide to spot a silver metallic Audi A6 Sedan move into a reserved parking slot. He sees a woman exit. His face dances in delight. He quickly gets out of his car to move her way. "Madeline, it's me Jim." He walks as fast as he can to get closer.

She turns in surprise of the unexpected call out. It does not last long as she recognizes the man moving on foot toward her. "Jim?"

In only a fraction of a second he responds. "Yes, I have to see you."

She stands motionless until he gets closer. "What are you doing here?"

He takes in a deep breath. "I'm in a bit of a bind, and I need your patience."

"Of course, what is it?"

He lets silence run its short course and then says, "I've got some unexpected travel coming up and I might not be around to be with you as regularly as I've been. I'm sorry, but it's business."

She pauses and adds, "Oh, that's not so bad."

"I knew I could count on your understanding."

"But why are you here so early. Couldn't you have told me tonight, at dinner?"

"No, that's the problem. I'm leaving now and I didn't want to say it on the phone."

She grabs his face and kisses him deeply with no resistance on his part. Then she wraps her arms around his neck as he lowers his hands to her waist. They remain embraced for a few more seconds. Then, she pulls away and asks quietly, "So the real question becomes, when do you return?"

"Maybe after a week from today. I'll call you every day."

"OK, I can work with that. But I'll miss you every day."

"Not more than me missing you."

"Can I water the plants? I'd love to see your place. You've never asked me over."

"That's taken care of. The lady who cleans my place does all of that. No need to worry."

««»»

By now, the local and national news channels broadcast the house explosion labeling it **The Big Bang on Barkley Street**. Left unsaid but implied is the blast was intentional.

Agent Le Boeuf makes her way to another residence in the neighborhood where the explosion took place.

"Do you think the arsonist is planning to blow up another house in the neighborhood?" The elderly woman wrings one hand with the other. Her head bobs a wee bit.

"There is no reason to believe that the unfortunate situation was caused by a person or persons. Our most recent evidence suggests there was a faulty gas pipe." Le Boeuf manages to lie convincingly.

"I hope so. I live alone and wouldn't know how to defend myself."

"My advice is to call the utility company to recheck all your gas connections. They'll do that free of charge if you call them. Here, take this card with their local phone number." She lays on top of a coffee table a business card with the name and phone number of the local utility company.

"Yes, yes, that makes sense." She looks at the card for a few seconds.

"Can you tell me anything that you might have heard or seen before or after the explosion?"

"Are you sure it was an accident?"

"Yes I am, but it is my duty to check all possible angles just to be sure." Le Boeuf smiles to move the conversation along.

The elderly woman has another direction she wants to pursue. "Gayle Balentine said a woman was inside the house when it happened. I guess she didn't have a chance."

Horizontal wrinkles cover Le Boeuf's forehead. "Who's Gayle Balentine?"

"She's the news anchor on Channel 7. I only watch Channel 7 news. You can always trust what Gayle Balentine says."

"Oh, I see, but I really can't discuss any details with you since we are still investigating the matter."

"Yes, of course, confidentiality is a must." The elderly woman pauses for a split second. "Did the woman own the house, or maybe she was renting it?"

Le Boeuf looks at her, and takes a deep breath of air. "Again, that's all confidential for the time being."

"Those crime fighters on television all solve the crime very quickly. Maybe you should talk with some of them to help you out. I mean, it wouldn't hurt, would it?"

Le Boeuf almost snaps back but catches herself in time. Calmly she says, "Let's get back to whether you saw or heard anything before or after the explosion."

"I go to bed around nine o'clock. I take one sleeping pill to make sure I have a good night's rest."

"So, are you saying you did not see or hear anything unusual until the explosion? Is that what you're saying?"

"Yes, I was soundly sleeping."

Le Boeuf realizes she's gotten all the useful information from the elderly woman that's possible. She stands. "Thank you for your time. Be sure to call the utility company to check the gas lines."

«‹›»

Agent Le Boeuf puffs out a breath of air after stepping outside the elderly woman's house, frustrated that she has found little evidence beyond the sketchy description given by Joe Messerle. She figures one more residence to check before returning to the office.

She walks to the house across the street, rings the front door bell, and waits to see who opens.

A woman in her early twenties, dressed in a white cotton shirt and tight fitting jeans answers the call. She wears little makeup, unnecessary since her skin is smooth and without blemishes. Her natural red hair is pulled back into a pony tail. She is barefooted. "Hi, what's up?" Her voice is animated and playful.

Le Boeuf shows her badge. "Hello, I'm sorry to bother you. I'm investigating the explosion in the neighborhood a few days ago. Can I come in?"

"Sure, I need a break from studying." She steps aside to let Le Boeuf enter. "Sorry about the way the place looks. I'm only renting it and simply despise cleaning."

"I totally understand. I put off my cleaning to the very end."

"Let me move this stuff out of the way." She walks towards a wooden table that is in the middle of the largest room in the house. Piles of books and papers are piled high on the table and one of the two chairs. No other furniture is evident and the walls are bare of pictures.

"You're a student?"

"Yeah, at Lincoln School of Law."

"Impressive."

She lifts her shoulders slightly, "I guess so, but thanks for the compliment anyway."

"What year?"

"Second, and then only one more to go."

"Do you know what field you'll get into?"

"Employment law, I find that to be the most fascinating."

"Mine was criminal law, and now I'm an Agent with the F. B. I."

"Oh, that's great. Where did you go?"

"Marshall School of Law."

"Congratulations, that's one of the toughest to get into." She finishes cleaning enough room for them to sit and talk. "That should do it. Have a seat."

Le Boeuf gets to the point quickly, "Were you home two nights ago?"

"The night of the explosion?"

"That's correct, the night of the explosion."

"I usually get up around five in the morning to study for about an hour before going to class. I had classes that morning. After classes I went to the School's library for a while, met friends for an early dinner and then drove straight here. I got in about sunset. I was planning to study a little more before going to bed. As I drove down the street I noticed a dark colored van parked on the opposite side of the street where this house is. There was a man sitting inside the van, I'd say about my age or maybe a little older, say thirty max, wearing a gray wool hat. He just sat there as I passed by. Anyway, I pulled into my driveway, got out of my car and came inside. Then, I'd say about twenty minutes later I went to the mail box at curbside to pick up my mail. The van was empty. I actually didn't give that much attention, so I came inside to look over my mail. It's mostly junk mail these days." She rolls her eyes. "However, there were a few bills I had to pay so I took care of them. Then I took the bills and the junk mail outside. I threw away the junk stuff in the garbage and put the bills inside my mail box." Her eyes light up. "That's when I saw him again. He was sitting inside the van. I can't give you the exact time, but it was definitely dark by then. I came inside, and began to study. I was in bed by nine but I heard the explosion. It woke me up."

Le Boeuf is not able to hold back a grin. "This is what every investigative Bureau Agent hopes for."

She cocks her head to the side. "What's that?"

"Someone like you who accurately remembers important things that matter."

"I'm so happy I'm of some help."

"Could you come down to the Bureau to describe again to a sketch artist the details of the man you saw in the van?"

"Certainly."

CHAPTER 7

Later that week Area Director Law calls a meeting early in the morning.

"Some of you are investigating the house explosion that killed one woman, and some of you are working on the Ranger case. I believe these two incidences have a bearing on each other and therefore the more everyone knows about what's going on with both the quicker we'll solve them both." He looks around at those seated at the rectangular table.

"We believe we know who set the explosion at Ranger's rental property that killed one woman."

An assistant passes around folders to everyone.

"Inside your folder are photos of three people. One is Jim Ranger, the man we are after. His photo is marked with his name. He's the con artist who's scamming money from unsuspecting people. He's got a record longer than anyone's arm and he's been in prison before. He's set up an organization in our city repeating what he's done elsewhere. One of our Agents is planted inside the organization. The Agent's identify is only known by me and I'll keep it that way until I decide otherwise. That Agent will receive a full briefing as done here. Another person, who was close to Ranger, had agreed to work with us in exchange for immunity. However, that person, Vince Allen, was killed. We think Ranger did it himself but have no proof. Ranger owes money, lots of it to a lone shark. That's where the second photo is important. It is the one marked as Mr. Xia. There is a third photo marked Zhi Yan, who works for Xia. He's one of Xia's collectors and the one we believe is responsible for exploding the house in hope that Ranger would be inside. It didn't work out as planned. Ranger is on the loose. He's not been at work for almost a week. We believe he's in hiding. The plan is to lure him out of hiding. I've had the house explosion case transferred to our jurisdiction so now the Bureau is the central clearinghouse of everything. Translate Bureau to mean me."

There are a few chuckles from those sitting around the table.

"I want to know at once when anything turns up, even if it seems irrelevant. Do what you have to do. Am I clear?"

All heads nod without uttering a word.

«‹›»

He runs as fast as his legs allow, lifting and extending each one to get away, pumping his arms in rhythm. He is separated about fifty yards from them. When he takes a quick glance back at the men in blue who chase him, he slips on a wet spot in the alley. The fall to the ground tears his jeans at the right knee and cuts his skin. He gets to his feet quickly as he recovers to escape. Tommie cuts the next corner too close to the building. His shoulder hits the structure's edge. His body flinches back a bit. The disruption is momentarily as he recovers to move on.

"Stop," yells Officer Weber.

He ignores the police officer's command. "Fuck you," Tommie replies. "You're not gonna get me."

Officer Weber shouts again, "Stop!"

Tommie's body skims a trash can. His momentum tips the garbage can over so that its contents spill on the concrete. "Take that!" he yells. He continues moving forward, but suddenly he stops. His eyes widen in shock. There is a building directly in front of him. He is at a dead end. He at once looks around. At first he does not see another way out, but then he catches sight of a fire escape ladder. He moves quickly toward the metal stepladder. With one hand he grabs hold of the nearest step to lift his body slightly off the ground. Then with the other hand he pulls himself to safety.

Officer Weber commands, "Stop right there!"

Tommie ignores the order. He climbs onto a small metal platform to run away.

Officer Weber repeats, "Stop!" Then he adds, "Or I'll shoot!"

Tommie doesn't hear the directive. He looks around to find a window or any other opening he can crawl through. His heart pumps wildly. He suddenly freezes in place. A window is solidly boarded up preventing him from crawling through. Then he slowly turns towards two police officers standing on the ground, guns pointed his way.

Officer Powers says, "There's no way out. Get down!"

Tommie gulps as he looks down at the two police officers.

"Get down," Officer Powers repeats. "It's over."

Slowly, Tommie climbs down the metal steps.

Officer Powers grabs Tommie by the shirt. "Turn around." He cuffs Tommie's hands behind his back.

Officer Weber faces Tommy. "You got a gun?"

Tommie smirks without a remark.

Officer Weber says, "I guess I've got to look." He checks for weapons, patting down Tommie. His eyes widen. "Well, what do we have here?" He pulls out a weapon, looks at it, and then frowns.

Officer Powers asks, "What did you find?"

Officer Weber holds a black toy gun in the air. "It's a kid's toy!"

Officer Powers replies, "But he used it as a real weapon. Let's take him in."

Tommie shouts, "You've got nothing on me." He struggles to pull away but is pulled back by the police officer.

««»»

Later the same day Tommie is placed in a lineup with six other men of comparable age, height, hair and skin color, and race. They all wear similar types of clothes. They stand behind a white line on the floor. Printed on the wall behind each suspect is a number that ranges from 1 to 10. In the middle of the floor in front of the men is a white circle. Sitting in a darkened room are observers who can see and hear the suspects in the lineup but who cannot be seen or heard by them. Among the observers are Officers Weber and Powers as well as the officer in charge of conducting the lineup, Captain Giles.

Captain Giles begins. "Number 1, step into the circle."

All seven suspects remain still, no one moves.

Captain Giles repeats, "Number 1, you at the end, step into the circle on the floor. Do it now."

The man at the far end of the lineup looks around at the other men standing to his left, and then points a finger at himself. "Me?"

Captain Giles answers, "That's right, you're number 1. Step forward into the circle."

The man identified as number 1 steps into the white circle.

Captain Giles asks, "What's your name?"

Number 1 says, "Paul Andrews."

Captain Giles asks, "Where do you work?"

"I'm in between jobs."

"So you're unemployed, is that it?"

"Yeah."

"Are you collecting unemployment?"

"No."

"Why's that, aren't you due to get it?"

"I don't know, maybe I am."

"Do you know why you're here?"

"No sir, I have no idea."

Captain Giles looks at a piece of paper in his hands. "Ever been arrested before?"

"No sir, never," he swipes his mouth with the back of his hand.

"Unless this is a misprint, I have your rap sheet in front of me. Do you want to change your answer?"

"Whatever you've got is wrong. I've done nothing wrong."

"You never robbed a jewelry store in Austin, Texas and spent one year in jail? You never robbed a bank in Austin, Texas and spend two years in jail? Is that what you're saying?"

"Never been to either place. You've got the wrong man."

"Do you have access to a vehicle?"

"No."

Captain Giles looks at Officers Weber and Powers.

Both police officers shake their heads, no.

"OK, Mr. Andrews, you can step back. Number 2, step forward into the circle."

The man identified as number 2 steps into the white circle.

"What's your name?"

"Blake Cetter."

Captain Giles asks, "Where do you work?"

"I'm self employed."

"What do you do?"

"This and that."

"Can you be more specific?"

"Odds and ends, whatever I can find."

"Do you know why you're here?"

"It's a mystery to me."

Smirks appear on the faces of the other men in the lineup.

Captain Giles looks at a piece of paper in his hands. "Ever been arrested before?"

"I was an alter boy."

"That wasn't my question. Have you ever been arrested before?"

"I don't remember."

"So, you might have been arrested, you just don't remember. Is that what you're saying?"

"Yeah, that about sums it up." He grins. He rubs the thumb and index finger of his right hand against each other.

"You never were arrested for stealing from others' pockets?"

"What are you saying?"

"I'm not saying, I'm asking if you were arrested as a pickpocket."

"Impossible."

Captain Giles looks at Officers Weber and Powers.

Both police officers shake their heads, no.

"Do you have access to a vehicle?"

"No, and I don't drive."

"OK, Mr. Cetter, you can step back. Number 3, step forward into the circle."

The man identified as number 3 steps into the white circle.

"What's your name?"

"Tommie Gray."

Captain Giles asks, "Where do you work?"

"Precious Metals Investments."

"What do you do?"

"I sell."

"Are you making a decent living?"

"It depends what you mean."

"How would you define it?"

"A million dollars."

"So, are you making a million dollars?"

"That's personal. I'm not going to answer it." Tommie guts his jaw forward.

"Do you know why you're here?"

"I do not." His voice suddenly turns shaky.

Captain Giles looks at a piece of paper in his hands. "Ever been arrested before?"

"No."

Captain Giles looks at Officers Weber and Powers.

Both police officers shake their heads, yes.

"Have you ever taken money that wasn't yours?"

"I might have when I was younger, very young."

"But you can't remember, is that it?"

"Yeah, I can't remember."

"Do you know why you were arrested earlier today?"

"I didn't realize I was arrested. What did I do?"

"You stole money from a bakery and smacked the owner of the bakery with a gun. Then you took off. Two police officers caught up with you. You tried resisting arrest. That's what you did."

"You're mistaken, that wasn't me."

"We have your finger prints on the weapon, a toy gun that looks like a real one, the weapon that you used to hit the owner of the bakery."

Tommie feels perspiration form on his forehead. He swallows deeply. "So what if I stole a few bucks."

"Why would someone like you who works in sales making a million dollars steal a few bucks? I don't understand that."

"I never said I was making a million dollars."

"But you're working at a job. Is that right?"

"Yeah."

"I don't understand why you would steal if you're working at a job. That just doesn't make sense to me. Can you explain it?"

"It was only a few bucks. What's the big deal?"

"The big deal is the man who you struck died. You killed the man. That's more than petty theft. It's murder. What do you have to say about that?"

"I want an attorney."

"You're going to need one."

«»»

Mr. Xia's choice of venue takes Jim Ranger to All Souls Cemetery. He drives his car as far deep into the graveyard as he can. Then he steps outside to continue following directions on foot as given to him by Xia. "If someone really wanted to find me, this is not the place," Jim whispers softly. He stops several times and then glances over his shoulder at every sound he hears. He manages to finally make his way to the specific grave site Xia indicated. He stops, stares, and reads the inscription out loud. "Life Is Just One Darn Thing After Another. Louis Oliver. Died In The Nick of Time." Jim frowns, clueless as to the relevance of the message. Then his thoughts are interrupted by a voice behind.

"Mr. Ranger."

Jim slowly turns. He recognizes the voice and feels his leg muscles start to tremble. He manages to keep under control the sound of his voice. "Mr. Xia." He notices additional men nearby. "I see you've brought others with you."

"One can never be too careful. Don't you agree?" He combs his straight long gray hair with a comb. "It's good to see you."

"Yes." Jim pauses, and then asks, "How did you find me?"

"It's my business to know these things. Did you bring the money you owe me?"

"Not exactly." Jim tilts his head to the side and turns both palms upward.

"I thought we agreed that I would spare your life in exchange for full payment."

"I have ten thousand dollars. I promise to repay the rest by the end of the month with five percent interest."

"Oh. Is that all your life is worth, five percent?"

"No, Mr. Xia, it's worth much more to me and to you."

"To me, why to me?" Xia cocks his head to the side.

"Because you know I'm an addictive gambler. You'll be making money off me until the day I die. I think we both know that."

"Is that all there is to it?"

"No, there's the obvious."

"And what is the obvious?"

"I don't want to die."

"That is important to both of us."

"Then we have a deal."

"Yes, we have a deal. Give me the money."

Jim reaches into a coat pocket to pull out a large envelope containing ten thousand dollars. "Here it is." He hands Xia a brown packet. "Count it yourself to be sure."

"Oh, I will. Don't go anywhere."

The blow comes from directly behind Jim, the sound of the metal objective hitting his head, toppling him over onto the ground. He clutches his head to avoid another whack. Through the blood spilling out of his head onto his face and covering his hands, he is not able to see the assailant. He quickly curls up in a fetal position to protect his entire body. He lies on the cold ground, now yelling in pain. He waits for another round of wallops. The wait is not long.

Two men take their turns in kicking Jim on his sides and legs.

Jim tries to swing an arm or leg to fight off the attack but his efforts are futile.

"Enough," shouts Xia.

The assault ends as quickly as it began.

"Let this be a lesson, Mr. Ranger. Do not breach any future commitments with me. Am I clear?"

Jim feels his stomach heaving, his throat cottony, and his reasoning ability to be impaired. Dizziness sweeps his mind making it difficult to reply. Yet he manages to nod his head and grunt, "Yes." The next second his belly heaves up undigested food lodged in his stomach.

Xia says, "You'll recover. Think of the positive. You've survived another day." He walks away followed by the men in black clothes.

Jim hears only the sounds of nature. "Hello?" He waits for a response to confirm he is alone. He manages to stand, albeit wobbly at first. "At least I'm not dead, but close to it." He looks around to confirm that he is by himself with no-one else. Then he hears a sound nearby. He freezes in place. "Who's there?" He looks around again but sees no one. "Is anybody there?" He waits for an answer that does not come. Seconds go by as he stands motionless in place. Then he whispers to himself, "I'm OK. I'm alive." He looks around again to get his bearings. He is disoriented and not sure which way to walk. Finally he figures out the way to his car. He limps in that direction. A few minutes later he spots his car. He begins to feel relieved that he's now safe. As he approaches the car he notices something unusual. The car is jacked up at the rear and both back tires are missing. "Damn it," he says in disbelief. He manages to gather enough strength to slap his hand on top of the car's hood.

««»»

Teddy Deaton, marketing executive, heads for a table at the back of the conference room. He looks over the liquor selection, and then grabs a Haig and Haig bottle to pour a scotch. He places two ice cubes inside the crystal glass. To his right he takes a quick glimpse at the variety of cold sandwiches, salads, and deserts. "Where's the hot food?" He moves the glass to his lips for a sip. "We used to have hot food when Jim was here. Where's the hot food?"

"We've got more to worry about than having hot food." Reggie Ward, finance executive, shakes his head sideways. "You're worried about the food selection when our revenues have leveled."

"Where is Jim?" Marshall Crum, chief legal executive turns to David Shea, security executive. "You talked with him last, didn't you?"

David Shea taps his fingers atop the conference table. "Yeah, a few days ago, but I haven't heard from him since."

"Is he taking a vacation, or has something happened to him?" Marshall narrows his eyes.

David answers, "I don't know, and I don't know where he is. But he's counting on us to continue the operation. I'm sure of that."

"There's money missing from our account." Reggie speaks slowly and purposefully. "He and I are the only ones who have access to it, and I didn't take any money."

"What are you saying?" Teddy points his right index finger towards Reggie.

"I'm saying there's money missing from the account," Reggie flatly answers.

"How much money is missing," asks Teddy. He takes another sip of scotch.

"Ten thousand dollars," Reggie replies. "It is his company and he can do whatever he wants with his money." He shrugs his shoulders.

"I don't like this one bit." Teddy walks towards the conference table. "It smells fishy."

"Listen, we're going to get through this. My sense is Jim is having some personal problems and he needs some time to work it out. Let's give him the benefit of the doubt. I mean, he's treating us well, very well." David looks around at the others.

The room is silent.

Reggie leans back in his chair.

Teddy takes a seat on the couch.

Marshall looks down at the table top.

David continues. "Let's move on with our meeting."

Reggie agrees. "As I was saying, our revenues have leveled. Three of the five reps are doing well, but two are not. I think we've got to decide whether to keep them or move them out and get replacements."

Teddy asks, "Who's on top, the best one?"

"That would be Matt. He's got everything we were looking for, aggressive, convincing, and durable. We need more just like him," A little smile squeezes out of Reggie's face.

"Who are the two duds?" Marshall stands and then heads for the liquor bottles.

"Tommie and Sarah," answers Reggie, "at least that's what the numbers say."

"Maybe they need more training? It is David's turn to head for the liquor bottles.

"They've never done this before, so maybe they do." Marshall stands and then stretches his arms to the side.

"Vince is too good, too thorough. No, I don't think lack of training is the problem," Reggie says.

"By the way, has anyone heard from Vince?" David looks around at the others in the room.

The room is silent.

David frowns, "I guess no one has."

"Let's get back to Tommie and Sarah." Marshall pours three fingers worth of Jack Daniels into a crystal glass. "What do we do with them?"

"Since Vince isn't here to fix the problem, as he should be, I say we get Matt to coach them. Isn't he our best rep?" David stares at the liquor bottles, undecided which one to take hold of.

"Won't that take him away from selling? Isn't that what we hired him to do, to sell not to train?" David finally reaches for the bottle of Haig and Haig. He smiles, and then pours two fingers worth into the crystal glass. He turns to Teddy, "Need a refill?"

Teddy waves him to come closer, "Only if you insist."

David walks towards Teddy, "I insist."

Reggie chimes in, "I don't think that's a good idea. Revenues are flat and Matt's our best performer. We can't take our best performer off the phones. Revenues could drop if Matt isn't selling." He gets up to walk towards the liquor bottles. He stares at each bottle for a few seconds, and then picks up a bottle of Beefeater Vodka.

"Just like a finance guy, only focusing on the numbers. We've got to get Tommie and Sarah up to speed fast. So, it's either Matt or one of us. I don't see any other way." David finishes filling Teddy's glass.

The room goes silent again.

David looks up at the men. "If there isn't any further discussion or options, we need to decide what to do."

Reggie takes a sip of Vodka. "OK, I'll agree for Matt to provide remedial training for Tommie and Sarah, but for only two days. If they don't improve then we should get rid of them. I say we cut our losses." He takes another sip. "What about it?"

Teddy nods his head, "I agree." He looks at Marshall. "What about you?"

"OK, I'll go along."

Finally David says, "OK, it's settled. Which one of us is going to talk to Matt, Tommie and Sarah?"

Reggie lifts his head towards David. "You, I think you should tell them. It was your idea."

David has the same opinion. "OK, I'll do the talking, but we all should be in the room with them. I don't want anyone to think that I'm running the place. We all are."

Marshall is of the same mind. "I'll get them now." He looks around at the others who nod their heads in agreement.

««»»

Inside the conference room, David asks, "Where's Tommie?"

Matt and Sarah look at each other, eyes open wide, lips tightened.

"Come on, somebody say something," persists Reggie.

Matt says, "I haven't seen him today. I don't know where he is."

Sarah is consistent with Matt. "Me too, I don't know where he is."

David grunts. He looks squarely at Matt and Sarah. "We've brought the both of you here to talk about a revenue situation. It includes Tommie but we'll deal with him at another time." He shifts his look to Sarah. "Sarah, according to our performance dashboard, you and Tommie are below expectation. This executive group considered a few options that included termination, but eventually we reached a decision that you and Tommie will be given one more chance to improve. If improvement doesn't take place quickly, we'll let you go." He turns to Matt. "This is where you come into play. You are the star performer, congratulations by the way," The executive group applauds. "We want you to coach Sarah, and the same with Tommie if and when he returns, for two days. Show her how you do what you do. We realize this is not part of what you were hired to do, so we will compensate you at double the rate you normally earn during the remedial training." He turns to Sarah, "Then after two days of remedial training, you'll be on your own. We will then expect you to at least meet your performance goals, or else face termination. "He returns looking at Matt. "Are you in agreement with what I've just offered you?"

Matt nods his head, "Totally. I'll do whatever it takes."

David moves his look towards Sarah, "And you? Are you in agreement with what I've just said?"

Sarah consents, "Yes."

David folds one hand over the other. "That settles it. Tomorrow starts the remedial training." He turns to the Reggie, Teddy and Marshall. "Is there anything you'd like to add?"

Reggie says, "The numbers will tell us all we need to know."

"I'm confident that this will work out," says Teddy.

Marshall sees eye to eye, "That's how I see it. Good luck."

David ends the conversation as he faces Matt and Sarah. "That's all. You can leave."

««»»

"This is awkward." Sarah's head is tilted downward, eyes slightly glazed in astonishment of the way things are turning out.

Matt grins, happy what is taking place. "It's not so bad. I can teach you a lot about many things, not just selling." He touches her shoulder.

She flinches at the sensation. "Don't touch me!" She looks up, eyes now glaringly angry. "Don't ever do that again, I mean it, never again."

He backs away, "Whoa, don't be so sensitive. Remember the other night? You liked the way I touched you, at least that's what I thought. Was I wrong?"

"That was then, this is now. The relationship has changed. I intend to keep it business only."

"Whatever." He raises his hands, palms facing her. "You win."

"Hey, what's going on?"

Matt and Sarah turn towards a recognizable voice. They see Dick standing behind Karen.

Karen steps forward, "What were you two doing inside the conference room?"

"Oh, that?" Sarah flicks her head toward the conference room.

Dick asks, "Yeah, that. Are you guys in trouble?"

Matt answers, "No, just an impromptu meeting to get focused on our selling goals."

Karen does not buy the answer. "That's too general. Tell us what really happened in there."

Matt turns to Sarah, "Do I explain or do you want to explain? It's your call."

Sarah pinches her lips. "OK, here it is." She clears her throat. "We were called in because the executives don't think I'm selling enough."

Matt interrupts, "Not just you, but Tommie as well."

Sarah clarifies, "Yeah, that's right, Tommie and me. Evidently we are not selling enough but you guys are. It's Tommie and me who are below our quota."

Dick wonders aloud, "Did they fire you and Tommie?"

Karen wonders about something else, "Where is Tommie? I haven't seen him today. He's usually one of the first in."

Matt shakes his head sideways, "I have no idea. The executives were wondering the same thing, because he's below quota."

"I hope he's OK," Karen adds.

Dick twists his face a bit. "He told me he was having some financial problems and probably would be looking for a second job."

Karen's eyes widen slightly, "So maybe he's interviewing now."

Dick offsets the comment, "Or maybe he's working a second job now and is late."

Matt responds with an idea of his own, "Or maybe he got into some trouble."

Sarah wrinkles her forehead, "Why would you say that?"

Matt raises his shoulders, "It is a possibility."

Dick returns to the original conversation. He looks at Sarah. "Did they fire you and Tommie?"

"No, but they gave me a warning," Sarah's eyes are blank looking, feeling little at the moment.

Karen asks, "What kind of warning?"

Sarah turns to Matt and then back to Karen. "Matt is going to coach me for a few days, actually two days, as a way of improving my techniques."

Dick asks, "That's it, two days of coaching?"

"Well, not exactly," Sarah answers. A slight smirk peeks through. "If I don't improve after the coaching, then I'm history."

Nonchalantly Dicks says, "Oh."

Karen has another question, "Why Matt? Why is he coaching you?"

Sarah turns to Matt, "You tell them."

Everyone turns to look at Matt.

Matt coolly says, "They said I am the top performer. I guess they think I have some tips that Sarah can use. I guess."

Dick asks Matt, "What are they, what are your tips?"

Matt lifts his shoulders without saying a word.

Sarah says with indifference, "I don't know either, but whatever they are, he does it well. He's the top performer."

Karen's eyes brighten with an idea, "Maybe all of us can be coached by Matt. That way, we'll get the benefit of his pointers."

"Ah, I don't think that's possible." Matt shakes his head.

"Why's that? Do you and Sarah have something going on together beyond the office?" Dick squeezes his eyes closer together.

"No, no, nothing like that," Matt defends. He looks at Sarah and then back to Dick and Karen. "The executives only gave me the go ahead with Sarah and Tommie, no one else."

Karen tilts her head to the side, "I just might ask them to include me. I want to be the top performer."

Dick juts out his jaw, "Yeah, me too."

Matt suggests something, "Then ask them, not me. I only work here." He stares at Dick and Karen. Then he hears his cell phone buzz. He grabs it from his pocket, and when he looks at caller ID his eyes open wide. He connects quickly, his eyes widen. "Dad?" He listens for a few seconds. "Be right there! What are you driving?" He disconnects. As he walks away he says, "I've got to go. I'll be back this afternoon sometime."

Sarah looks at Karen and Dick, "I guess he needs to see his father."

"It appears that way," echoes Karen.

Dick decides to walk away without comment.

"Please excuse me. I have to use the women's restroom." Sarah walks away leaving Karen standing alone.

««»»

Once inside the women's restroom, Sarah bends over to check for legs inside each of the stalls. Convinced she is alone she calls Area Director Law. "Hey, this is Sarah. Something just happened that I think you should know about, although it could be nothing."

"You sound anxious. What happened?"

"Do you remember the sales guy named Matt?"

"Yes, the others are Dick, Tommie, and Karen, besides you. What's with him?"

"He's been assigned by the executive group to coach me for a few days in order to improve my sales numbers or else they'll fire me." She takes a breath of air to compose herself.

"What's the problem? That sounds good to me in that they still don't suspect you. There's got to be something else. What is it?"

"Yes there is. Matt just got a cell call from his dad that sounded urgent. Matt looked very worried. It could be nothing, as I said before, but this could mean something."

"Do you suspect him of anything, maybe of being an accomplice of some sort?"

"I can't imagine that. I mean, he's about my age. No, I'd put that idea aside."

"Then why are you calling me? I don't understand."

"I think you should follow him to see who his dad is, and what they're up to."

"What's the motive? I'm still unclear."

"He just looked very jumpy when he got the call. That's all I've got."

"We've got undercover in the lobby and in the parking garage. I'm now pulling up his photo on my computer. What type of car does he drive?"

"A new Honda Crosstour EX."

"And how do you know that?"

"I followed him home one night."

"And . . .?"

"We played a computer game."

"A computer game, is that what you said?"

"Yes I did."

"I didn't realize you were into that sort of thing."

"Actually, I'm not, but let's get back to him."

"Go on, I'm listening."

"Like I said before, this may lead to a dead end, but then again, it could be something. All I'm doing is my job, keeping you up to date."

"Sarah, I appreciate that, really I do. I'll have him followed. Is there anything else?"

"No there isn't."

"OK, I've got to hang up to take care of business. We need to talk again, soon, for a more full report."

"I'm available when you are."

"I'll get back to you this week. Be safe."

Before Sarah leaves the women's restroom, she looks at herself in the mirror. The reflection shows a sharp contrast with someone her age who has not been subjected to her life's experiences, both personal and career. She steps closer to the mirror's image, leans over to get a better view. She blinks a few times in response to the bright light above the wash basin. Then, hesitantly, she gently touches her face with one finger as if worried something horrifying would happen with the action. She strokes her skin. She turns toward the touch and moves her lips. "My God," she whispers. She takes in a deep breath, steps back from the mirror, and puts aside the thought. "I've got a job to do." She walks out of the women's restroom.

«‹«»›»

Sarah moves to her workstation, sits, and stares at the packet of leads printed on three-by-five cards in front of her. She is temporarily detached from the moment, still thinking of the image of herself in the mirror, just a few moments ago. Inner thoughts are interrupted. She senses someone nearby, so she slowly turns around in her chair.

"We're worried," Karen says.

"Yeah, both of us are," Dick agrees.

Sarah slowly transitions out of her state of self-concern. Her face slowly turns into a tiny smile as she draws back her mouth at the corners. She keeps quiet for a while, and then asks, "I'm sorry, I was preoccupied with another thought. What did you say?"

"Are you OK?" Karen asks.

Sarah is confused. Wrinkles appear on her forehead. "Why would you ask that?"

Dick chimes in, "You just look worried, maybe even a little sick."

Sarah shrugs off the matter. "That's just how I look when I'm concentrating. Sorry about that, there's nothing wrong with me."

Dick looks warily at Karen, "OK, if you say so."

Karen gets back into the conversation. "But we are worried."

Sarah asks, "If not about me, then who or what?"

Karen glances at Dick who says, "Go ahead Karen."

Karen continues. "We don't think this place is what it claims to be. There's something fishy going on here, but we can't put our finger on it. We know it's just our feelings, but haven't you had feelings that you couldn't explain, but that had meaning?"

Sarah nods her head, "Of course, everybody has."

Dick eagerly adds, "That's what we're saying about this place."

Sarah wants to know more. "Give me an example. That could help."

Dick speaks first, "Take for the example Vince Allen, the guy who trained us. He was supposed to be one of the big shots around here, but right after the training he disappeared. Nobody talked about him, they still don't. It's as if he never existed. I sensed he and Jim Ranger were real close to one another, but Jim never mentioned a word about his whereabouts."

Karen interrupts, "And then Jim Ranger disappeared. Isn't he the owner of this place? Where is he?"

Dick quickly butts in, "And what do you make of the security checks? Come on, what's so secure in this building that we've now got to have security checks? Don't you see how this all adds up?"

Sarah asks, "What does it add up to?"

Karen voices the weak point in their argument, "That's it, we don't know."

"On the other side, they seem to want to save Tommie and me from getting fired. Why would they ask Matt to coach us if they don't want us to succeed?"

"We're not disputing they don't want us to succeed. Come on, if we sell, they make money. That's not what we're saying," Dick is convinced he is making a strong enough line of reasoning.

"Where's Tommie? He's now disappeared." Karen continues to make a case for Dick's and her point of view.

"It's all circumstantial. But that's just my opinion." Sarah nods her head sideways. "I'm sorry, I don't buy it."

Dick gives it one more try. "What was so important that Matt had to leave so quickly?"

"We all heard him talk with his father. It sounded like an important family matter. If a family member called you in an urgent sort of way, wouldn't you drop everything? I would, and I think so would you." Sarah's voice is not as convincing as she would like, not confident sounding, just middle-of-the-road.

CHAPTER 8

"Everyone does something in their life that they regret. Some people kick their dog. Some people lie in their resumes, whatever it is that people do when they're upset, confused, or desperate. You know what I mean?"

Tommie Gray stares downward at the floor, unwilling to say anything until his appointed lawyer shows up.

Detective Gatto continues. "I'm not totally sure why people kill other people. That's always been a mystery to me. You know what I'm saying?"

Tommie keeps quiet.

Gatto resumes. "I know this is an awfully difficult time. You don't have any previous arrests, so something must have triggered this. You know what I mean?"

Tommie makes a fist with one hand and grinds it into the other hand.

"I assume you don't have any enemies at work, at least those that you know of. At least that's what I think. You know what I'm saying?"

Tommie feels the rhythm of his heart pick up.

"Or that you owe some loan shark a few thousand dollars that you can't pay because you've got a gambling habit. You know what I mean?"

Tommie feels a little weak in his arm muscles.

"Or maybe your lady is asking for more than what you can afford. You don't want to lose her because she's good to you. You do what you gotta do. You know what I'm saying?"

Tommie begins to bite his fingernails.

"Maybe your lady really isn't the lady you thought she was. You found out she's some slut, she's been sleeping around." He smacks his lips. "Huh?"

Tommie's muscle weakness turns into shortness of breath and sweating.

"Maybe she left you but you still gotta pay child support for the kid you had with her. You know what I'm saying?"

Tommie's face turns pale, his pupils dilate, and he falls forward onto the floor losing consciousness.

««()»»

Area Director Jackson Law heads to **The Body Shoppe**. He parks in a crowded parking lot across the street and makes his way inside the place.

Deep in his own thoughts for the moment, he barely is aware of the pole dancers entertaining the crowd. He doesn't stop for a few minutes to watch the women as his custom, nor does he fantasize about spending an hour or so with anyone of them as done many times before. He looks to the back of the room where two large men are stationed to screen on who enters and who is kept out. Law recognizes both guards. He heads their way.

"Hi, Anthony and Philip." Law stops in front of the two men. "You've got a decent night going."

Philip nods while Anthony answers, "After a while they all seem the same."

"Can you let me in to see Crystal? I'm expected."

Anthony nods OK to Philip who opens the door.

As Law walks past the two men, he says, "Thanks, have a good evening."

Law enters a dimly lit room, a place he's been to many times before. The door behind him clicks shut. He takes a few steps to the left in spite of the darkness. He smells a mixture of scents that are intended to arouse one's sexual desires. He suppresses his own cravings for the time being.

Out of the shadows he hears a voice. "Jackson, I can smell your presence. Come here, join me."

Just at the sound of her voice, he feels his hunger for her increase. His body warms up. Yet, he resists losing control. "Crystal, I've never figured out how you do it."

"You're too inhibited to be emancipated from your restrictions. You'd be a better cop if you would only loosen up."

"It's not as easy as you make it out to be."

"Nothing is impossible to a willing heart, mind, and soul." She tosses something to him.

He extends his hand to catch the object. He looks at the ornament, and then wrinkles his forehead.

"It's a violet star Italian love charm."

He looks up, "Why this for me?"

"You're missing love in your life. You know it, I know it, and we both know it isn't going to be found here."

He walks close enough to Crystal to kiss her on the cheek. "If things were only different," he says with exasperation.

"Don't try to change what you cannot change." Her eyes sparkle and her mouth is drawn back at the corners. "What brings you here?"

He takes in a deep breath, clenches the love charm in his hand and begins. "I'm looking for someone who might frequent **The Body Shoppe**. I was hoping you'd help me."

"Now, now, Jackson, we've gone over this before. I don't snitch on my customers. They come here anonymously and leave the same way. Otherwise, it would ruin my business."

"I respect that, I really do, but this is an exception, a one-time exception that I hope you'll agree to. Let me explain."

"OK, but I am highly biased against it. Let me make that perfectly clear." She leans back into an oversized chair that is covered with a silk cloth wrapping of red roses. "Go on, I'm listening."

"His current name is Jim Ranger, although he's had many other names. In a nutshell, he's a con artist, an experienced expert in scanning money from naive investors, mostly the elderly. He's set up an operation in town and I'm trying to close him down."

"What an asshole! Why can't people make money legitimately! What does he look like?"

"He's 47 years old, in good physical condition with broad shoulders and a square jaw. He's about six one to six two, with blue eyes and straight teeth. He wears contact lenses. There are no noticeable scars or tattoos that I'm aware of. He dresses very stylish. His personality is over the top as he appears to be honest and earnest, but deep down he's a snake in the grass!"

"You sound emotionally fixated on this guy. Why so attached?"

"He's a crook that takes advantage of people, especially those who can't afford to make a financial mistake. He doesn't care one bit."

"OK, Jackson. I'm going to make an exception this one time only. I'll have the guys keep a look out for him, but to be honest, I don't think we'll find him here."

"Why do you say that?"

"He doesn't fit our customers' profile."

"You're created a customer profile?"

"Jackson, please. I've got my M. B. A. in Marketing and Psychology from Northwestern University Kellogg Graduate School of Management. I know who my target market is. Hell, I'm a businesswoman who's got to differentiate from my competitors. Just come into this place any day of the week, Sunday through Saturday. We're packed to the gills. I offer people, mostly men, something they want. And I do it better than the competition. Please, give me some credit."

"I didn't mean to offend you, I just meant . . ."

"I know you didn't mean to offend me, none taken." She smiles. "Now that our business is settled, can I do anything else for you? You look awfully stressed. Maybe I can relieve some of the tenseness, my way." She places her hand on his knee.

««»»

Agent Castillo sits inside his unmarked car, spots Matt leave the lower level garage parking elevator to walk towards a dark blue Honda Crosstour EX. He hears the sound of car doors unlock prompted from an electronic device, and then watches Matt climb into the car. Castillo turns on the engine of his vehicle.

Too engrossed in other thoughts, Matt does not notice Castillo follow him close behind.

The drive is short, not over five miles, but too long to walk. Matt pulls into a jam-packed parking lot that serves a local grocery store. He circles the lot a few times until he spots a late model Chevy Camaro with a white cloth dangling outside the driver side window. He smiles, "That's my dad." Unable to find an open space close to the Camaro, he stops along the vehicle. "There's a spot two aisles over. I'll park and come back." He sees his father nod, and then he drives off.

Through a high powered camera lens Castillo watches at a distance. At the right moments, he takes several digital photos.

Within a minute Matt jumps into the passenger side of the Camaro. Slightly out of breath from excitement, he says, "What's going on? You sounded concerned, very concerned." He stares at his father. "You look like you lost a fight, big time, what happened?"

Jim Ranger gives his son a big smile. "Nothing to worry about. I should have weaved instead of bobbed." He returns the stare at his son. "It's good to see you. How are you doing?"

"I'm doing fine. The question is how are you doing?" He looks closely at his dad and then fixates at the open cut on his dad's head. "That's looks cruel. Does it hurt?" He points to the gash.

"Just a slight bruise, I've got to be careful when I walk underneath ladders." He forces a smile that doesn't fool either one. "I've got more important matters to talk with you about. First, does anyone suspect who you are?"

"No, I'm positive. Why, do you?"

"I'm not yet sure, but there is a distinct possibility. What's going on with the business, the executive group, and all the sales people?"

"You know I don't have access to the financial records, but I do know that one of the sales reps is going to be coached by me to improve, or else the executive group says she'll be history."

"Which one, Sarah or Karen?"

"Sarah."

"I'm surprised, Vince thought she was going to be one of our superstars."

"That honor belongs to me, your son. Evidently I'm number one in sales, the others are acceptable, but Tommie and Sarah are below expectations."

"You're not coaching Tommie?"

"Funny you should ask that. He's AWOL, didn't come to work today. Nobody knows where he is. It's a mystery."

"I'm not surprised about Tommie. I told Vince that I didn't think he should pass through. His personality just seemed a bit unstable and his work history too erratic. But, I gave into Vince's assessment. He has been usually correct in the end. I now don't think Tommie is going to return, so I wouldn't worry about coaching him."

"Whatever happened to Vince? He's not around. We sales people sort of miss him, he was good to us."

"Loyalty, my son, loyalty."

"Huh?"

"He switched loyalties. I uncovered disturbing information about him, someone who had been my long time friend and ally. At first I was shocked. When I got over it, I was angry. Then finally, I had to get even. He's gone and won't return ever again."

"Why won't he return?"

"He won't be able to."

Matt pauses for a second, and then his eyes widen, "You killed him!"

"There's only one way to solve a cancer, you have to totally get rid of it so that it never comes back. That's just how it's done."

"Oh." Matt's opened eyes remain frozen.

"Don't be shocked."

"I guess I am. I mean, I never thought people would actually be killed in what we do."

"Well, that's how it is."

"Yes, I understand that now." He swallows deeply. "You didn't kill him, did you? Someone else did, right?"

"It doesn't matter who did it, it's done, so forget about it. Tell me about Sarah. Have you slept with her?"

His eyebrows rise. Matt looks surprised from the unexpected question. His jaw noticeable drops as if there is no tension around his mouth. For a fraction of a second he is speechless, followed by slight confusion.

"Come on son, she is an attractive young woman. Have you?"

He gets over being startled, "Yes, once."

"Do you have future plans for her?"

"Why does that matter?"

His father gives a grim stare. "Just give me an answer."

Matt keeps quiet.

Jim's scowl is now threatening looking.

Matt finally answers. "Not at the moment."

"Don't confuse business with pleasure, they rarely mix. Call this exchange a coaching moment between father and son."

Matt settles down. "I understand."

"Stay away from her. She'll hurt you."

There is a moment of silence that slices through their conversation.

Matt asks, "When are you coming back to work?"

"I've got a few more things to take care of before I return. I think Reggie, Teddy, Marshall and David are running the place OK for now. I'd guess in a week or two."

Matt isn't sure whether to hug his dad or shake hands, so he waits for a cue to come.

Jim puts a solid hand on Matt's shoulder. "I'm counting on you to stay loyal, we're family and that matters a lot to me."

"Of course, there's no other way." Matt feels his throat constrict a wee bit.

"Alright then, you better get back to work to start coaching Sarah. But keep your distance from her. Remember what I said." He gives a grin. "I'll be in touch."

Matt waits for some further physical contact that does not materialize. "There's nothing else you want to say to me?"

"Why, should there be?"

"I don't know, but when you called I just figured there was something you wanted to tell me."

"Can't a father just talk with his son?"

"Of course, of course."

"Don't let on to anyone that we talked. Do you understand?"

"Perfectly, I understand." Matt swallows with some discomfort. "I still think you should have a doctor take a look at the cut on your head, it looks nasty."

"I'll see what I can do. Now go."

Matt turns his face away so that his dad does not see moisture form at the corners of his eyes. He then opens the door to get back to his car.

««»»

As Castillo keeps a close eye on both men he calls his boss. "You won't believe what I saw!"

Area Director Law says, "Don't keep me waiting."

"Matt met with Jim Ranger. I wonder what their connection is to each other. Do you want me to follow either one?"

"Matt met with Ranger, are you positive?"

"I couldn't be any surer. I've got the photos to prove it. What do you want me to do next?"

"Follow Jim Ranger. Find out where he currently lives. See if he meets anyone else. Then report back to me once you're done."

The phones disconnect as Castillo starts his car's engine to follow Ranger.

The drive takes about thirty minutes to complete. After leaving the parking lot, Castillo goes south on Tanager Drive for about six miles towards Hummingbird Road. Within less than a mile he turns right and then a quick left onto Batiquitos Drive. He follows Ranger for about three and a half miles before he turns right onto El Camino Real that eventually merges into Mesa Blvd. This stretch goes for about five miles until there is a left turn onto Shawline Street, and then after a half mile onto Ronson Road. The road at this point becomes Cardin Street and it is lined with fully grown trees on both sides. He notices Ranger's car slow down, so he duplicates the move. He stops about two houses from where Ranger pulls into a driveway.

Castillo grabs his camera and quickly gets out of his vehicle. He finds a spot behind a tree to hide in the hope that whoever resides at 7192 Cardin Street shows his face so he can take a few photos. The wait is short. An attractive black-haired woman in her late forties answers the door. She and

Ranger hug before he enters the house. Castillo manages to click off five photos to take back to his boss.

Castillo is unable to delay telling his boss about the news. He calls him immediately from his cell. "I'm in my vehicle, outside 7192 Cardin Street. An attractive, I mean very attractive woman met him on the steps. They hugged and kissed, and then they both went into the house. I've got five photos to prove it." He waits for a response, but the only sound he hears is his own breathing.

Law recognizes the address, he knows who lives there. It's the same address he's been to a few times in the past when he and Madeline Courier were more than just friends. He can't believe his ears. "What's the address again?"

"7192 Cardin Street. The house is about fifteen years old, while stucco exterior, . . ."

"I don't need that information." He is irritated, his voice sounds harsh and severe. "Get back here as quickly as possible. I want to see the photos."

"I can send them electronically if you want."

"No, I don't fully trust the Internet. Get back here now."

Castillo knows when his boss is upset about something, but in this case he doesn't know exactly the cause. "Yes sir. I'm on my way now." He hears the phones disconnect.

««»»

Law is furious about the surprise, a real eye-opener. He bangs his fist on the desk. Not in a million years would he think that Madeline and Jim would hook up. "I should have taken the opportunity with her a long time ago. Stupid me, stupid!" He shakes his head, incensed. His thoughts turn to various ways to get to the bottom of it, to track down Jim Ranger in order to put him away for a very long time, and to get the full picture of what she sees in him. He considers turning the tables on both of them right now, to go to her place to confront them. He would demand that they tell him everything. He stands to walk around his office, to calm down, to better figure things out.

By the time he circles his office a few times he settles down. "What the hell am I thinking about. I'm acting like an adolescent who's hurt because his former girlfriend is seeing another guy. Christ, how juvenile is this?"

Once he stops walking he notices an unlit table lamp in the corner of his office. He walks towards the fixture to turn it on but the bulb remains unlit. He stares at the bulb. "Fuck you."

Law returns to take a seat behind his desk. He taps his fingers against the desk's top and then pulls out a side drawer. He reaches to the back of the drawer to withdraw an unmarked envelope. Slowly he opens it to take a look at a photo of him and Madeline happily together during one of their past vacations in the mountains. He draws a long breath of air and slowly lets it out. His fingers clench the photo tightly, a reminder of their good times together. He stays in the emotional state of mind for a few more seconds, and then he snaps out of it. He places the photo into the envelope, and then returns it to the same safe place, hoping in a weird way to forget her and the way it was between them.

CHAPTER 9

Later that night, Sarah drives to her one bedroom apartment after an hour of intense physical exercise at an all-night gym. She heads for the mail box to see if there is anything of interest. "All junk mail," she says aloud as she flips the mailings into a nearby trash can. Next, she heads to the front door, anxious to shower in her own place rather than at the one in the gym. Her mind returns to the conversation with Karen and Dick earlier in the day. She wonders if she's missing something that is so obvious to them, in spite of her knowing what really is going on in the office. "I need real evidence, not hunches." Her head starts to buzz with a bit of confusion. She opens the front door and walks inside.

Her route to the bathroom where the shower is located takes her past a small table where she places her keys and cell phone. She stretches her arms above her head to pull the kinks out of her muscles and reset her bone joints. She hears a few clicking sounds that signals the self-adjustment worked. She feels a bit relieved from the exercise.

Sarah undresses, tosses her clothes on the floor, too tired to be tidy for the moment. She twists the shower's knob to let the water heat up to the right temperature before she steps inside. The warm water pulsates in just the right way to make her feel good. She stays under the liquid stream for a full fifteen minutes before stepping out of the shower to wipe her body dry.

She heads for a wicker basket near her queen sized bed to grab a large light blue colored cotton pullover. She pulls it over her body, and then takes a deep breath of satisfaction. Now staring at her bed, she grows restless. Her mind returns to the earlier conversations at work. She heads for the kitchen.

Sarah opens the refrigerator not looking for anything in particular, which is exactly what she finds, not much of a selection to choose form. "Pathetic," she shakes her head. She shuts the door and stares at it for a moment. Then something pops into her head. She turns to open a cabinet door underneath the sink. "Yes," she spots a single bottle of Croix de Marsan Bordeaux, 2010. With hesitation she takes hold of the bottle and looks at it with slight apprehension. "Maybe I shouldn't." She begins to return the bottle to its original spot, yet continues to stare at it. "Only one drink, that's all I'll take, one glass of wine." While her words suggest one attitude her face shows skepticism.

Within minutes she sits in a kitchen chair sipping the wine. Then her cell phone rings. The unexpected sound almost causes her to drop the glass onto the kitchen floor. She glances in the direction of the sound, speculates at who would be calling her at this hour of the night. Sarah walks toward the cell phone, stares at it, thinks over what to do. She does not recognize the caller ID. Part of her wants to pick up, but part of her says to let it go to voice message. The phone rings another time and once more. She picks up. After only one glass of wine her speech is slurred, "Hello?"

There is subdued music in the background, yet she hears no person on the other end of the call. "Hello, who's this?" Again, there is a muffled sound, and then a click as the phones disconnect.

««»»

Matt looks at his cell phone, and coughs. A tear forms at the corner of his left eye. With his other hand he lifts a glass of Jim Beam to his mouth to take a long swallow. His face is twisted in a desperate looking expression. "Bartender, give me another." He is drunk.

"Don't you think you've had enough?" A woman in her early fifties walks closer to him. "I can call you a cab to take you home."

"I . . . don't . . . wanna . . . go . . . 'ome." Matt's stare is glassy.

"I think you've had enough. I'm calling a cab."

"No, don't."

She turns her back to reach for a nearby phone to make a call.

In the meantime, Matt wobbles away from the bartender, almost trips over his own feet. Within a few seconds he falls against a chair inside the bar and topples onto the floor. He passes out.

««»»

The next day Matt makes it to work, although his mind is not functioning fully, the remnants of last night's drinking binge keeps him off balance. Noticeable weariness is in full view as he slowly walks to his workstation, his eyes are partially open and puffiness is evident just beneath his eyes. He lets his body flop in the chair, and then he lets out a grunt.

Sarah turns towards him. "You look like crap." She gets a whiff of alcohol that still clings to his body. "And you smell worse." She is not feeling her usual self after finishing off the entire bottle of wine last night.

"One of those nights," he mumbles. "You don't look so great yourself." His stare is a blank look and his breathing is deep and painful. "I need a cup of coffee." He stands too quickly, he almost falls over. He steadies himself by placing a hand on top of the desk. Slowly, he walks towards a coffee making machine.

Sarah's forehead wrinkles, wondering if she should offer help. In the end she leaves him alone until he returns. She massages her forehead to relieve some tension.

With a cup of coffee in each hand, he offers one to Sarah. His hands wobble just enough to spill some coffee on the floor. "Here, I brought this for you." He sits in his chair, and then takes a sip from the paper cup. He closes his eyes as the beverage makes its way down his throat. He lets out a slight sigh of relief.

"Is there something you want to tell me?"

He keeps silent for a second, and then shakes his head, "Nothing. Is there something you want to ask me?"

"Yeah, when are you going to train me? I don't have much time. If I remember what you said, I only have a few days. Time is running out."

"Two days, that's the amount. Two days." He raises two fingers in the air.

"We're in day one and it appears to me by looking at you that you're not in the best shape to start training me."

"It'll be OK. I'm good at what I do." He takes another sip of coffee, this time it's bigger. "Did I mention that you don't look so great yourself?" He clears his throat. "But, I'm feeling better already."

She puts aside his observation of her. "Does that mean we're starting now?"

He turns to face Sarah. "Yeah, but there is something I've got to tell you. Follow me into the hallway." He stands, coffee cup still in his hand, and heads for the office door.

She grabs her cup of coffee and follows close behind.

Now in the hallway where no one else is around, Matt begins. "This isn't easy for me to say, but I've got to say it." He takes another sip from the cup.

Sarah maintains a blank stare all the while.

"I called you last night from a bar. I was blitzed beyond belief."

"So that was you!" Her stare is no longer neutral looking, closer to anger. Her eyes widen.

"Yes, I'm sorry."

"Go on, why were you calling me, to apologize for something?"

"Not exactly, I was reaching out for help." His voice is toned-down and serious sounding.

"Oh."

"This has to be between us, no one else. Will you promise me?"

She puckers her lips, not sure she wants to agree to anything before she hears him out. "Tell me first, and then I'll decide."

He looks away and then back towards her. His eyes now look sad and gloomy. "I think my father has done horrible things." He starts to cry. His hands shake almost to the point of losing a firm grip on the coffee cup. Fortunately the cup is almost empty so no harm is done to stain the carpet below.

Surprised, Sarah extends one hand to touch him. "Oh."

He takes in a deep breath of needed air and then resumes. "I think he killed Vince. I have my suspicions about his reasons so I'm not totally sure."

Her mouth opens wide, surprised to hear. "Do you know what you're saying?"

"Yes I do. I never thought my father would do something like that, kill another man. I mean he hasn't lived a wholesome life, I know that, but to kill someone . . ." His voice trails off.

"Do you have any proof?"

He shakes his head, "None, other than Vince isn't around here."

"Why are you telling me?"

"I don't know who else to turn to."

"But me, I'm not a cop. I'm just trying to earn a living by working here, just like you."

"There's no one else I trust."

"Who's your father?"

"You know him."

"I do, who?"

"Jim Ranger, he's my father."

"No!"

"Yes."

"Was he the one who called you yesterday, that took you away from the office so unexpectedly?"

"Yeah, that's him."

"And that's when you figured out, or maybe just assumed, that he killed Vince."

He looks squarely at her, "Yeah."

"Are you asking me a question or do you want me to do something? I still don't know why you're telling me this."

"There's more."

She breathes in through her nose and slowly lets out the air. "Go on, I'm listening."

"I think he'd kill again, anyone who gets in his way. I'm afraid he might kill me if I stepped out of line."

She twists her nose to the side. "Why you, do you know something that you've got to keep secret?"

"I never thought it would get to this point. I mean, taking money from people is one thing but killing is something else."

"Matt, what are you saying?"

He waves one hand around, "This place."

"What about this place?"

"We're stealing money from unsuspecting people!" His voice climbs to a higher volume.

"Stealing, is that what you said?"

"Stealing, swindling, cheating, call it what you want, but that's what this operation is all about. We're being dishonest with everyone we talk to. There's no financial payoff for the people we call, nothing. It's a con game. That's what my father does, that's who he is. He's been that way all his life and he got me hooked into it. I'm as guilty as him."

She recovers quickly from hearing his admission. "Then go to the cops. That's what I'd do. Tell them everything you know."

"I'm afraid of what may happen to me."

"I'm sure they'd offer you protection and a reduced charge if you cooperate with them."

"How do you know that, are you a cop?"

She puckers her lips and then confidently says, "Come on, do I look like a cop?"

"I don't know, other than those in uniform, I've never met one, especially an undercover cop."

169

"Matt, be assured that I'm not one of them, but I think you should go to the police."

"I've got to think about that. It might be best that I keep my mouth shut or else take off to hide."

"Could you live with yourself if you did either one? I mean, you seemed very upset when we first started talking, but now you want to forget about it."

"I guess I'm not sure."

"What about the others?"

"Who are you talking about?"

"The others who work in the office," she waves her hand toward the office door. "According to you, they're all involved in cheating people out of their hard earned money. Are you going to let them continue doing that?"

"What they don't know won't hurt them. They're all getting paid to do a job. I've got to take care of myself, to think about what I should do."

"What about the executives, are they in on it as well?"

"Of course they are, but they don't know about me."

"What's that supposed to mean, about you?"

"They don't know I'm his son. You're the only one who knows that, only you."

"And what about me, how do you think I feel knowing that I'm swindling people?"

He forces a half-grin, "You're not doing a very good job at it, so I wouldn't worry. You can always quit."

"It isn't that easy."

"Why?"

"I've got ethics, a conscience, I know right from wrong. I couldn't continue doing it if I believed it was wrong, both legally and ethically."

"Then you should quit right now. No one will question you since you're already on a sort of probation."

"It's not that easy. I know what I know because you told me. How do you know I won't tell the cops?"

"You don't have any proof, no evidence, nothing, only what I've said."

She turns her face away from Matt and then back towards him. "I'm taking a sick day today to think things over. At least I'll have one day to figure out what I want to do before the two days are up."

««»»

Early the next morning, Saturday, Sarah's cell phone rings. She turns over in bed to check the time, 2:30 AM. She rolls back to her other side and pulls the bed sheet over her head. The cell rings again. "Shit." She stays motionless in the hope that she can will the caller to hang up. It doesn't work out that way as she hears a third ring. "Go to voice mail," she says. The ring sounds a fourth time. "Crap, this better be good." She extends her arm to reach the phone. Groggy and with an unsteady voice she asks, "Yeah, who's this?" At first there is silence, but then there is the sound of someone crying. She repeats the question, "Who's this?"

"I'm sorry to call." The voice sounds weakened and confused.

"Who is this?" She sits up in bed.

"I should never have told you anything. It's my fault, all my fault."

"Matt, is this you?"

"I just want to say thanks for listening to me. You didn't have to but you did. You won't see me again."

"Matt, what do you mean?"

"It's all going to end."

Suddenly, Sarah gets his point. Her eyes open wide. "Don't do anything foolish. Wait until I get there."

"There's no more time, no more talk, there's only action."

"Please, don't do it!"

"I'm hanging up."

"Please, wait until I get there. Then we'll talk."

He slowly points the revolver at his head. "Good bye."

"Matt, wait!"

Bang! The instant the bullet enters Matt's head he is dead.

"Matt, talk to me!"

Silence.

"Matt, are you there? Talk to me."

Silence.

Sarah disconnects the phone to call 911.

««»»

When Sarah arrives at Matt's apartment complex there is an ambulance, two clearly marked police cars, and two reporters from the media. A crowd of apartment dwellers mingle outside the building. She parks a little away from it all to avoid any attention to herself. She recognizes Officers Gabnowski and Sabatini from an earlier situation at Ranger's house. She walks directly to them. "Hi, I'm Agent Noble." She shows them her badge.

Gabnowski looks at the emblem, a bit surprised. He does not recognize her. "What's with the F. B. I.?"

"Could be nothing, but we were informed of a suicide that might have some relevance to a case we're working on."

Sabatini peeks at her badge, and then glances at Gabnowski. Finally he looks at Sarah. "If it were me, I'd turn it over to you."

She raises both hands, palms towards the two officers. "Oh no, I'm not asking for it. I'm just here to observe."

"We know as little as you do as to what happened here. It seems a guy took his own life. Somebody called it in. We were the closest so we got the call." Gabnowski turns to Sabatini, "Isn't that right."

Sabatini nods his head, "That's about what happened."

She studies their faces as an automatic reflex. "Mind if I look around?"

Sabatini replies, "Sure. If you find something relevant, let us know. Will you do that?"

"Cross my heart." She smiles and then walks towards Matt's apartment.

Standing outside Matt's apartment door is a third police officer. She stops. "Hi, I'm Agent Noble. Mind if I step inside?" She takes out her badge.

The officer is a big man with a barrel chest, large hands, and dark brown eyes. An assortment of police gear around his waist accentuates his girth dimension. He takes a look at the badge. "Be my guest." He glances in the direction of the door. He appears disinterested at first.

As Sarah walks past him, he keeps his eyes glued to her.

Now inside the apartment she quickly scans its interior to see it to be tidy and neat, just as it was when she was with him the one time. About to move to Matt's bedroom two paramedics get in her way as they carry out a body-bag containing a corpse. She steps aside to let them pass. No words exchange between her and them. After they leave, she enters Matt's room alone to look around. "Damn," she says softly, "what a shame." She notices blood on the bed sheets and some splattering on the wall. She spots an opened pack of gum, an opened bottle of Jim Beam, and a dirty glass on top of a night stand. She breathes in some air and then shakes her head sideways. "Damn."

"Hey, Agent Noble, you gotta go now. Sorry, but I've got my orders." The big man with the barrel chest stands at the bedroom door.

She looks up, "Sure I understand." She walks towards him. "Terrible isn't it that a person takes his own life."

He shrugs his shoulders. "It happens more often than most people think. There are more suicides these days than fatal car accidents. It's on the rise for some reason. My guess is that some people are so desperate that they believe they have no other choice."

"I don't think I'd have the guts." She says.

"I guess that's the difference between you and him."

««»»

She checks her watch, 3:45 AM, not sure of the value to call her boss about what's happened. Moreover, she's not emotionally ready. She gets into her car to drive around a while to collect her thoughts. An early morning film of moisture gently floats across the road. She feels chilled inside the car, so she turns on its heater to warm up. Gradually the car's inside temperature reaches seventy-two degrees.

As Sarah drives she looks back into the rear view mirror, something she's got accustomed to since becoming a F. B. I. Agent, a security measure the Bureau's Chief Instructor told her would reduce exposure to danger. No one is behind. The streets are mostly empty at this time of morning.

She catches a glimpse of a van that slows down in front of various retail outlets and then speeds up. Through the driver side window the driver tosses a plastic bag that contains promotional marketing literature at each doorstep that will most likely be tossed in the garbage before reading. Although she is not familiar with this neighborhood she suspects this is a daily or weekly routine. She drives on.

Up ahead she notices a diner that is bustling. The parking lot is jammed. She quickly calculates the odds are slim of finding an empty parking space, so she considers driving on. She has no intention to park blocks away or even circle back a few times in hope that a space would open up. Then, by chance, a driver pulls out of a spot. She swerves her car into the lot to park.

After shutting off the engine, she sits still for a few seconds, watching through the diner's front windows the goings on inside. People are talking with one another in a happy manner. They seem to be in good spirits. She suddenly feels sad that she does not share their joy. The corners of her mouth depress downward.

As she continues to survey them a man wearing a blue shirt with an insignia below the left pocket exits the place. His pants are navy blue and he wears black shoes with rubber soles. He stretches his arms above his head and turns his head in a circular motion. He puts his hands into his pants pockets, smells the morning air, and then walks towards a truck parked next to her.

She now recognizes the emblem as two crossed golf clubs with the phrase, **Manager - La Costa**, written below.

He nods his head her way. He appears calm. His face is darkish with rounded features that are framed by short closely cut dark curly hair. His skin is blemish free. His physique is muscular and he appears in good shape. He is about six feet tall with brown eyes. A handsome man, but in a crowd he would not stand out. The sound of his voice is deep toned with clear articulation. "They've got a new special. You've got to try it while it lasts."

Sarah smiles but keeps silent, not sure what to say even if she wanted to.

He gets into the truck. Within a few seconds he pulls away.

Sarah's loneliness and sadness continues for another few seconds. She takes in a deep breath, and then slowly lets out the air. She decides against entering the diner. She'd rather feel bad by herself, alone, with no one around. She checks her watch again, 4:05 AM, not much time has passed. She restarts her car and pulls out of the lot to figure some other way to get rid of the blues she's feeling.

She reaches to turn on the radio for some company. An early morning talk show host is explaining his conspiracy theory of an attack on Earth from beings of another place in outer space. Sarah quickly presses the radio's **SCAN** button for alternative stations. Each choice is worse than the former. Frustrated, she shuts the radio off.

She eyes the rear view mirror to spot a large vehicle approaching at a fast speed. Red lights swirl on top of the truck and then she hears sirens. She pulls off to the side of the road to allow the fire truck to safely pass followed by an ambulance. Her curiosity is not heightened at the moment, so she chooses not to follow the vehicles, but rather to drive around for a while before she calls her boss. She pulls away from the curb and drives a few miles.

She drives around for another hour.

Up the street she spots another all night diner. In contrast to the place she just left, there is only one parked car, a late model white Ford Galaxy, in front of this place. There is nowhere to park behind the building. The diner appears empty of customers. A defective neon sign above the small building blinks erratically yet she makes out the name,

McHale's. She opts to find out what's cooking at *McHale's*. She parks next to the Galaxy.

A bell rings as Sarah opens the door to walk into *McHale's*. She surveys from one corner of the place to another. No one seems to be around. "Hello, anybody here?" She touches her revolver strapped in a hip holster, an automatic reaction when she senses the possibility of threat. "Hello, anybody here?"

A sleepy sounding voice from behind a wall is heard. "Yeah, be right there."

She looks in the direction of the voice. Then she quickly moves her jacket to cover the gun and holster.

A stout man with gray hair opens a door. He rubs his eyes and then looks at Sarah. "Hi doll."

Sarah stares at the man as if she knows him from someplace but cannot put her finger on it. She steps forward.

The stout man meets her half way. "What's a nice looking girl like you doing out this time of the morning. Coming or going?" His smile shows off pearly white dentures. He rubs the stubble on his chin as he gives Sarah a good look over.

"Have we met before?"

"Sure would like to say yes, but unfortunately for me, I don't think so."

"You look awfully familiar, as if we've met before, sometime ago, somewhere."

"I get that a lot." He tilts his head to the side towards a photo of a man in a U. S. Navy uniform.

She takes a good look at the photo. "Is that you?"

"Don't I wish it was me," he grins her way. "I wouldn't be here, that's for sure, if that was me."

"But I've seen that man before, I know I have."

"See many movies, the old ones, not the crap that's out today?"

"I like the old television ones, great stories with great acting."

"That's exactly what I mean. No special effects, nobody's ass or boobs flopping around. Yeah, exactly what I mean." His face lights up.

"So spare me the guessing game, who's that in the photo?"

"Remember **McHale's Navy**?"

She hesitates and then quickly recovers, "Yes. That's Ernest Borgnine."

"You earn an A grade. Next question, what was McHale's first name?"

"You've got to be kidding. I have no idea."

"Quinton, he was Quinton McHale, the commanding officer of the naval ship that was stationed on a Pacific Island Base called Taratupa."

"You're a bigger fan than me."

"I almost have no choice." He points at his face. "I look like the guy so much that I can't disappoint others who are curious."

"So you're not related."

"That would be nice."

"You need to take advantage of the similarities between you and him. I mean, you can ramp up advertisement to make this place hopping."

He shrugs his shoulders. "It takes money to make money, something I don't have much of. I'm not into social media but I know it works." He twists his face.

"I wish I could help you out, but that's not where my skills are."

"What do you do?"

Sarah hesitates, not willing to tell the truth. "I'm a student."

He seems interested. "Where?"

"It's an online university, one I'm sure you haven't heard of."

"Online, that means the Internet and computer stuff."

"Totally, it's not for everyone."

"You can say that again."

There is a pause, and then he resumes. "What are you doing out at this time in the morning?"

"I just finished posting a paper online and I'm still keyed up so I thought I'd take a drive around. I can't fall asleep."

He frowns.

"What I mean is I had to submit an academic paper to my instructor who is way across the country. There is a place where I can send it so that he can read it, grade it, and give me feedback. It's all done through the Internet."

"Oh, I see."

She realizes technology is not his strong point, so Sarah changes the topic. "I'm a little hungry. Can you fix me something to eat?"

His face lights up. "What'll you have?"

"What's your specialty?"

It takes him less than a split second to answer. "Frittata."

She wrinkles her forehead. "That's Italian, are you?"

"You don't have to be one to cook like one. There was this guy who I served with in the Navy, his name was Vincent Verrigni, a real wiry kid but wow, could he cook. His strong suit was Italian omelet. He'd throw everything and anything into the pan, always used a dozen of eggs at a time."

"I'm getting hungrier as you talk."

"Are you going to tell me your name and what you really do?"

"I told you I'm a student. I'm Lela."

"Right, I know it's none of my business, so I'll back off. It's hard to fool somebody like me." He turns around to head for the kitchen. "What'll you drink? Black coffee goes perfect with frittata."

Sarah pauses to reconsider telling him the truth, but in the end keeps it to herself. "Black coffee sounds great."

"If you want to come back here with me while I'm cooking, that's OK with me. I don't expect any other customers for a while. You can see how a master does it."

Her eyes open wide to consider the offer. She decides to take him up on the offer. "I'm coming."

"It can get quite hot back here, so you might want to take off your jacket."

She walks into a room smaller than she imagined. The space fits one person nicely but two makes it a tight squeeze. "I'll keep it on. I like the feeling of being warm."

"Open the refrigerator to get me six eggs. I'm hungry all of a sudden. I'll cook enough for two." He pours a quarter cup of extra-virgin olive oil into a twelve-inch skillet that he heats up over a medium-low gas flame. "While you're at it, find some milk. There should be a quart at the back on the second shelf."

Sarah carries out the order without a word. She places the items on a counter top. She watches him dice a half-clove of garlic that is tossed into the skillet. Quickly, the smell of garlic fills the air.

"Do you like peppers? There's a red pepper in the bottom pull-out shelf. I like red peppers."

Without commenting, she returns to the refrigerator to grab the vegetable, and then back to the counter top.

"Slice the pepper into slivers, remove the seeds."

She looks around for an appropriate knife, finds one and starts the process.

He walks to a back shelf to grab a fresh bag of Espresso Coffee Beans. "When you're through with the pepper, grind these beans to a fine grind. That's how it needs to be done. The coffee machine is over there." He nods his head to the left. Then he moves to the refrigerator to take hold of a sealed packet of imported asiago cheese, and finally to a shelf where there is a can of parsley. He shreds a cup of cheese with a hand held grater.

Sarah smiles with joy, fully enjoying sharing the tasks. Other thoughts have been sent to another part of her brain for temporary storage. She feels as if she's been given a peak at Heaven but can only stay a short time.

He looks at the color of the garlic simmering in the heated olive oil. He nods his head to give permission to proceed with the next step. He reduces the heat to low before he adds the sliced pepper to sauté for a short time. He beats the eggs and milk together with a whisk until the mixture is fluffy. Then he pours the egg mixture into the skillet to let cook until the bottom is light brown while the top slightly solidifies. He smiles at Sarah. "This is going to be great." He places a cover over the skillet.

She finishes fixing the coffee to look up. She returns his smile with one of her own. "Yes it is."

Burbling sounds are soon heard as fresh water makes it way over the coffee grinds. Then the smell of freshly brewed espresso coffee fills the air.

"The first cup goes to you. It's good luck." He turns to check on the progress of the frittata. He lifts the cover to take a look see. He grins with pleasure, and waits in silence for a few more minutes. Then he replaces the cover over the skillet.

"Here's your coffee." She hands him a full cup.

His smile stays glued to his face. He reaches for the cup and then raises it at shoulder level, "Salute."

"You sure you're not Italian," she jokes.

He sips the coffee slowly, letting the full flavor touch every taste bud to the fullest amount. "We make a good team, you and me."

She finishes the first sip and then looks directly into his eyes. "You're a good teacher."

They drink their coffees in silence for a few more minutes.

With one hand still holding the coffee cup he moves towards the gas range to check on the food. With his free hand he lifts the cover, leans over to smell the aroma. He places the cover and the cup of coffee on top of a nearby table, only to return to the gas range. He turns off the heat, sprinkles the cheese over the egg mixture, and then gently folds the frittata at three edges careful to bring each edge to the center. He carefully turns the frittata over so that the folded side is down. Silently he counts to ten. His lips barely move. Lastly he slides the finished omelet to a large platter with a final touch of parsley sprinkled on top. He glows at the masterpiece.

"It's looks almost too good to eat," Sarah says.

"It's never too good to eat. Grab two plates, take your coffee, and follow me to a booth. I'll cut it in half. Do you want bread or anything else?"

"No, this is perfect."

They settle into a booth, sitting across from each other. He slides half of the frittata to a plate and gives it to her. "That's yours." He slides the remaining half onto a second plate. "Eat up."

"Buon appetito," she replies.

He looks up, eyes widen. "You speak Italian?"

"Not really, just like you, only a few phrases." She takes a bite, slowly eats, savoring each morsel. "This is wonderful."

He takes a mouthful, and he then leans back in the bench, jaws chewing. His eyes brighten with delight. He swallows and then takes a sip of coffee. "It sure is."

They eat in silence for a short time before Sarah looks at both cups. "I need a refill, how about you?"

He nods his head, "Yes, thanks."

She leaves the table to refill their drinks.

"Do you want to talk about it?" He cuts off another piece of food.

Finished with filling the two cups, she stays put in the kitchen. Sarah clears her throat, "What do you mean." She waits for a response before moving on.

"I'm pretty good at reading people. You're easy to read."

"I don't know what you're talking about."

"Sure you do, there's something bothering you. I saw it immediately in your face when you first came into my diner." He places a piece of the frittata in his mouth to chew.

She slowly walks towards him, "Really?"

"You're settled down quite a bit now. I'm sure it had to do with getting it off your mind. Cooking is one of the best therapies for working out problems."

"Is that right?" She sets both cups on top of the booth's table, and then slides into the bench.

He reaches for the filled cup of coffee, "Yes, that's right." He sips the coffee. "I'm not pressuring you, don't get me wrong, but if you want to say something then just say it. It won't go any further than you and me."

She is not about to reveal the source of her problems, at least not to him, someone she really doesn't know very well. "Everyone has problems, you included." She wonders if he noticed her gun and holster when she first entered the place.

"Of course, but not everyone has the sort of problems you have, me included."

She takes a long sip of coffee to think. She is still not sure it is good bet to talk about anything personal or professional with him. "I don't even know your name."

"What's in a name? Sometimes the best people to talk with are strangers, someone who might have similar interests as well as similar problems. Sometimes the anonymous person is a good listener, more objective, can see things more clearly. You know what I mean, I know you do."

"And you're that type of person, the anonymous third party?"

"I didn't say that, but I could be. You don't know until you try."

"It's personal, something I don't want to get into. Can we drop it?"

"Definitely, not one more word from me." He takes another sip of coffee. "Can I tell you something personal that I haven't told anyone, I mean it, not a single person?"

Relieved the pressure is off her, she says, "Sure, if you want to."

He sets the cup on top of the booth's table. "It was a long time ago, very long ago when I was in the Navy. I had just re-upped because I loved being a sailor. There was nothing else I wanted to do with my life." He pauses to look away and then goes on. "Up to that time I never had to kill anyone, the enemy. I knew though that it was only a matter of time before my luck would run out. It always does, that's what they tell you. So you have to be prepared for the unexpected." He hesitates again. "Anyway, it happened to me when I least expected it. Some sailors are trained to be sharpshooters, like I was, a gunner's mate. You never know when an unidentified boat might try to ram your ship. Sometimes you've got to take them out." He looks directly at Sarah, eyes unblinking. "We were off the coast of Somalia, and got contacted that assistance was required to neutralize a threat on land. There were some Marines who were in trouble, surrounded by the enemy. There was no helicopter support and no other U. S. military force was close enough to assist, except us. This meant a landing force was required. The Officer in Charge took a team of six, himself, a Petty Officer who was me, three seamen and a radioman. Our job was to take out any and all enemies in order to save our fellow warriors. Neutralize them or kill them, whatever it took. I wasn't the only one who was scared as hell, but we went ashore just as we were ordered, just like we were trained. That's what you do, you obey orders without question. Anyway we made our way to where they were pinned down. We spotted the enemy. We knew what we had to do. But guess what?" He pauses.

Sarah's eyes widen. She lifts her shoulders and then slowly lowers them.

He continues. "The enemy was a group of kids with rifles and enough ammo to last a very long time. They were kids who had those Marines cornered. Kids! Can you believe it! Anyway, I crawled alone around behind them, got myself ready to do what I had to do, what I was ordered to do, what I was trained to do. My rifle was ready for fire, but I couldn't do it! I couldn't pull the trigger." He takes in a deep breath of air, and then blows it out. "I could have taken them all out, killed them right then and there." He pauses again for another breath of air. "You know what I did next?"

She shakes her head, no.

"I fired my gun into the air several times as I yelled to them to get out, to get away. I waved them to leave. I don't know if they understood my words, but they understood my meaning because they dropped their guns and ran like bats out of hell." He tilts his head down, eyes now starring at the coffee cup. "I was a coward. I was told to neutralize the enemy, but what I did was save them from being killed. Nobody knew exactly what I did, nobody up until now. I was by myself. Yet, I was awarded a Silver Star. Can you believe that, for courage and bravery? I wasn't a hero at all. I was a scared coward." Slight moisture creeps into his eyes. His head stays tilted downward.

Sarah is speechless for a while. Then she says, "But you did save their lives, didn't you, the Marines."

"I also saved the enemy's lives."

"You said they were kids."

"Kids, adults, what does it matter? They all have the capacity to harm someone else. Those kids were trying to kill Americans, but I let them go."

"I think you did the right thing. You saved the lives of those Marines. You did what you were ordered to do, to neutralize the enemy and to save the Marines. You did both. You got the enemy to leave and the Marines were saved."

"I guess you don't understand, or else you would never say that."

"I guess I don't." She feels the urge to cover his hand with hers, to comfort him, but in the end puts it out of her mind. She looks away, through the windows, to notice the early morning darkness now is partly light. She checks her watch, 6:20 AM. "Want more coffee?"

"No, I've had enough." He stands, piles the individual plates on the platter, and then places the forks and knives on a plate. "I've got to clean up." He walks away.

"I still think you did the right thing."

"Bring the cups to the kitchen sink."

Sarah joins him in the kitchen. "I'm sorry you feel the way you do. I wish I could have been helpful. I wasn't."

He gathers himself together. "It is what it is. Thanks for listening." He places the dishes and utensils into a metal sink. "I'll wash them later." He turns to grab a damp cloth. "I've got to clean up the booth." He walks away.

"I wish I could stay longer, but I've got to go."

"Yeah, more papers to write, I guess."

"This was a great time. Thanks. I'll stop by again, soon, I promise."

"Yeah, a great time," he sniffles a wee bit.

"I think you should consider promoting your place on the Internet, you know like with Facebook and Twitter."

"I have no idea what you're talking about."

"Maybe I can help, not myself personally, but I might know some people who can do it. It wouldn't hurt for me to ask around."

"Yeah, some of your classmates or college professors might be interested."

Sarah decides now is the time to make a clean break. She walks towards him as he continues to swab the booth's table top.

Finished, he stands erect and turns, now face to face with Sarah.

She puts her arms around him, tightens as much as possible. "Thanks for everything. I won't forget you."

He feels moisture creep into his eyes. It feels good, so he does not interfere. "I won't forget you either."

Sarah drops her hands, and finally walks out of the place.

««»»

As keyed up as Sarah is, she is not yet ready to call her boss for an update. The recent time at *McHale's* is something she tells herself she won't be able to put out of her mind for a long time. It's hard to stop thinking about a Navy veteran spilling his guts out to someone younger with dissimilar life experiences. She tries not to dwell on it, but it isn't easy. She wonders if she should have told him about some of the crap she's dealing with. Maybe he would have understood, maybe not. It's too late for any of that; too bad, and too sad.

She thinks about others she knows who might be dealing with issues of greater importance than hers such as those close to Matt who will certainly miss him once they find out about his death. Then there are the victims of the scams that Ranger is responsible for. They'll probably never know it was him who was behind it all. There are of course many others, too numerous to name who have felt or who are feeling some sort of pain more severe than her.

She concludes after all her inner dialogue that she isn't that bad off. She continues to drive around for another thirty minutes before she heads back to her lonely apartment where no one waits for her to return.

CHAPTER 10

The next day over lunch at a small inconspicuous place Sarah updates Area Director Law about the latest incidences.

Silently he thinks about what he has just heard, not revealing what specifically he may be mulling over. He continues to sip on a bowl of minestrone soup as Sarah picks on her salad. "Pass the sticks, please," he says as he nods his head towards the bread basket.

As hyper as she feels, Sarah silently shoves the basket his way.

He snaps the stick in half with one chomp of the baked bread. He chews it until there is nothing left in his mouth. Then he takes care of the second half with the same competent proficiency. He leans back in his chair. "If I hadn't been around the block a few times, I'd conclude this is all far-fetched, more in line with a good novel or movie. But that's not how I'm thinking." He pauses, takes another sip of soup, and then resumes. "What would you do if we switched shoes?" He tilts his eyes towards her.

Turning the table surprises Sarah, yet she quickly starts reflecting on the situation. "We've got to look after the victims so they can get their money back, and we have to shield future people from being scammed."

"That's good thinking. That might just be the real long term problem. But more immediately, we've got to put Ranger behind bars." He pauses and then repeats his idea. "That's really our immediate problem. The question is how do we best to it? What do you think?"

"It seems the more time that passes, the greater chances are that Ranger will disappear. I mean, we don't know where he is right at the moment, do we."

He tightens his lips, unwilling to tell her of the photos he's seen of him and Madeline. "That's right, not at the moment."

"Eventually, Ranger is going to find out about his son's suicide. My hunch is at that time he's going to make a run for it, to get away all together." Her voice quivers.

He looks squarely at her. "Look at me."

She raises her eyes to meet his head-on. "What?"

"Are you alright?"

Her lips shiver and her vision blurs. "I don't think I can go on."

He frowns, "What does that mean?"

"I don't think I can continue as an undercover Agent. It's getting to me."

"What happened?"

"Matt's suicide, I think that's what did it." Her face looks desperate.

"A transfer, is that what you want, to some other case, maybe a desk job, is that what you want?"

"You were right all along. I'm not cut out for this. I've been fooling myself."

"Can you hang in there until we get Ranger? It shouldn't be long."

"Are you saying you can't do it without me?"

"What I'm saying is that you're the only one inside who knows what's really going on. If you pull out now, they'll suspect something and disappear. We're so close, so very close."

She takes in a deep breath of air and slowly lets it escape. "OK, but this is it. No more undercover after this case. Promise me."

Relieved, Law agrees, "You've got my word on it."

Sarah lets her shoulders drop, liberated from future similar assignments.

Law quickly gets back to the case. "We also have to worry about the others, Ward, Deaton, Shea and Crum."

She takes a little time to restart her engine before she backs up his idea. "I see your point, they too may take off."

He quickens the pace of the conversation to keep her engaged. "And we'll never know about Allen."

In a short time she is up to speed. "And we'll not be able to make whole those who were scammed."

"Sarah, they may never be made whole regardless if those responsible are found guilty."

"What do you mean?"

"Somebody has to pay the victims their lost money. If the company Ranger is operating doesn't have the money for whatever reason, then there is no way they will be reimbursed. The Government isn't their banker."

"So what you're saying is we have little time before we act."

"Right, we have to ramp up our resources now or else these guys will be gone, moved on to some other place to start all over again."

Sarah looks at her salad, uninterested in picking and choosing any more to eat. "I've lost my appetite."

"It happens." His eyes look a little sad at what he thinks she is feeling. "Nonetheless, while we are not desperate to do just anything to put him and the others away, we are getting real close to a critical point when it might be too late to do anything."

"I have an idea." She leans forward. "Promise to let me finish before you say anything."

He resists rolling his eyes. He's got to keep her immersed in the case for a while longer. "I've got time to listen, if you've got time to talk. What's your idea?"

««‹›»»

Area Director Law calls an emergency meeting of all available F. B. I. Agents at 2 PM, Sunday. Everyone is dressed in a mixed bag of casual clothes.

Standing at the head of a large conference room table, he looks around the room to see unhappy faces. "I'd like to say I'm sorry for calling you in on a weekend, but I won't do that."

He glances at each and every face to see a mixture of anger, annoyance, and downright disgust. He knows it's directed at him. "I've interrupted time with your family, golf, tennis, and whatever you were doing at the time. I know."

He continues to scan each and every face looking his way. "When each of us decided to be part of the Bureau's family, we all took an oath to earnestly, firmly, and without hesitation support the F. B. I's national security mission. I won't take the time to repeat word for word what that is because I know all of you are aware of and understand it."

He takes a sip of water from a glass nearby. "In order to be successful we must understand the specific threat, identify specific resources to be used to defuse the threat, and integrate all our intelligence from within and outside the Bureau. Our ability to investigate and eliminate networks that might harm us is often times a slow and frustrating process. Yet, we cannot abuse the power we have by acting capriciously. I, personally, over the years been involved in a wide variety of cases that have ranged from terrorist organizations to domestic financial scams. Of course, predators lurk not only in the animal jungle but we also find them among our fellow human beings. Some people will always look to make a dishonest dollar by preying on another person's trust or by cheating the system. And their crimes affect all of us."

He looks down at the table for a second and then glances at Agent Le Boeuf. "With all your footwork in the field, you haven't come up with much to put Ranger away. I know you've done the best you could do, but it hasn't been enough. I think you'd agree."

Le Boeuf keeps silent. She knows he is not asking her to engage in any type of discussion, nor is he putting her on the spot to embarrass her in front of her peers. She's lived through enough of his meetings to understand that's just how he acts, nothing more, nothing less. He's not making it personal.

Law then looks at Agent Castillo. "The photos you shot are important, but again, there's nothing illegal about a father and son talking with one another or a man and woman being together." He feels his throat constrict a bit so he takes another sip of water. His eyes rapidly blink a few times.

Castillo nods his head to agree with the statement. He too understands Law's communication ways.

Law continues. "This leads us to essentially no place, to nowhere, with nothing to use against Ranger."

He gives Sarah a momentary look and then shifts his eyes to the entire group. "All of you may not know Agent Nobel." He points a finger her way. "Stand up to let everyone see you."

Sarah takes a quick look at the table's edge before she stands, surprised of what she's been asked to do. She looks around the room with as neutral looking of a face as she can muster. Yet she sees everything but neutral looking eyes her way, leery and suspicious is more like it.

"Agent Noble has been undercover at a telemarketing operation that is taking money from innocent hard working people. The man responsible is Jim Ranger. He has a lengthy criminal history of doing the same thing in various States over the past several years. Agent Noble probably knows him better than any one of us in this room."

He looks at her again, "You can sit down now."

A few barely audible mumbles come from the group.

Agent Spentz whispers to Agent Rock, "Is she filling an affirmative action spot?"

"Maybe the boss is taking a personal interest in her." Rock grins.

Spentz murmurs, "Quid pro quo."

Law does not clearly hear the conversation between the Agents but nonetheless does not appreciate idle chit chat during his meetings. He gives them a peeved look. "Is there something you want to tell me or the other Agents?"

Spentz and Rock stop talking all together. They both shake their heads, no.

He continues. "Within the last few days we've found out that Ranger's son was an employee at the firm. Matt, that's his name, was in a sales position, and it was likely that his role was to secretly monitor what each of the other employees were doing, and then report back to his father.

Then, according to Noble, there was an emergency call from Ranger to Matt to see him. Matt took off. We've got some photos of them together. After that meeting Matt returned to work for a short time, just enough to ask Noble to talk with him, actually she essentially listened to him. He was in a state of distress. Matt then took off again, but later called Noble a few times. She said he sounded beyond distressed, sort of tormented in a way. Then finally, he took his own life. He's dead."

Agent Larson asks a question, "What was weighing him down so much that he committed suicide?"

Law turns to Noble, "Why don't you answer that one."

"He believed that his father killed Vince Allen, the one guy who allegedly was closest to him, because he believed that Allen was a snitch. Further, Matt believed that his father would kill anyone who betrayed him. Matt told me he feared for his life as well if his father ever thought that he was disloyal to him."

Larson looks at Law. "Sir, is it true about Allen?"

Law nods his head, "Yes, we got Allen to agree to feed us information in return for leniency towards him. I guess Ranger somehow figured it out."

"But how was that possible?" Larson looks puzzled.

Law shakes his head, "I have no idea."

Castillo asks, "What do you think is going to happen when Ranger hears of his son's suicide?"

Law turns to face Sarah.

Sarah glances at Law for a yes nod to go on.

Law gives her the go ahead with a head shake.

"I think I might be the best one to answer that one. I don't think he'll care too much one way or another. He's got blood of ice, and you're either with him or against him. At least that's how I read him."

Law raises his head, "Any more questions?"

Le Boeuf says, "I suspect there's something else in addition to this update that caused you to bring us here all together on a weekend."

"Yes, there is something very important. Agent Noble has offered a plan to get Ranger. It isn't without risk, but there isn't anything that is riskless. I want her to explain it." He looks at Sarah. "Come to the front of the room to map out your idea."

As before a few barely audible mumbles come from the group, yet this time Agents Spentz and Rock keep quiet.

Sarah takes in a deep breath as she scans the skeptical faces of the other Agents, doubtful that she is up to the task because of her youth and inexperience. She clears her throat. "Most of you don't me, I know that. Most of you might also be wondering why I'm involved in this case. In other words, does this kid have what it takes to go undercover? Those are all good questions, and to be honest I've wondered at times about myself. I suspect all of us have at one time or another."

Out of the corner of her eye she sees Law move uneasily in his seat, so she changes the topic to the specific set of circumstances. "This case involves the Bureau's criminal responsibilities, specifically, telemarketing fraud. Ranger has set up a simple scheme. He uses well known actors who are clueless about what they're pitching on television. The advertisements ask people who are interested in knowing more about the specific financial investment mentioned on television to request further information by simply calling a number to leave their full name, city, state, phone number, and best time to call back. What these naive people don't understand is that they're being set up to become a victim of a telemarketing fraud. They will be lured into believing that they can make a quick return on an investment that seems too good to be true."

She looks around to see nodding heads of the Agents, so she continues. "Some of the phrases the telemarketers use are: you must act now or the offer won't be good; you have won a free gift, vacation, or prize, but you have to pay for postage and handling or other charges; you must send me money, give me a credit card or bank account number, or I'll have a check picked up by courier; you can't afford to miss this high-profit, low-risk investment opportunity; this offer is limited and will not be available for much longer, so you have to act now."

Law interrupts, "They don't need a briefing on telemarketing fraud since they know that already. Get to your plan."

"Yes sir." She feels her face flush a bit. "My . . . the plan . . . proposed plan is for me to get very close to Ranger in order to gain his confidence."

Agent Crawford asks a question, "How close, in what ways?"

"He's made a sexual pass at me before, so I assume he finds me attractive."

Crawford adds his own interpretation, "Maybe he's just horny; his testosterone level is working overtime."

Several laughs are heard from the group.

She feels her face get redder. She waits for the laughter to subside. "You're probably right. I'm just the newest target on his list."

The group settles down.

"Whatever it is, he wants to get into my pants." She grins in a deviant way to head off further disagreement."

The comment puts an end to the group's banter.

"Doc Shure has written a preliminary psychological report on Ranger. Area Director Law has the full report, but the main points I remember are that Ranger suffers from delusions and paranoia about his peers, specifically that they are out to get him. He expects to be deceived by others, reads hidden threatening messages into most everything, and questions the loyalty of others. This leads him to trusting very few people, if anyone at all. His entire life has probably been and most likely still is composed of only a small circle of people he trusts. He is erratic yet at times functions at a normal level."

Crawford asks, "I hate to be the only one who's asking questions, but what makes you think he'll trust you?"

"I think he's overconfident. I'm hoping to get him to fall in love with me in which his feelings for me are so strong that he'll tell me anything and do anything for me."

The room is quiet and then a loud burst of laughter erupts.

She waits until they stop before she clarifies. "Do any of you have a better plan?"

Le Boeuf raises a hand, "So you're saying you're willing to have sex with him?"

Sarah stares at Le Boeuf and then glances around the room, "I really hope it doesn't come to that."

Le Boeuf is persistent, "That's not what I asked. Are you willing to have sex with this man if that's what it takes? It's a simple yes or no question."

Sarah swallows deeply. "Yes." She feels her legs shake a little.

The room is dead silent for a short time.

Le Boeuf raises her hand again. "You'll have to excuse me, but let's be honest, the plan is weird, I mean very weird.

It's as if you are putting yourself into an experiment that could easily backfire in so many ways."

"For example," Sarah asks. She moves closer to the edge of the conference table to feel its edge against her thigh. The touch settles her down.

"For starters, you could actually fall in love with him."

A few mumbles are barely heard.

Sarah asks, "What else?"

"Or he could fall in love with you, but in his way. He could possess, control, manipulate, dominate, or think of any other word that fits into this category. He'd have his way with you and you'd be unable to defend against yourself."

Sarah looks around the room, "Any other possibilities?"

Castillo says, "He could find you out, and then kill you."

She looks around for further comments. The room is quiet, so she replies. "Yes, any of those three are possible, I guess. But unless we have another plan, I'm willing to take the risk. If Area Director Law agrees with the plan, then I'll need everyone's support, whatever that may mean. I can't and won't go it alone."

Castillo asks, "How long do you expect your mo-jo to work on him, a day, a week, a month, when?"

Sarah gets right to her answer without offering an explanation, "I have no idea."

Law looks around, assessing if there is any value to continue with the questions. He finally steps in to end the meeting. "Is there anything else you need to know?" He continues looking around to see disappointed and confused faces. "I haven't made my decision yet, but I'll do that by tomorrow. You'll be kept informed. That's all. This meeting has ended."

As the room clears, there are indistinct murmurs from most of the Agents. Le Boeuf remains seated in the back of the room.

With the room now empty except for Law and Le Boeuf, he waves her to follow him into his office.

《《》》

"Be honest with me, do you think it'll work?" Law's face is unsmiling with a dour appearance.

"Are you crazy?" Le Boeuf shakes her head. She sits in a chair. Her mouth remains slightly opened in wonderment.

"Maybe, but do you think it'll work?"

"Is she stable, mentally and emotionally?"

"Probably not, but are any of us?"

"You're putting her at risk, not to mention the case. You do know that, don't you?"

"Listen, we've both been around here long enough to understand how things work. Some do and some don't. At times it's a better bet to hit the slot wheel in Vegas than to . . ."

"That's not the point, and you know that. You are intentionally putting her and the case at risk. There has to be another way to get Ranger."

He slaps both hands to his sides, "Fine, tell me. Give me another option. I'm all ears."

"I've never heard you sound so desperate and appear so agitated. You're usually calm and unruffled. There's something else going on. What is it?"

He turns away to look through a large window. He rubs his face with both hands and lets out a puff of air.

She continues, "And you've been grumpy the last few times I've seen you."

He keeps his back to her. "I know where he is, or at least where he most recently was."

"That's good news, isn't it?"

"I guess so, but I'm not sure if he's still there."

"Give me the address. I'll check it out. I can do that."

"He's probably gone by now."

She stands and then walks towards him.

He feels her warm breath on his neck, and then her hand grabbing his arm. Slowly he responds to her touch.

"Talk to me. You can say anything to me, you do know that."

He puckers his lips as tightly as he can. He appears firm to keep quiet.

She moves her hands to stroke his face. "What's the matter? I've never seen you like this before."

She touches a chord with him. "He was with Madeline."

She pulls her hands away and steps back. "Madeline?"

"Castillo took the shots. It's her with him, I'm positive."

"You're not over her, but I thought you were. I was positive."

"So was I. I'm sorry."

"I'd say that changes a few things about us. Doesn't it?"

"I don't want to lose you. You've been too good to me and have put up with a load of my crap." He steps forward to take her in his arms.

"No, back off. This definitely changes our relationship." Her mouth freezes into a narrow even line.

"To what, what does it change it to?"

"I'm not sure yet. You can't be with me when you want to be with her. That's for certain. You have to make up your mind which one it will be."

He feels his throat constrict a bit so he swallows to lubricate it. "Can we get back to the case?"

"I'm sure that's safer for you."

He lowers his head realizing he's been humiliated. "OK, how do we get Ranger if you don't like Sarah's idea?"

Part of her wants to come into contact with him, to feel his arms tightly wrap around her body, to kiss him deeply so that they almost get out of breath, to emotionally go back to how it was only moments ago. However, the logical part of her tells her to separate her feelings from him, to focus on working out a plan to get Ranger. In the end, she bases her decision on reason. "The photos of them together are only suggestive. They do not tell the entire story."

His eyes brighten. "Go on."

"He could be playing her like he's played everyone else. It's a temporary bond to satisfy a short-lived need for something."

"So you're saying he might be using her until he passes onto someone or something else."

"That's exactly what I'm saying."

"Assuming that's true, how does that help us get him?"

"Redirect Sarah to confront Madeline, not Ranger."

Wrinkles form on his forehead. "What will that do?"

"It will prevent him from suspecting that we're on to him, and it will protect Sarah."

"Hmm, that makes sense." He pauses to look away, and then back to face Le Boeuf. "Sarah doesn't know anything about Madeline, who she is, what she does, or who . . ."

"That's right, who she was intimate with at one time, namely you."

"She can ask any question she wants because she is on the investigation."

"Are you sure Sarah does not know of Madeline's Deputy County M. E. position and has no clue about you two?"

"Positive, there's no way."

"All of it might come out eventually."

He wrinkles his forehead again.

Le Boeuf clarifies, "You and her."

"That was a while back."

"I don't believe you, but if you're OK with it, then it's OK with me."

He stays quiet for a few moments before going on. "I'm OK with it."

"I can actually work with Sarah since I'm more experienced working in the field than she is. We could actually partner up together."

"Are you sure you're OK with that?"

"Why wouldn't I?"

"I mean, what we've just talked about."

It is Le Boeuf's turn to frown. "Oh, you mean me and you, you and Madeline, the three of us. Is that what you mean?"

"Yes."

"Don't worry about me. I can stay emotionally disconnected. I've done it before and I can do it again."

"I'm just, well, don't want you to get into something that . . ."

"Like I said, don't worry. I'm good."

"OK, that settles it. I'll set up a meeting for tomorrow morning with you and Sarah together to work out the details. And then after that's finished, I'll inform the other Agents. Have I missed anything?"

"I can't think of anything right now."

"Look out after Sarah. She's in a fragile place right now."

"Look out in what way, and explain what you mean by fragile."

"She wanted out of the case, actually to leave undercover work."

"And I bet you convinced her to stay in until Ranger is caught, to stay loyal to the Bureau, or said something that sounded patriotic."

"That's my job, to get the bad guys, to motivate the Agents, to . . ."

"Cut the crap with me. You know that I know better than that."

He steps forward to reach out with both hands to hold her.

She puts up both hands, palms toward him, "No, that's not a good idea. Let's keep this professional."

««»»

The next morning Law meets with Le Boeuf and Sarah. Instead of starting out the meeting with cordialities Law gets right to the point. "This may be our last chance to bring Ranger in. Up to this point he's been crafty just enough to be a step ahead of us. It's up to the two of you to make sure he's caught."

Sarah shifts a glance at Le Boeuf and then returns looking at Law. "Two of us, I thought I was the one to bring him in?"

"That's too much for one Agent to handle. Le Boeuf has many years of field work. She knows what to look out for."

"Am I the Lead Agent or am I now in a support role?" Her face hardens.

"Don't let your ego get in the way. You are both Lead Agents and I expect you to be a team, equally sharing whatever it is you do."

Le Boeuf keeps silent throughout, giving the impression of having been informed of the arrangement beforehand.

Sarah turns to Le Boeuf, gives her a good look over, and decides not to argue about the deal. "I'm OK with it if you are."

"He's the boss. I'm good."

Law continues. "That's how it's going to be. Castillo took photos of Ranger and a woman together a few days ago. We know the address of the place. It appears to be a residence, probably of the woman. The odds are that he's staying with her. If that's not the case, then she might know where he is. I want the both of you to interview her to find out what she knows." He looks at both Agents to detect any confusion.

Sarah says, "So it seems the shift in the plan is to target the woman to get to Ranger, not for me to get to him directly."

"That's right. That's the plan, it's settled."

Sarah tightens her lips for a few moments and then asks, "What do I do about the telemarketing job? I can't just disappear."

Le Boeuf joins in, "She's got a good point. If she doesn't show up for work, they'll suspect something."

Law's face is expressionless. "I hadn't thought about that."

"I've got an idea." Sarah's voice sounds euphoric as if she's just won the lottery. "I'll go to work today, act normally."

She looks at Law, "In the meantime you ask the local authorities to make a call into their office to speak with Ranger. We all know he won't be there, so the call will probably be transferred to one of the executives. However the conversation goes, the local authorities should say that Ranger's son has been in a horrible accident, and that Matt's father needs to be contacted. I'm not sure if they all know that Matt is Ranger's son, but if they don't now they will know then. In the meantime, I'll casually ask any one of the executives where Matt is since he's supposed to be training me, but that I haven't seen him. I'll act as if I don't want to be fired from the job, that I need the training. I'll get worked up over it. I'm sure I'll be convincing. Hopefully, they'll say something to me that I'll be able to interpret as worrisome. I'll point blank ask if Matt is OK. Let's hope they tell me that Matt isn't coming in for a while. Then I'll go to pieces and claim that I need some time off to recover from whatever is making me feel stressed." Her face continues to look proud of the idea.

"This might work, and give you and me time to talk with the woman." Le Boeuf smiles towards Sarah and then turns to Law, "I like it very much."

Satisfied that everyone agrees, Law turns to Sarah. "I'll get a hold of The Chief of Police, Max Monaco to make the call in an hour. That should give you enough time to get to work."

Then Law shifts to look at Le Boeuf. "You'll just have to wait until she leaves work. Figure out how you two will meet up with each other."

CHAPTER 11

Sarah enters the office building within an hour feeling a little jumpy. Everything has to work as planned or else there could be trouble for her. She passes through security without a hitch and walks at a hurried pace to reach the elevators. She hears a bell ring signaling the doors are about to close. "Hold up," she shouts. She sees a foot break the plane of the two closing doors just in time to stop them from closing. "Thanks, I'm a little late for work." She keeps her head face down to avoid any eye contact that might give away her uneasiness.

"Me too, I'm usually ahead of schedule, but a long distance call took up more time than I had anticipated." His voice sounds fine and delicate like a slow drizzle of rain at just the right pace to cool off a hot summer's day.

Now unhurried and no longer trying to race she looks up. She sees a cinnamon looking face, soft brown in color with clear and sparkling brown eyes. He looks tranquil with just the right amount of proper posture to embody respectability. She is unable to hold back a smile.

The man slightly parts his mouth with an evocative smile. He extends his hand, "Good day, I'm Neptune Aes."

Without conscious thought she extends her hand to meet with his. His skin feels warm and refined to her touch. "I'm Sarah Noble." There is more than a filament of desire to hold onto his hand as long as possible. However, the elevator bell sounds to break up the mood.

"That's my floor, I've got to leave." He pulls his hand away from hers and gracefully walks out of the elevator.

As the elevator doors close she gets a whiff of an aromatic spice flowing her way. The sound of the door's meeting each other snaps her back to reality. "Hello, what was that about?" Moments later the elevator doors open.

She steps into the hallway and then walks towards the office door.

««»»

Sarah steps inside, looks around to see people at their workstations not paying any attention to her arrival. She proceeds towards her work area and then sits down. Before she is able to turn on her computer Dick and Karen are by her side.

Karen speaks at a fast pace. Her eyes look troubled. "The executives have been in a meeting for close to an hour. Something is up!"

Dick agrees, "I think big time, something's going down."

"It's just a meeting, why are you guys so worked up?"

Dick's face is uneasy looking and his voice sounds as if he is pleading to be understood. "We all know when something bad is going to happen. Come on."

"The only thing I'm worried about is not getting trained. I have no idea where Matt is, and he's the one who they chose to train me."

««»»

Inside the conference room the executives argue.

"Where the hell is Jim? I don't like this one bit!" Teddy walks around, head down, hands in his pockets.

"He's got some personal things to take care of. I've already told you that." David tries to stay calm but his stomach muscles tighten.

Reggie says, "You don't sound very convincing. You're worried just like the rest of us."

Marshall stays quiet for a while as he sizes up the situation.

"And why are you the contact person? Doesn't he trust any of us?" Teddy stops pacing to look at David.

"You're sounding paranoid. Calm down." David's hands begin to sweat a little.

Teddy glances toward Marshall.

"And you, you're quiet. What are you thinking about?"

Marshall takes a deep breath and slowly lets the air out. "I'm just as perplexed as you are. First Vince is gone someplace to do something that we really don't know anything about. Then Jim takes off, allegedly to care of something personal. We tell Matt to train Sarah but I haven't seen Matt around either. And then there's Tommie, where is he? Has he left too? Yeah, I agree this place is becoming something like a circus. I don't get it."

"Who knows what's going to happen next?" Reggie stands to refill his coffee cup.

"Maybe we should close up this operation and get out?" Teddy looks around at the others.

Reggie pours coffee into his cup. "We're making money. I don't see any financial reason to shut down."

Marshall joins Reggie at the coffee pot to get a refill himself. "It's more than making money."

Reggie turns around to look at the others. "Like what's more important than making money?" He takes a sip of coffee.

Marshall says, "Like not going to jail."

"Who said anything about joining to jail?" Teddy lifts his chin.

Marshall clarifies, "All I'm saying is that whatever we do we must be cognizant of avoiding going to jail. We all know what that's like, and I suspect no one wants to go through it again. That's all I'm saying."

Silence slices through the conversation for a few moments. Then the telephone rings. Everyone jumps at the unexpected interruption.

"I'll get it." David walks towards a phone sitting on a nearby table. "I thought I said no phone calls unless it was an emergency."

David listens for a few seconds, and then his eyes widen. "Put him through." He looks around at the others who are attentively watching him.

"Yes, Chief Monaco. I'm David Shea, head of security. How can I help you?" He shrugs his shoulders towards the others.

"No, Mr. Ranger is not available at the moment. He's on a business trip. Can I help you with something?"

The others walk closer to David.

"Oh, that's terrible. I'll try to get hold of Mr. Ranger but when he's away on business it's often very difficult to contact him. But, I'll do my best."

David's eyes widen with anxiousness.

"Yes I will. Thanks for calling." He slowly replaces the phone to its cradle. Then he turns to the others.

Before David utters a single word, Teddy asks, "What was that about?"

"That was the Chief of Police, Max Monaco. He wanted to talk with Jim, but you heard what I said."

Teddy pushes on, "Go on, what else?"

"Jim's son has been in an accident, a very bad one according to Monaco. He was calling to tell Jim about it."

Marshall asks, "Why would a Chief of Police do that? That is typically done by lower ranked support staff, not the Chief?"

"He didn't cover that. I don't know."

Reggie asks, "Did Jim have a son? I didn't know that?" He looks around at the others.

Teddy adds, "Me neither."

Marshall says, "Nor me."

The three look at David with a smidgen of suspicion on their faces.

"It's Matt, that's who his son is."

"Are you serious?" Teddy is doubtful.

"Very. Jim didn't want anyone to know about it."

Reggie asks, "But he told you."

David nods his head, "Yes he did. To my understanding I was the only one. Not even Matt knew that I knew."

Teddy raises his voice, "What else do you know that we don't?"

"Don't get paranoid?"

Teddy says, "It's not paranoid, it's annoyed. I've just about had enough of this crap. I thought we were all equal partners in this operation, but now we find out that you are the chosen one."

"You're misinterpreting everything. Jim thought that in this instance, it was best to limit the number of people who knew about this situation, only this situation, nothing else."

Marshall tries to shift the conversation to another topic. "Let's move away suspecting David. I'm willing to accept the fact that Jim asked him to keep something personal a secret." He turns to David, "Do you know where Matt is?"

"I have no idea, and that's the truth. We never talked outside of the office and only talked about his role as an employee when he was in the office. Not even Matt knew that I was aware he was Jim's son."

Reggie asks, "How badly injured is Matt?"

"Monaco didn't say and didn't seem to want to tell me anything else."

Reggie adds, "It makes sense to keep the details for family members only." He pauses. "Hey, but how did the Chief of Police know that Matt is Jim's son and that this is where to find Jim?"

David answers. "He didn't say and I didn't ask. But Matt might have given him this number."

Silence wedges into the conversation for a few moments.

Reggie puts an end to the stillness. "I don't like the sound of this, I really don't."

Calmly David says, "What do suggest we do?"

"I wish I knew," Reggie shakes his head.

Then, Marshall asks, "Whatever we do, we have to stay calm." He looks around to the others. "Do we keep this quiet, or tell anyone else in the office?"

Teddy offers his opinion, "Keep it quiet."

Reggie agrees, "Yeah, the less people who know the better it is."

David offers a slightly different idea. "Maybe just Sarah since she's the one Matt is supposed to train."

Marshall cautions, "I'd just say that Matt is not feeling well and that we'll allow her to continue working here until he returns. Keep it as brief as possible."

David looks around the room, "Everyone agree?" He sees their heads nod. "Do we have any other business to conduct?" He keeps looking at them.

"I still feel uncomfortable about what's going on. It just doesn't feel right." Teddy shakes his head.

Reggie agrees, "Me too."

"We'll get through this. It's only a speed bump." Marshall's voice sounds reasonable and calm.

Reggie sets his cup on the table, "We're still making money. Maybe that's all I should care about."

"Ok. I'll let Sarah know. If anyone hears from Jim, tell him about Matt."

««»»

As the executives leave the conference room, David walks towards Sarah. He sees Dick and Karen sitting alongside her.

He smiles, "Hello everyone." He turns to Sarah, "Matt hasn't been feeling very well these past few days, so he's taking some time off. This means the training that was to take place will be delayed until he returns. Don't worry about anything."

Dick glances towards Karen without saying a word.

Sarah says, "Oh, I'm sorry to hear about Matt. Do I still have my job?"

"Yes, of course. We certainly can't penalize you for something you had nothing to do with, can we."

"I'm relieved, but I'm sorry about Matt. Do you know when he'll be back to work?"

"Not for sure, but I can't imagine no more than a few days." David keeps smiling, although the more he holds it in place, the less sincere it becomes. "Just keep making your calls until he returns." He turns to return to his office.

When David is out of range of hearing their conversation, Dick asks Sarah, "Do you believe that?"

Karen frowns, "What do you mean?"

Dick turns to Karen, "First it was Tommie and now it's Matt. Why are these people vanishing?"

Sarah jumps in, "Please, you're sounding like this is a Twilight Zone episode. Nobody's vanishing."

Karen agrees, "I go along with Sarah, I think your imagination has gone wild."

Sarah voices another point. "At least I've still got my job."

"I'm going back to work. I've got a bunch of calls to make to reach my quota." Karen walks away.

"Me too, and so should you." Sarah stares at Dick.

"I get the message." Dick leaves her alone.

Left alone at her workstation, Sarah makes a call on her cell to Le Boeuf, "I'll meet you in fifteen minutes."

««»»

As Le Boeuf drives, she asks Sarah, "They received the call from Monaco?"

"Yes. I wasn't in the room when they got it so I don't know how they reacted. All I was told that Matt was under the weather and that I should continue making my calls the best I can for now."

Le Boeuf continues to drive. "I would have liked to have been a fly on the wall. I can't imagine they took the news calmly."

"David Shea who's in charge of security sure appeared in control with me. Two other employees were at my workstation when he told me the news."

"What did they say?"

"Dick thinks something is up but he can't put his finger on it while Karen seems to have settled down a bit since we last talked. The place is not easy to figure out especially since all of us sales types are new."

"But I think we can now assume that the executive group knows that Matt is Ranger's son."

"I think that's a safe bet." She thinks for a second and then continues. "But I don't know if they all knew before the call from Monaco. It wouldn't surprise me if that was pretty hush-hush."

"We're almost there. The GPS indicates it is 2.3 miles from where we are."

There is silence for a few moments before Le Boeuf resumes talking. "What I'm about to say I don't want you to take offensive. OK?"

Sarah turns to face Le Boeuf. "Sure."

"This is between us girls and it's my opinion only, so take it for what it's worth."

"Sure."

"Don't ever sell your body to anyone for any price. It cheapens you."

Sarah's neck muscles tighten as the rest of her body stiffens from the out of the blue comment. "I don't quite understand what you mean."

ANTONIO F. VIANNA

"During Law's powwow with the Agents this past Sunday, Castillo asked you about having sex with Ranger. Do you remember that conversation?"

"Yes I do. What about it?"

"You said you would be willing to have sex with Ranger if it got you what you needed to bring him in."

"Like I said, I remember that. What's your problem?"

"You don't think you cheapen yourself as a woman if you are willing to sell your body?"

"It's not like I'm going to enjoy the sex with him. It's the price I'm willing to pay to put a scumbag like Ranger away for a long time."

"That's a pretty hardened view. The ends justify the means, whatever it takes to get the job done."

Sarah looks the other way, through the passenger side window. She sees her tightened lips through the window's image. "If that's what it takes."

"You're hardened much further beyond your age."

Sarah turns to face Le Boeuf. "Are you saying you wouldn't?"

"Put bluntly, yes, that's exactly what I'm saying. There are some boundaries I won't cross. Maybe this has to do with our age difference, maybe something else. All I'm saying is that personally I wouldn't do it, and professionally I'd find another way to put Ranger behind bars. I think it demeans and belittles me personally and professional as a woman to resort to sex."

Sarah faces the window again, this time without uttering another word.

Le Boeuf continues. "I've worked hard to get where I am, probably harder than most others. I'm not about to let my gender be a factor in how I'm evaluated at my job, and quite honestly, it really, I mean really, pisses me off when I see that happen, be it a man or a woman. I'm older than you, I know that. And I don't want to sound like I'm preaching to a child, but I am very serious about this issue. When gender is put into the mix, it clouds other's perception about whether we have what it takes to make it."

A few more minutes of silence settles between them.

Sarah's voice sounds limp, "I understand."

Le Boeuf glances towards Sarah, shakes her head slightly, "I hope so, but I doubt it."

"What's that supposed to mean?" Her voice hardens a little, but not much.

"You heard what I said, but you're still not convinced. It's in your voice and in your eyes."

Another round of silence comes to roost.

"There's the place." Le Boeuf pulls the car to the side of the road, and then lets the vehicle idle as she continues to talk, "How to do want to handle it?"

"Uh," she shrugs her shoulders. No clear plan comes to mind.

"I think we should both act normally. I'll park here and then we should walk to the front door to ring the bell. If someone answers other than Ranger we begin to ask a few questions about where we might find him. We should keep this low keyed, initially, and then if we need to we'll ratchet the conversation little by little. What do you think?"

"Uh, yeah, sounds good to me."

"What's wrong? You've lost focus."

"I'm sorry. I'm stuck on what you said earlier, about cheapening me as a woman and as a professional. I wasn't expecting that at all."

"Is that all that's bothering you?"

Sarah snaps back, "Yeah!"

"Maybe I came on too strong."

Sarah settles down. "No, I'm glad you did. I've got some thinking to do."

"OK, but you've got to get back to the moment at hand. Are you ready to proceed?"

"Yes, I'm ready."

"Get out of the car and follow my lead."

««»»

Both woman walk towards the house, Le Boeuf much more confidently than Sarah. Le Boeuf pushes the door bell. Its chimes are heard outside the house, but no one answers. She gives it another press with her thumb, yet again there is no response. "Let's walk around back to see if there is an opened window or door."

Sarah notices three waste cans to her left, each with a different colored lid. She stops, lifts the lid off the one with a dark blue top that is labeled **Recyclables**, and takes a look inside. She reaches into the reinforced plastic container to grab a handful of paper and then she takes a serious look at what's in her hand.

Le Boeuf continues walking ahead, unaware of Sarah's find.

"Hey, I think I've got something."

Le Boeuf turns to notice Sarah reading a piece of paper, so she steps closer. "What do you have there?"

"It seems to be a handwritten note."

"What does it say? Read it to me."

Sarah smiles as she reads the words. "Madeline, to the love of my life. Jim." She turns to Le Boeuf, "That's sweet." She hands the note to Le Boeuf.

Le Boeuf silently reads the same words on the note. Her lips move without a sound. She ignores Sarah's commentary.

"If Jim is Jim Ranger, it shows us he was here with her, Madeline. That's useful news." She hands the note back to Sarah. "Anything else inside?" She looks at the same container.

Sarah reaches inside the plastic container once again to pull out more paper. "Here, you look through this and I'll grab the rest."

Silently, each Agent sorts through the rubbish.

"Nothing here except third class mail and a few magazines addressed to Madeline Courier. I guess she's the owner of the place. It's a nice-sounding name, sounds French."

Le Boeuf tosses what's in her hand back into the waste container. "Nothing here either." She looks at the two remaining containers, one with a gray colored lid for **Trash** and one with a green colored lid for **Green Waste**. You look into the one with the gray lid and I'll take a look at the green one."

She grins. "Rank has its privilege." She opens the cover to take a look inside. "There's nothing but garbage that I can see, and not much of it at that."

Le Boeuf's observation mimics what Sarah sees, "Same here." She closes the top. "Let's see how we can get inside this place." She walks towards a sliding glass door with Sarah close behind. She shades her eyes with her hand to see what she can see through the glass. "Nice place."

Sarah stands alongside copying Le Boeuf's move. "She must have money. I wonder what she does for a living."

Le Boeuf keeps silent about what she knows of Madeline. She grabs the door handle to shove the door open. "The door is locked."

"Maybe there's an open window. I usually keep my small bathroom window open to let in the fresh air. I wonder where the bathroom is." She lifts her head to give a good once over of the back of the house. "That could be it." She moves ten yards to her right. "It's on the second floor, too far to get to without a ladder."

"I'll boost you up." Le Boeuf squats close to the ground. "Here, take my hands and step on my shoulders."

Sarah twists her head to the side, "Really?"

"Do you have another idea? Maybe you should lift me?"

"I like it your way." She jokes, "Just don't drop me. I'm real fragile."

The significance of the word as applied to Sarah does not go unnoticed by Le Boeuf whose eyes open wider than normal. With Sarah carefully balanced on Le Boeuf's shoulders and their hands tightly clasped with each other's Le Boeuf slowly stands.

"Whoa," Sarah says as she slightly sways from side to side.

"Steady yourself," Le Boeuf calmly replies. "I'm going to walk close to the house. Tell me when you can reach the window."

With one hand freed from Le Boeuf, Sarah touches the exterior side of the building. "We're very close. Stay steady while I reach for the window." With her second freed hand Sarah makes contact with the building's side. Slowly she extends her body to stand straight. She wobbles a bit but quickly recovers. "I've got to punch the window screen open." She hauls her right fist with as much force as she can into the screen. "Ouch!"

"What happened?"

"The screen's cut my knuckles."

"We're close, you can go on."

Sarah takes in a deep breath, licks the blood off the finger joints and takes a second crack at it. This time the screen pops away to fall in the bathroom floor. "I did it."

"Can you climb through the window?"

"It's small but I'll manage." She grabs hold of the window's edges to drag herself inside.

Le Boeuf feels the weight of Sarah lift from her shoulders. She steps away to look up to see Sarah's feet dangling over the window's frame. "Great, you did it."

Sarah finishes climbing inside and then sticks her face outside the window. "I'll be right down."

"Don't touch anything. You've got to clean up any blood you might have left."

"What about the screen? It's got my blood all over it."

"We'll take it with us and then toss it somewhere."

"This isn't legal what we're doing, is it."

"Now's not the time to think about that. We probably don't have a lot of time to check out the place, so we've got to hurry. Now go, get downstairs to open the door."

Minutes later Le Boeuf and Sarah stand inside Madeline's house.

"You check the upstairs and I'll check down here. Remember, don't touch anything and don't forget to clean up the bathroom. Wipe away any places where you might have touched. That includes the exterior window frame. Use a towel. We'll take it and the screen with us when we leave. OK?" Le Boeuf looks at Sarah to find out is she understands.

"So this is really how it's done."

"Yes, and that's why Law wanted you to work with me. Now go upstairs and do what I've asked."

Sarah turns around to start examining the rooms upstairs.

««»»

Twenty minutes later Le Boeuf and Sarah sit inside the car.

"How are those knuckles?" Le Boeuf looks at Sarah's right hand that is wrapped with a towel.

"They hurt but I'll be fine."

"What did you find upstairs?"

"Men's clothes and grooming accessories. I took a used razor blade and a toothbrush. Maybe there's a way to match whatever is there with Ranger's DNA."

"Smart thinking, but you know we can't legally use that evidence."

"I understand but it might help us understand the situation better."

"There's no argument with me. Anything else?"

"No, nothing that I could find. What about you, did you find anything?"

"A few coffee cups inside the dishwasher that I took. I'm sure one is Madeline's and hopefully the other is from Ranger. Let's hope our people can pull off something from what you've got and what I found."

"Too bad we didn't enter the house with a warrant."

"Too bad, so sad, but that's just between the two us."

"Would you say we've been successful?"

"I'd say absolutely, we did great."

"I wonder who Madeline Courier is, and how she knows Ranger."

Le Boeuf hesitates, unsure if she should be the one to tell her what she knows or let that fall on Law's lap. "My experience with the Bureau has taught me one thing for certain."

Sarah quickly asks, "What's that?"

"Things are rarely what they seem to be. There's always a surprise someplace."

"Hmm, that's interesting." Sarah delays further talking for a short time. "Do you want to know something?"

"Sure, what's that?"

"I think you know something that I don't know about Madeline and Jim, but aren't yet willing to let on. That's what I think."

"It's complex. In due time, but not from me."

"Aren't most things complex?"

"Yes, but they don't have to be. People make it more complicated than it is or has to be."

"Then when will I be told and from whom?"

"I'd take it up with your boss."

"Area Director Law?"

Le Boeuf nods, "He's our boss, yours and mine."

««»»

Later that night, Madeline returns home from work. She notices Jim's car is not nearby. She isn't surprised since he's always been a mystery to her since when they first met. She heads for the refrigerator to pour a glass of Chardonnay. With a full glass of wine in hand, she walks up the stairs to take a shower before fixing something to eat.

As she turns the corner from her bedroom to the bathroom where the shower is located she suddenly stops, almost dropping the wine glass. She immediately notices the screen at the small bathroom window is missing. Immediately she thinks it must have come loose somehow and fallen outside. She stretches her neck through the open window to look around. Her eyes carefully inspect the backyard but do not come up with the item. She pulls her head away from the window and then skims the area nearby her feet. Again, there is no screen. It then dawns on her that there might have been a break-in. She sets the wine glass on a nearby table and then starts the process of examining places where she keeps valuables.

First she heads to a safe that is out of sight within a clothes closet. She pulls the lever but the safe door does not budge. She moves to a jewelry box on top of a dresser. Again, after going over what's inside, she realizes nothing is missing. Lastly, she looks underneath her bed to see a shoe box. She extends an arm to pull it closer. Upon opening the box, all cash money seems to be accounted for.

Perplexed as to what might have caused the window screen to vanish, she returns to the bathroom where she grabs the wine glass to take a sip, and then another. She sits on the edge of the bathtub for a few seconds. Nothing fresh comes to mind so she places the glass on the table to get ready for a warm shower.

Slowly she removes the rest of her clothes, turns on the shower faucet to allow the water to warm up. She returns to the glass of wine for a final sip before she walks beneath the shower's warm water's spray. Then, out of the corner of her eye she gets a glimpse of a red spot just underneath the window's edge. She frowns, at first not sure what to make of the speck. She leans her body closer to the spot. Then suddenly it dawns on her that the smudge might be someone's blood.

With a great amount of poise and self-control, she reaches inside a nearby drawer to pull out a fingernail file and a sterile band aid. With utmost precision she removes the red spot from the window's edge and transfers it to the band aid. "If this was a break-in, and if this is the blood of the intruder, then I might be able to get a DNA match."

Slowly she moves to the safe once again, but this time her intention is to pull out a small hand gun. With the weapon in her hand, she quietly begins to inspect the rest of the house for any signs of the housebreaker. It takes her fifteen minutes to complete the check. She forgets to check the back glass door that was left closed but unlocked after Sarah and Le Boeuf left the place. Relieved to be alone, Madeline goes upstairs to take a shower.

CHAPTER 12

Late in the afternoon the next day, Area Director Law makes a visit to the County Morgue. As he pulls into the parking lot, he notices Madeline's silver metallic Audi A6 Sedan parked in her assigned spot. He mumbles to himself a few words of encouragement to keep the discussion all business.

He steps inside the building assuming to be greeted by the receptionist just as before. However, the area is vacant. He glances around the room to spot someone who might help him, but there is no one. Law decides to walk directly to Madeline's office without an escort.

He spots Madeline sitting in her office with another woman, so he hangs back a while until she is alone. The delay is only a minute.

Law gently taps on the door frame to announcement himself. "Madeline, can I have a few minutes with you?" His voice sounds a bit timid.

Surprised to hear his voice, she looks up. Her eyes are opened wider than normal.

Law does not wait for a response. He steps inside her office. "I'll keep the door open unless you want it closed."

Wrinkles crease her forehead, "What are you doing here?"

"It's not personal, if that's what you're thinking."

"I didn't imply it was or wasn't. I asked why you are here."

"It's Bureau business."

"Everything seems to be Bureau business these days."

"What's that supposed to mean?"

She waves her hand to brush off the comment. "Forget about it. What do you want?"

"I think you've unintentionally got yourself into a situation that you need to get out of."

With obvious sarcasm, she says, "Oh, really!"

He takes in a deep breath and tells himself to stay calm. "I'm here because I don't want to see you get hurt or get into any trouble."

"That's a first on both accounts."

"Please, don't make this harder than it is." He takes a seat.

She points to the chair he sits in. "Please, make yourself comfortable." Sarcasm continues.

"I don't know why I care about you but I do."

"I thought you said this wasn't personal."

"Alright then, let me get right to the point."

She applauds, "Finally."

"One of the cases assigned to the Bureau centers on a specific person who is swindling people out of money, big money. He's spent most of his life doing this and we are close to finally getting sufficient evidence to arrest him."

Madeline's face turns somber, but remains silent.

"We believe the name he is using is Jim Ranger." He doesn't have to wait long for a response.

"Who?" The name lingers in her ear that no one else can hear.

"That's right, Jim Ranger."

Horizontal wrinkles deepen across her forehead and her jaw remains dropped so that her lips and teeth are parted.

"While I can't divulge how we know this, it is a fact that you know him and that he is temporarily living at your place."

The surprise Madeline felt just a moment ago is followed by confusion. Her eyebrows are momentarily raised so they are curved and high. She is speechless.

"I don't want you to get involved with him. He's dangerous. We believe he's already killed someone whom he believed double-crossed him."

"I don't believe you."

"Why would I make up something like this?"

She folds her arms over her chest, "To get back at me."

"Please Madeline. Do know how juvenile that sounds?"

"I still don't believe you." Her voice is harsh sounding.

"He's running a telemarketing scam operation in our city. We have an undercover Agent working there. We have proof."

"Then why are you telling me? Just arrest him!"

"It's not that simple, and you know that. I've got to follow the law to the letter or else the case will be thrown out."

"Then why are you telling me this? Why did you really come here to see me?"

"There are two reasons. One, I don't think you know the kind of person you are spending time with. You could get caught up in this mess. Second, I want to wire you."

"That's preposterous. It's not going to happen!"

"What can I say or do to convince you?"

She narrows her eyes, "Nothing, absolutely nothing."

"Then, at least distance yourself from him for a while. Take a vacation or go to a conference, but take off somewhere so that when this comes down you aren't around."

"I'm not going to run away based on your suspicions. You haven't given me one iota of real evidence to support your claim. It's all been conjecture."

"Listen Madeline, you know I can't disclose much evidence with you during the investigation. In fact, I probably shouldn't be here right now talking with you."

"But you are."

"Yes, and that should tell you something about how serious this is." He keeps a firm stare towards her, unblinking and unwavering.

"There could be another Jim Ranger, not the one I know."

"That's always a possibility, but the Jim Ranger we're looking for is the one staying at your place, the man who's swindled hard working people out of their money."

"How do you know that it's him?"

He pauses, looks away from her stare, and then back to face her. "I've got photos of you and him together?"

"What?"

"Yes, you and him together."

"Where?"

"At your doorstep."

"You had your people poke their nose in my personal affairs?"

"It's not like that."

"Then tell me, what is like?"

"We were following him. He took us to your place. It's that simple."

"This is outrageous!"

"Actually, it's very good investigative work."

"You know what I mean."

"I'm trying to be honest with you."

"Surprise! You've had a change of heart!"

"Don't bring up old stuff that no longer matters. What happened, happened."

"Sure, just forget about all the times when you disappointed me." She looks away. "But I guess that's easy for you to do, isn't it."

Frustrated he's not getting anyplace with her, he puts up his hands high in the air. "I give up."

"That sounds familiar." She pauses and then continues. "The Jim Ranger that you know, the terrible and ruthless person, is not the one whom I know. Definitely not the one you're looking for."

"How sure are you?"

"Positive."

Law stands, slaps his hands to his sides. "Have it your way. But, don't say I didn't try." He turns and starts to walk away.

"Hey!"

He stops and turns around, lips are tightly sealed.

"Was it your people who broke into my place?"

"I don't know what you're talking about. Someone broke into your place? When did that happen?"

"Don't get smart ass with me. It was your people, wasn't it."

"I said I don't know what you're talking about. You should report it to the police."

"I just might do that. I've got a sample of blood taken from the place of entry that just might match someone, maybe an Agent. That would be awfully embarrassing, I imagine."

"I don't know what you're talking about."

"You know I do."

Law lifts his eyebrows and shrugs his shoulders. Then he turns around to leave her alone.

««»»

All hell breaks loose outside the conference room.

"Where is she?" Teddy's shoulders are curled in, his body slouches forward. "Where is Sarah?"

Startled, all personnel in the office stop working and look in the direction of the angry sounding voice. Everyone keeps quiet.

Teddy looks around at the staff. "Doesn't anyone know where Sarah is? Huh? Anyone?"

Silence continues for a short time until David appears. "What's the commotion about?"

Teddy glances at David. "She's not here. Where is she?"

David remains composed. "Calm down. Maybe she had a doctor's appointment or is just running late."

"Doctor's appointment! She knows she's supposed to let us know before she takes off for anything personal. She knows it."

David answers. "Maybe it was something unexpected. Come on, Teddy, settle down." He puts his hand on Teddy's shoulder.

Teddy quickly moves away. "Don't touch me, don't ever touch me."

Reggie walks into the open space to get into the conversation. He steps forward. "What's going on? I'm trying to balance the books."

"Teddy is all shook up because Sarah isn't at her work station."

"I'll speak for myself." Teddy switches glances between David and Reggie. His eyes stick out as if they are swelled. "She's supposed to be at work eight hours a day. As one of the executives of this company, I have a right to know why she isn't working and where she is."

Marshall finally comes forward. "Let's talk about this with less emotion. Come on, we've got to settle down in order to figure this out. No use in disturbing the office staff. What do you say, come on." He walks towards Teddy, nods his head, and finally puts his arm around Teddy. "Teddy, come on, we'll iron this out with rational thought. Let's all go to the conference room."

Reggie and David silently nod toward Marshall and Teddy.

The walk to the conference room settles everyone down.

««»»

Now inside the conference room with closed doors, Marshall looks directly at Teddy. "What the fuck was that all about?"

Teddy's shout is almost at the level of a loud scream. "This place is going to pieces, it's out of control!" He licks his lips and is short of breath as he rapidly inhales and exhales air.

Marshall continues, "Lower your voice. We don't want the others to hear. They've already heard enough." He puts his finger across his lips. "What do you mean, out of control?"

Fear defines his pale face. "Marshall, please, look around, what do you see?"

"Evidently, it's not what you see. Tell us, all of us, what you see."

He gulps another hunk of air. "First Vince disappeared, then Jim took off someplace, next Tommie went missing, then something happened to Matt, and now Sarah is nowhere to be found. I don't know what's going on, but this isn't right."

Reggie comes to his rescue. "He's got a point."

"How do you explain it?" asks David.

Marshall says, "I can't, but let's put this into perspective. We're not running a conventional business, are we?"

Teddy settles down a wee bit. "If it were my decision alone, I'll suspend the operations and disappear. It doesn't smell right to me."

David asks, "You mean just walk away?"

"That's exactly what I mean. I'd walk away right now while we have a chance."

Marshall looks at Reggie, "We'd be leaving a hell of a lot of money on the table, wouldn't we?"

Reggie nods, "Oh yeah, significant sums for each of us."

David wonders aloud, "Isn't there a way to transfer money to each of our separate accounts before we disappear?"

"Of course that's possible. I could make that happen today if we all agreed." Reggie looks around at each of the others.

Teddy asks, "Then what happens with Jim's portion?" His forehead shows droplets of perspiration.

Reggie already has a ready response, "I have his account number. I could transfer his portion accordingly."

"Then let's do it now!" Teddy is raring to go with the suggestion.

Reggie asks, "Shouldn't we talk this over with Jim?"

Teddy asks, "Why? He's not around. Nobody knows where he is. Haven't you been listening?"

Reggie continues, "Well, it is his organization, and he did bring us into it. I just think we should put it out to him."

David finally voices his opinion. "The problem is we don't know where Jim is or how to contact him."

Marshall recommends a solution. "Let's do this. Each of us will sleep on it for two days. We'll convene a meeting at that time to vote. Since there are four of us, excluding Jim, majority will rule. In case of a tie we'll stay as is for a month. Then we'll go through the same process again until there is a majority one way or another." He looks around at the others.

Teddy asks, "Who's going to tell Vince?"

David answers, "Jim knows where he is. That'll be up to him."

Reggie is the first to agree, "OK with me."

Teddy huffs out a big breath of air, "That's not my first choice, but OK."

All eyes turn to David.

"I'm in."

««»»

Le Boeuf and Sarah set up a meeting to talk with Law.

"That about sums it up," Le Boeuf keeps her eyes on Law for a short time and then glances at Sarah. "Is there anything that I left out?"

She shakes her head, "I think you covered everything."

Law looks at Sarah. "How are you doing with the way this case is turning out?"

"I'm not sure what you mean?" Her glance between Law and Le Boeuf is not convincing.

Law puts aside the failed attempt of naivety for the time being. He takes on a more important matter. "You didn't entirely go by the books when you broke into her house and took evidence without a warrant."

She squirms in her seat, uneasy about the comment. She settles on looking at Le Boeuf.

"I'm OK with it, but you have to settle on what works for you." Le Boeuf is matter of fact.

Sarah says, "At first it was a little uncomfortable, but then I made up my mind that it was the only way."

Law keeps his stare at Sarah for a while and quickly glances at Le Boeuf right before he turns his back on both Agents. He realizes Sarah will most likely leave the Bureau once this case is put to bed. "Back in the days, there was a more trusting view of what our Government did and didn't do. Looking back, the notion was naive. Americans wanted to believe in truth and justice. There were movies made to support that belief, even the comic books had their heroes, such as Superman. But that's changed a whole lot. Nobody is above suspicion, no one is safe anymore. Those heroes of yesteryear could not make it in today's world."

He turns to look squarely at both Agents. "It was inevitable that everyone would be subject to scrutiny. Today, the inspection is often so intense that it seems to be a crime if you can't find some dirt about someone."

He lowers his head and shakes it sideways a few times. "Breaking the rules has always been done in the Bureau, even before I became an Agent myself. That's not surprising. How can we expect to play by the rules when the bad guys throw them out? That's not playing on an even field."

He pauses and then looks at Sarah. "But there are unspoken rules that we must comply with, and the biggest unspoken rule is this. Act as if everything is hunky-dory. Don't let on to the public or to other Agents that things might be out of control, or that you're having a bad day due to some personal problems. That isn't our job. Don't break character. The only exception is to keep me informed of what you're doing, preferably before you do it, so that I can cover your back. Eventually I'll trust you more and more as we get to know each other better, just as I trust Le Boeuf." He smacks his lips together, "So now, Sarah, how are you doing?"

She realizes the high stakes involved with her answer. "I'm doing fine."

Law grins, "I'm happy to hear that. Is there anything else I need to know?"

Sarah looks at Le Boeuf who signals to her with a lift of her head to answer. The question is directed to her. "What do you recommend we do next?"

"Le Boeuf, any ideas?"

"I think we should make a visit to Madeline Courier at her place of work to hear what she has to say."

Law asks, "What if she puts it together that your unexpected visit and the house break-in are connected somehow?"

"We'll deny knowing anything about the break-in, and only say that we're paying her a visit with regards to the photos of her and Ranger that were taken by the Bureau. We avoid saying anything about the break-in."

"Sarah, do you know Madeline's position with the County?"

"I'm afraid I don't."

"She is the Deputy County Medical Examiner."

"Oh, is that it?"

"Yes it is, but don't you want to know the importance of this information?"

"I guess I should."

"She is a Government County employee whom we often work with on cases. She is very good at what she does and I don't want her to become antagonistic towards the Bureau."

"So you want her to be handled with kid gloves?"

"Actually, the only special consideration is not to get ruff or argumentative with her, but don't back away. She is very good at taking the offense when she thinks she's being confronted or criticized. She'll try to get you out of character in order to push you away or to find out something about you or the case that she has no need to know. Yet at the same time, I want the truth from her about Ranger, where he is, why she was with him, and if she has any involvement with any of his illegal schemes."

"That's clear enough."

"Just remember the biggest unspoken rule."

"Act as if everything is hunky-dory. Don't get out of character."

««»»

Sarah and Le Boeuf walk side by side towards their car in the underground parking garage. Sarah is the first to speak. "That meeting took me by surprise."

"Why's that?"

"I figured we'd just update him on what happened at Madeline's house and then move on."

"His meetings are usually more than the subject of the meeting. He usually drops pearls of wisdom along the way. He's great to work with. He's taught me a lot."

"I can see that. I hope you become the first female Area Director of the Bureau." Sarah grins.

"Is that so?"

"You seem surprised."

"Why not you?"

"I don't think I'm cut out for that."

"And you think I am?"

"Could be, if that's what you want." Sarah pauses, not sure if she should continue, so she moves to another topic. "What's the plan with Madeline?"

"I don't know specifically. Do you have any ideas?"

"In addition to keeping my cool with her I don't know, maybe just play it straight up like we said in the meeting, without revealing anything about the break-in."

"Do you want to take the lead?"

Sarah turns to Le Boeuf, "Really, you'd agree with that?"

"I'm comfortable with it. What do you say?"

"I'm in."

They walk together in silence until they reach the parked vehicle.

Le Boeuf speaks. "I don't think we should call before. Let's catch her by surprise at the Morgue."

"Sounds like a plan."

««»»

They reach the County Morgue within thirty minutes. Le Boeuf pulls the vehicle into the parking lot and then comments to Sarah. "Check out what she drives."

Sarah stretches her neck to take a look at the Audi A6 Sedan. "Nice if you can afford it. I wonder what she makes."

"It's all public record, so that's easy to find out. My guess is high nineties as a Deputy County M. E., maybe slightly more. But that's just my guess."

Sarah curves her mouth and then blows air outward to make a whistling sound.

"There's an empty spot in the corner to park."

Once they exit the car, they walk confidently towards the front door.

A receptionist sits behind a high counter. "Good afternoon, how can I help you?"

Sarah pulls out her badge. "I'm Agent Noble and this is my partner Agent Le Boeuf from the F. B. I. We'd like to speak with the Deputy County Medical Examiner Madeline Courier."

The receptionist reaches to touch each badge for inspection. "Yes, I'll tell her you're here. Do you have an appointment?"

"No, I'm sorry we don't." Sarah glances towards Le Boeuf and then back to the receptionist. "I guess we should have thought about that before coming. I hope this isn't any inconvenience."

"Oh, no, don't worry." She waves her hand to brush off the matter as inconsequential. She uses a four digit phone extension number to notify Madeline. "Yes, it's me. There are two F. B. I. Agents who'd like to talk with you." She pauses, "No, I don't know what about, I didn't ask." After another pause the receptionist moves the phone away from her mouth to ask Sarah a question. "The Deputy is asking what it's about."

With poise Sarah answers, "It's confidential, you know Bureau work."

"Of course, I understand." The receptionist repositions the phone close to her mouth. "They say it's confidential." She frowns and then after a pause says, "I'm sure it's very important or else they wouldn't be here." A final pause ensues before the receptionist hangs up. "Yes, that's settled. You can come with me. We'll need to walk through that door." She lifts her chin towards a nearby door that indicates **For Official Use Only**.

The walk to Madeline's office is short.

"That's her office just ahead. I guess she stepped out for a second, I don't see her."

Le Boeuf mentions in a casual manner, "We can wait for her. There's no need for you to stay."

"Thanks. I've got a few things to catch up with before I leave for the day. Just take a seat." She points to two chairs that are stacked with piles of paper. "Let me move the papers so you can sit down." She steps forward to clear the papers away from both chairs. "There, that should do it. It was nice meeting you. Goodbye." The receptionist walks away.

Sarah remarks, "Cheery and professional, wasn't she."

Le Boeuf replies showing a slight grin, "The sun before the rain."

Both Agents glance around the messy office putting a temporary end to their conversation.

Sarah comments. "She's making us wait on purpose, isn't she?"

Le Boeuf grins, "That's my guess."

Moments later Madeline walks into her office. She stands, legs slightly parted, at the door way. She gives them a thorough look over before silently walking toward her desk. She takes a seat before talking. "What's this about?" She sounds annoyed. Her hands lie flat on top of the desk.

Sarah keeps her composure. "Thanks for seeing us with no notice. We apologize."

"Get on with it, what's on your mind?"

"I'm Agent Noble and this is Agent Le Boeuf."

Both Agents reveal their badges.

Madeline ignores looking at them. "They're printing them younger and younger."

Sarah is unable to hold back a frown.

Madeline clarifies, "You're only a kid."

Sarah feels her body temperature heat up, but she resists getting shaken.

"Le Boeuf, you're old enough to be her mother. Why's a mother encouraging her kid to work for the Bureau?"

"Madeline, cut the crap. This is serious. Grow up yourself." Le Boeuf's voice is controlled and firm. "We've known each other too long."

"It's been a tough day. I guess I'm a little wound-up. Talk to me."

Sarah hesitates, not sure she should take the lead or relinquish to her partner. In the end, she forges on. "I'll get right to the point."

Madeline interrupts, "Good idea." She smirks.

Sarah continues. "What we're about to talk about is confidential. You do understand."

"That's all I work with, confidential matters. I understand."

"We're working on a scamming case where the suspect is taking money from unsuspecting people. We believe you might know the suspect, and can assist us in the investigation."

Madeline glares at Le Boeuf. She flashes back to the recent visit from Law. "Did Law send you here?"

Le Boeuf remains quiet to let Sarah answer. "If you mean Area Director Law, then yes because we work for him."

She turns toward Sarah, "I told him everything."

"Area Director Law?"

"Yes, that's what I said. He sat right where you're sitting only a few days ago. He asked me about a man, Jim Ranger. He told me he had pictures of Jim and me. Is this the same case you're working on?"

Sarah's confusion prevents her from speaking, so Le Boeuf takes over. "Yes, it's the same one."

"Then talk to your boss!" Her voice rises.

Le Boeuf replies, "Since we're here, can you just give us a run down on how you know Jim Ranger and where we can find him? We'd like to talk with him as quickly as possible before he disappears."

Madeline turns away from both Agents. Her face is tense looking and her eyes look like daggers. "Like I said to Law, he's not the man you're looking for. The Jim Ranger I know is sweet and caring. He wouldn't harm anyone."

Sarah jumps back into the conversation. "OK, then. When we talk with him we can iron all this out. But we first need to find him in order to talk with him. Where is he?"

Madeline swallows as she tries to keep up with her rapidly changing emotions. "He's temporarily living with me until he can find a permanent place to stay. We've got plans, big plans to settle down together. I love the man."

Sarah gives a quick glance to Le Boeuf and then back at Madeline. "The sooner you can tell us where he is, the better it is so we can settle all of this."

"I'll tell him about it and ask him to contact you."

"Oh, no, that won't work. Just tell us where to find him." Sarah hears her voice raise a pitch.

"To be perfectly honest, I haven't seen him in a few days. He travels constantly."

Le Boeuf asks, "When do you expect him back?"

"This may sound as if I'm hiding something from you, but I really don't know. That's the truth, honest."

Le Boeuf doesn't buy her statement. "There's no way you talk with him when he's traveling, is that what you're saying?"

"For all I know he could be in Schenectady or Sausalito. Like I said he travels a lot."

"You're not buying time so that you can alert him to us, are you?" Le Boeuf keeps on target.

"No, definitely not, I wouldn't do that, he's done nothing wrong."

Le Boeuf looks at Sarah. "That's all I've got. Anything else we should ask the Deputy County Medical Examiner?"

"I think that covers it." Sarah smiles as she turns to face Madeline. "Thanks for being so cooperative. If Jim Ranger contacts you, however, don't mention that we talked. But if you could let either one of us know when he returns, we'd greatly appreciate it. Would you do that?"

Madeline gives off a forced smile, "Of course."

CHAPTER 13

Eleven men sit on the warehouse floor, the same warehouse used before where a sign dangles, **Quality Is Our Middle Name**. The men's legs are crossed one over the other and they keep silent as they have been told. The smell of oil and grease still lingers in the air. It is just the right place for the meeting.

Suddenly a man's voice shouts out, "Mr. Xia."

Everyone quickly stands, to do otherwise would show disrespect.

Slowly Mr. Xia walks to be visible to the men now at attention, taking long strides in spite of his five feet one inch height. He takes a seat, the only visible chair around. He nods once.

"Sit." The same man's voice shouts out the command.

All eleven men resume their former positions.

Mr. Xia speaks with fervor, yet controlled. "I have brought you here together in a private gathering to provide you an important lesson for survival. I title this lesson, obedience. It is a lesson that all followers must learn. One of my responsibilities is to give orders, and what you have to do is to comply with those orders. Sometimes there are followers who do not carry out my orders. There may be a rationale explanation, there may not be. I know of five frequent reasons why orders are not followed."

He pauses to look over the men. He sees nervousness in their eyes. Satisfied he has their full attention, he continues. "One, followers might not correctly understand what I want done. Two, followers might not have the resources to carry out the order. Three, it might not be in the followers' interests to complete the order. Four, there may not be sufficient consequences, both positive and negative, to do what is ordered. Five, there may be unforeseen obstacles that appear which prevent the order from being achieved. I understand all of this. Yet some followers get infected with disobedience, like an overwhelming disease. In other words, some followers simply don't follow orders. Unless you recognize this within you, you too might be infected, and I know of only one cure, and cure is not pleasant."

He halts briefly before resuming. "I have an order that I want fulfilled. If you can accomplish this, you have nothing to worry about. If this order is not done then there will be a final cure."

This time he spends a few long moments before moving on. "Here is the order, so listen carefully. Mr. Jim Ranger owes me money. I no longer care about the money, but I do care about respect. He has disrespected me, and he must pay. I want Ranger found and put to death. I don't care what it takes or how you do it. Just do it. I am not interested in excuses, only results. You have five days from today."

Mr. Xia stands.

The eleven men at once get up from the floor and remain motionless while standing until he leaves the area.

««»»

"Where're Teddy and Marshall? Don't they know we've scheduled this meeting?" Reggie stands at the back of the conference room pouring a cup of coffee. "Do you want a cup?"

David shakes his head, "No, I've had enough this morning." He checks his wristwatch. "Marshall told me he was going to pick up Teddy this morning. He was concerned that Teddy might not come in."

"Why's that?" Reggie takes a sip of coffee.

"He was worried about him since Teddy wasn't actually in control of himself at our last meeting."

"Yeah, that was sure strange behavior, I agree."

"Let's wait a while before I call his cell."

Reggie looks at the extensive assortment of fresh fruit, pastry, and juices on the back table. "Maybe we should cut down on this stuff." His back is now turned away from David.

"It's really not that much. We get it wholesale."

Suddenly David's cell phone rings. He glances at the dial. Without looking up he says to Reggie, "It's Marshall."

Reggie turns around towards David.

"Hey Marshall, what's up? Have you forgotten about the meeting?" David listens for a few seconds. "No shit!" He glances at Reggie. "Yes, stay there until you're asked to leave. That's terrible. I'll let Reggie know. It's terrible." He shuts down the cell. David's face is pale.

"What's wrong, what happened?" Reggie looks intently at David.

"Teddy is dead." His voice is faint, almost impossible to hear.

"Oh my God, how did it happen?"

David takes in a deep breath of air, and then takes a seat in a nearby chair. His body starts to tremble slightly.

Reggie places the coffee cup on the back table and heads to be next to David. "Talk to me."

"It appears that Teddy died of an overdose of something."

"No, that can't be. I don't believe it."

"It was a tightly held secret. Very people knew, I think only Jim and me knew."

"I can't believe this."

"Twice previously that I can remember Teddy barely survived overdoses with drugs. He mostly used crack."

"No, that can't be true. You and Jim knew him before?"

"Yeah, a while back. Then we went our separate ways until now."

"Oh, I didn't know that."

"I suspected it was only a matter of time when the pressure got to him that he'd go back, and even overdose. I'm actually not surprised. It's tough to break the habit."

"No foul play involved?"

"That'll be up to the police to figure out. With drug deaths there's typically an autopsy. And, let's be honest, he wasn't in the business of making friends."

"No other health problems?"

"I think he had a difficult time breathing normally. I saw him once when his face and lips swelled from some sort of adverse reaction of the medicine he was taking."

"That sounds like emphysema. My mother had it, and not a pretty sight."

"Then you know how difficult it probably was for him to get fresh air into his lungs."

"Yeah, but still he took crack? That's stupid."

"I know."

"So, Marshall found him dead?"

"I guess so. He called 911 and when they arrived the paramedics couldn't revive him. I guess Marshall has to be questioned."

"Damn, that's terrible."

Now calmed down, David says, "We shouldn't say anything to anyone in the office about this. Agreed?"

Marshall agrees, "Completely."

"I also think we should keep the office open."

"Yes, no sudden moves. It might unsettle them." Marshall motions with his head to where the office personnel continue to work.

"If anyone asks where he is, we'll say he's traveling. No more."

"Yes, the least said the better."

"I'd like to hear from Jim. It seems since he left this place has been in turmoil."

"We're still turning a profit, and that's what matters, isn't it?"

"I'm not arguing with the financial return, I'm just saying that things haven't been the same. You have to agree with that."

"I'll give you that much, but I'm not worried one bit. This place could run itself because of the system we've set up. It's on automatic pilot and we're just riding the wave, in a manner of speaking."

《《》》

The door leading from the holding cell to the courtroom is reinforced metal. Tommie Gray wears an orange jumpsuit, something that will not be allowed should there be a trial. At the wrists, his hands are handcuffed and are secured by a chain around his waist. Further, there is a metal binding around each ankle that is linked by a two foot chain. As Tommie walks, the metal jangles. There are two security guards on each side of him to keep an eye on him.

Inside the courtroom there is a court administrator, a court reporter, the prosecuting attorney, the defendant's attorney, and the judge. All other chairs are empty.

Judge Albright starts it off. "The purpose of this preliminary hearing is to determine if there is adequate cause to require the accused, Mr. Tommie Gray, to stand trial for the offenses charged. In this case it is murder and robbery."

The defense quickly asks, "Your Honor, I request the restraints be removed from my client while he is in the courtroom."

The prosecutor quickly stands up, "I disagree. May we approach the bench?"

Judge Albright responds, "There's no one else in the court, so tell me what's on your mind."

"Your Honor, the accused is in a position to stand trial for murder. He is hot-tempered and highly unpredictable, and has been a problem during the waiting period for this hearing. I believe he will try to escape if his restraints are removed."

"There is no evidence of my client's personality as described. That discussion would occur should there be a trial. This is not the time to bring up such nonsense."

"That's not the point, your Honor. What if Mr. Gray tries to break out? Without the restraints he could cause all sorts of havoc."

"Your Honor, we have two trained guards standing inside the courtroom that are adequately prepared to subdue him, if that should ever happen. The doors are locked. How on earth could he escape?"

"Even if he didn't succeed, he could harm us. He's already killed one person. He has the capacity to kill again."

"Your Honor, that's simply an outrageous and irresponsible conclusion!"

Before more debate continues, Judge Albright interrupts, "Both of you give it a rest." He turns to Tommie Gray. "Son, do you have any intention to run out during this preliminary hearing?"

Tommie looks at the Judge eye-to-eye. Without showing any emotion in his face or feeling in his voice he says, "I'm not your son."

"Yes, I'm aware of that."

"I'm nobody's son."

"Would you care to answer my question?"

"I'm already planning my escape."

"Well, well. That demonstrates something about your attitude." He turns to look at both attorneys. "In my courtroom the restraints remain in place until I say otherwise."

««»»

Madeline sits alone at the bar drinking a classic Martini made from Boodles Dry Gin, a bead of Cinzanno Dry Vermouth, stirred and served straight up, with two olives. She slides one olive into her mouth, slowly chews it until it melts away. She stares at herself in the large mirror behind the bar. There is music in the background, low and gently sounding that is barely audible. In the mirror, she catches sight of the man she's been waiting for. There is a slight sigh of relief.

Law slowly walks towards her, looks around at the nearly vacant place, and then takes a seat at the bar next to her.

"Hi." His voice is toned-down all the while feeling in good spirits from her invitation.

She turns to him, "Thanks for coming. What'll you have? I've got a tab running."

He looks at the half filled drink in front of her. "Definitely not one of those, I'll have a Pinch neat."

She raises her voice slightly to call out to the bartender at the other end of the bar. "Joey, Mr. C will have a Pinch, neat. Give him a double."

Joey nods his head and gives her a smile to acknowledge the drink order.

"Is that me, Mr. C?"

"I'll explain shortly, but yes, it is."

"And who are you, or do you dare me to speculate?" He smiles at what seems to him to be a cute game.

She is all business, without her normal quick-wit and clever responses. "I'm Miss B."

He doesn't want the conversation to become serious so he proceeds, "Are there others, a Miss A or a Mr. A?"

"Yes there is. Mr. A is Jim Ranger, but don't mention his name to Joey. Trust me."

"Are there any Miss or Mr. D, E, F and so forth?"

"Of course there are."

"Who are they?"

"That's not important now."

The bartender appears before them with a double Pitch neat in a crystal glass. "Will you be having dinner tonight?" He looks first at Madeline but when she does not react he turns to look at Law for an answer.

Madeline is late in her response. "I think we'll have a drink first and then decide."

"Certainly Miss B," Joey says as he walks away.

"Madeline, what's going on?"

She raises her glass towards him. "Let's toast to good fortune." She forces a smile that does not fool either one.

He concedes for the time being, "Yes, to good fortune."

They each take a sip of their drinks.

Madeline beats Law at getting to the point of the meeting. "I asked you here because I've been thinking about something, very seriously."

"Oh," he straightens his posture in the stool.

"The two Agents you had pounce on me were the same two who broke into my place, weren't they?"

"I don't know what you mean, Agents Le Boeuf and Noble?"

"Cut the crap, I know they were the ones."

"I'll look into it, but I can't imagine they would break the law."

She lets out a puff of air, getting slightly disturbed by his attitude. "Anyway, it got me thinking about Ranger."

Law's body slightly jerks as he begins to listen more attentively.

"I guess I've got your attention."

"Go on, I'm listening."

"I know you are now. Anyway, I did some snooping on my own." She takes another sip of the cocktail before she continues. "We both know he's been living at my place, but just for a short time. Some of his clothes are still around while he's traveling. I found a few receipts from restaurants, hotels, and airlines. He's what they call a frequent traveler. He's accumulated thousands of miles. I found several different names on the receipts, not one is Jim Ranger. I hate to admit this to you, but I agree with you. He's not who he claims to be."

"Well, that's something." Law frowns, not sure what help the information might be to track him down.

"That's only part of it. There's more."

"Oh, what else is there?"

"That's where Joey comes into the picture."

"Joey the bartender, is that who you mean?"

"The one and only, Joey the bartender."

"What does he know?"

"I'm going to let the two of you talk while I go to the ladies room." She looks away from Law. "Joey, can you come here?" She curls her finger towards him.

He smiles as he approaches Madeline. He looks at both drinks, frowns, and then asks, "Miss B, are you ready for dinner?"

"No, not just yet, I want you and Mr. C to have a talk. My friend is very important and we'd both appreciate your help in something." She takes the Martini with her as she leaves Joey and Law together.

Joey looks squarely in the eyes of Law without blinking. "What can I do for you Mr. C?"

Law pulls out his badge. "Joey, I'm with the F. B. I." He pauses to maximize the surprise. Then he puts the badge away. "I understand you know Mr. A, is that right?"

Joey's eyes begin to blink a few times. "Yes, yes, he comes in here on a regular basis, sometimes alone, sometimes not."

"When he comes in with others, is there only one person or many, men or women?"

"I'd say all of the above."

"What type of business is Mr. A in, do you know?"

"Ah, no I don't."

"Joey, I know you do, tell me."

"Really Mr. C, I don't know."

"You've never overheard any conversations he's had with those with whom he's been with?"

"Well, just bits and pieces."

"Tell me the bits and the pieces, as best as you can remember."

"Is he in any trouble?"

"I'm just trying to talk with him about a few things. He travels a lot, you know, and I keep missing him. So, tell me what you've overheard."

"I don't want to get him into any trouble."

"You don't have to worry about that. Just tell me, what have you heard?"

Joey lets out a deep breath of air. He feels a little confused for the moment, but quickly settles down. "Oh, yeah, I remember a little."

"That's good. Tell me."

"I think he's a sales manager because he's always talked about motivating his sales team."

"What kind of sales, pharmaceutical, computer, clothing, or whatever?"

"I think he knows something about gold and silver investments."

"Joey, I think you believe he knows a great deal about gold and silver investments."

"Really, why do you say that?"

"Joey, remember who I am. I showed you my badge, so cut out faking what you know, tell me everything."

Joey swallows deeply and then continues. "That's what he talks about all the time. You know, the deflation of the dollar, the way the world's economies are going. You know."

"I see." Law pauses. "Have you invested in gold or silver?"

Joey leans over to whisper. "Between you and me, Mr. A gave me a special deal."

"Really, what kind of deal did he give you?"

"He told me about gold coins."

"What did he say about gold coins?"

"That gold increases in value, that it's a safe investment for someone like me who's newly married with a kid on the way."

"So you invested?"

"Of course, haven't you?"

"Not yet."

"What are you waiting for? Haven't you seen those television ads, you know the ones with the famous actors?"

"I don't watch much television."

"If I were you, I'd scrape up the money to do it. This opportunity is not going to last much longer."

"Is that what Mr. A says, that this is a limited opportunity?"

"Yeah, and I take his word on it."

"Do you have the gold coins stored in a safe place?"

"It's in the safest place ever."

"Oh, stored in a bank?"

"Not at all, they're with Mr. A's investment company."

"How do you know that?"

"Mr. A gave me an official certificate verifying it. He even signed it."

"I guess that's proof enough."

"Of course, very safe."

"Is he a nice guy?"

"Huh?"

"Is he a nice guy? Does Mr. A treat the people he's with well? Does he treat you well? Or is he mean to others? You get the idea."

"I've never seen him lose his temper, if that's what you mean, and he tips well. Hell, he told me about investing in gold."

"Do you think you'd recognize any of the people you've seen him with if they came into the bar without him?"

"Sure, I think so."

"Have you ever seen any of them come into the bar alone?"

"No, I don't think so."

"Is there anything about him that might seem unusual or strange?"

"Like what?"

"Like out of the ordinary, or something that surprised you, anything."

"No. He's really not unlike you or me. He looks like a common guy, nothing special about him, just a regular guy."

"When will he be back from his travels?"

"I don't know."

"Has anyone, other than me, recently been asking of his whereabouts?"

"Yeah, a few guys, my age, came in here a day or two ago, wanting to talk with him about investments."

"What did you tell them?"

"I said I didn't know where he was or when he'd come into the bar. But I said I'd pass him the message that they were looking for him."

"Can you describe these men?"

"It was a busy night, so I didn't get a real good look at them."

"Try hard."

"The guy who did the talking was grouchy. He was ordinary looking. The other two guys were quiet. One was thin and bald, while the other one was fat. That's really it."

Madeline approaches the bar. The Martini glass is empty. "Are you two done?"

Law turns to face her. "I think so."

She takes her former seat. "Good. Now I can have another drink."

Law asks, "How about dinner, are you hungry?"

««»»

Over dinner Law appears preoccupied with something, not concentrating on the conversation. Madeline speaks up. "What's on your mind?"

"It's Ranger and what he's doing to people. He's got Joey believing in him. The poor kid's invested in gold coins that probably are worthless or that don't even exist. He's doing this to all sorts of people. I can't let the bastard get away, I won't."

"I never knew, I should have, but I didn't. He was so kind and thoughtful to me. I thought he really cared about me, about us."

"You're speaking in the past tense."

"It has to be over between us, I can't let him continue in my life knowing what he's been up to."

"Does that mean there may be room for someone else?"

She smiles, but for a short time, and then her face is neutral looking. "Jackson, you were very important in my life at one time, and in a way you still are very special, but not in the way you want it to be. I'm sorry."

"I can change, I know I can."

"That's water under the bridge, let it flow, let it go." She takes a sip of the Martini in front of her. "What about Agent Le Boeuf?"

"Huh?"

"Agent Le Boeuf, you know the Agent that was with Agent Noble. Let's call them Miss D and Miss E, the two who broke into my house."

He raises his voice, "They didn't break into your house, so stop saying that!"

"Shh, lower your voice. I'm sitting right here. I can hear you."

"They didn't break into your house." He grabs the crystal glass in front of him to swallow the scotch. "Back to Le Boeuf, what does she have to do with us?"

"Miss D seems more your type, that's all I'm saying."

"And what type is that?"

"Listen Jackson, I'm not a social worker and I'm not a match maker. I'm just saying that Miss D seems right for you. I don't know why."

"Stop calling people by a letter!"

"Do you realize that we know each other, Miss D and me?"

His eyes are unblinking like a statue.

"There aren't many women in the type of jobs we have. We're a small number and we tend to get to know each other over time."

"Why are you telling me this?"

The harshness of his voice momentarily startles her. She flinches. "You've got a point, there's really no reason."

He jeers her way, almost in a taunting fashion.

She ignores the attempted intimidation as she takes a sip of the Martini. Then she asks, "Did Joey help you out?"

Law still lingers on her comment about Le Boeuf, puzzled over Madeline's assessment. "Huh?"

"I said did Joey help you out?"

"In a way."

"Care to tell me or do you want me to guess?"

"He's seen Ranger talk with other people about gold investments, maybe some of them were investors and maybe some of them were part of his team. He described him as an ordinary person but likeable, nothing that really stands out.

CHASE

And that's one of Ranger's greatest assets. He acts as if he's your pal who wants to help you."

"I guess you've got one of your biggest challenges ahead, finding him."

"No kidding."

"I'm starved, let's look at the menu."

"One more question, and then I'll stop."

"Sure, what is it?"

"What will you do now that Ranger is out of your life, as am I?"

"That's a great question, something I've been thinking about." She moistens her lips with a quick swipe from her tongue. "I think I'll leave the area, move someplace where no one knows me, and start up again. I think I need a change of scenery to rejuvenate myself. I've read about people my age re-careering."

"You can't be serious?"

"Oh no, to the contrary, I'm very serious. I take it you don't think it's a good idea."

"That's right. You're running away from your current situation, not towards anything specific. What's to say you won't wind up in the same situation elsewhere? Isn't it better to be pulled to a place rather than to be pushed away?"

"Normally, yes, but this isn't normal. I have to get away. That's just how it is?"

"What will you do and how will you earn a living? What kind of lifestyle will you live?"

"Elementary, Doctor Watson, simply elementary."

"So this might be our last supper, that's what I'm hearing."

"Oh, Jackson, don't be so gloomy. Be happy for me that I'm trying to figure a few things out, even at my age. I want you to be happy for me, to support me. Don't tell me why I can't or shouldn't do this, help me do it."

He takes a final swallow of scotch. "I'm not very hungry."

"It's not like this is our last supper together."

"It sure feels that way to me."

««◊»»

A short time after midnight the next morning Madeline tosses and turns in bed. She is alone, restless and unable to fall asleep for more than ten minutes at a time, at most. She sits up, moves the pillow against her back for support and stares at the open window nearby. The night's cool air glides through the room and across her bed, not cold enough for her to change the natural air conditioning. In her mind she rewinds the evening spent with Jackson, flip flopping with regards to making it clear enough she's determined to start a new chapter in her life that does not include him as one of the main characters. Yet, she wonders how much more obvious she could have been. "He's always been stubborn and probably always will." Her lips barely move as she speaks in an undertone to herself. She continues in a low voice. "I should be happy I've made this decision, but I'm sad in a way. I wonder why." She curls her shoulders in just the right way to release some tension that has been building up, and then she twists her head sideways a few times to loosen the muscles in her neck. "I'm not going to back off from my decision, it's final and that's that." She pauses with the inner dialogue for a few seconds. The intermission gives her the opportunity to pay attention to the silence that surrounds her. She smiles, comforted with the stillness. Slowly she closes her eyes, takes in a deep breath of air and lets her head rest on the pillow. She falls asleep, but the calm does not last very long.

Ranger unlocks the front door. The clicking sound of the lock's tumblers moving in the right direction is barely heard, but loud enough to wake Madeline.

Her eyes pop open while her body remains still. She listens for another sound.

He presses the door handle downward to open the door, and then closes it. The door strikes the wooden frame with sufficient force to announce its reunion. Ranger tip toes with the grace of a ballet dancer to keep the sound of his movement as minimal as possible. He makes his way up the stairs, unaware that Madeline is wide-eyed and alert.

He reaches the master bedroom, but hesitates for an instant, looking at her in bed. He immediately notices she is not asleep. He forces a smile that does not fool either one.

"Good morning Jim." Her voice is sharp sounding.

He remains in place for another second or two before he unhurriedly steps forward. He senses his own timidity and movement at a snail's pace. "I didn't want to wake you."

She wants to believe him, but down deep inside she now believes he's a liar. "Is that so?" Her eyes are unblinking.

Gradually he makes his way to her side, sits on the bed's edge, and reaches over to touch her. "I'm bushed from travel, I need a little sleep."

"I bet you do."

He quickly deciphers what she means, so he tries to shift the conversation, "You sound tired too. Are you working too hard? Maybe you and I need to get away together for a while."

"You've got part of it right."

He senses she's onto him, so to settle down he slowly breaths in and out. "I'd like to talk about this more, but I really need some rest. Can we have dinner tonight?"

"How much longer did you think you could mislead me?"

He plays the part of being confused. He cocks his head to the side and wrinkles his forehead. "I'm not following you."

"Your pretense, you know, putting on an act to pretend to be someone you're not."

He swallows without her noticing. "I'm still not following you." He figures the least said the better off he is.

"Let's start with us. Do you really love me, or are you using me?"

"Of course I love you. He reaches to touch her face."

She pulls back. "Don't touch me."

"If you have another man in your life then I should be the one who's put off, not you. Is there another man?"

"Nice try, don't switch it around. Answer my question, do you really love me or are you using me?"

"I love you and always will. I'm just having some business problems that are distracting me from giving you the attention you deserve. I'm sorry that's happening."

She feels disgusted at his obvious cover up. Yet there is something about him that wants her to leave the discussion to another time. She is close to falling for his well invented trap. "How much do you love me?"

He is not about to lose control of the conversation. "So much that I want to marry you as soon as possible." He creates tears at the corner of his eyes.

She does not pick up on the fabricated tearfulness at first, but then with just a little time to think about it she realizes he is making it all up. She purposely waits to hear what else he cooks up.

"You don't seem happy. I've just proposed to you, I thought you'd be delighted."

"It's all so sudden. My mind hasn't taken it all in." She figures two can play the same game.

He leans over to kiss her.

"No, don't do that. I've got a cold and I'm taking some medication. You shouldn't get too close to me. I don't want you to get what I've got." She holds her hands between his face and hers.

"Just a little kiss, that's all I need."

"I don't think it's a good idea."

He's not accustomed to a woman being frigid with him. "Come on, just a little kiss."

She gives in, albeit not wholeheartedly.

"Now, that wasn't so bad." He smiles more to himself for winning the battle than for showing sincere affection. "I suppose you want me to sleep in the spare bed."

"That's actually not a bad idea."

««»»

Several hours later the same morning, Madeline wakes up, tired from a restless sleep. She checks in on Jim to find him sound asleep in a spare bedroom. He looks content and at peace with himself. She wonders how he does it. Deceiving others to take hard earned money is something she could not live with. It would drive her crazy.

She readies herself for work, and then leaves without telling him goodbye or leaving a note. She intends to let Jackson know about where he is once she gets to work.

At the sound of the garage door opening and then closing, Jim steps out of bed. He looks out a nearby window to confirm that Madeline is driving off. He figures he has only a short time to gather his stuff and leave the place before he is found out. It takes him less than thirty minutes to complete the undertaking.

««»»

Thirty minutes later Madeline pulls her Audi into her assigned parking place. She reviews the tasks ahead for the day, prioritizing a visit with her boss to resign as the main item. Next is to tell her staff about her employment decision, and then to give a call to Law about Ranger's whereabouts.

"Are you sure you know what you're doing?" David Benadryl, the Medical Examiner, is surprised.

"I've given this much thought. I need a change of scenery to figure out the next chapter of my life. It's the right thing to do, I'm sure."

"You sound awfully confident. I wish I could detect some doubt in your voice but I don't. In a way I envy you."

"Why's that?"

"It isn't everyday that a successful person of good health and spirits changes her career. It takes guts, and I think more people should do it."

"That's how I see it, we only have one life. I appreciate your understanding."

"When will you leave us? I'll need to get Human Resources involved in finding a replacement, although no one can really replace you."

"Thanks for the compliment. Would thirty days be sufficient?"

"A year would be better." His smile is genuine and sincere. "But I know that's unreasonable. Yes, a month will do."

"I'd like to tell my staff as soon as possible before they hear it from someone else. May I?"

"Of course. Further, it you want me to say anything to them, just let me know. Also, I hope you realize that I'll give you an exceptional reference should you need one."

"That's very kind."

"Don't let on to Human Resources, they'll only step in to stop it. They'll want to control all communication."

"I completely understand."

««»»

"Are you positive he's still there?" Law's voice is a mixture of joy and surprise.

"I can't be one hundred percent positive of anything, but he was sound asleep when I left for work."

"How long ago was that?"

Madeline checks her watch. "I'd say about an hour ago, maybe a little more."

"This is the break I've been hoping for. Thanks. I owe you big time."

"Just be happy for me."

"Yes." His voice is cheerless sounding.

"I've got cases at the Morgue to act on, so I've got to go."

"Yes, again thanks."

As soon as the phones disconnect, Law gets a hold of Agents Le Boeuf and Noble to give them an update.

««»»

"We're going to put the bastard away for a long time." Sarah's eyes are opened wider than normal.

"You sound as if this is personal." Le Boeuf momentarily glances towards Sarah, and then refocuses on the cars in front. Her hands firmly grip the steering wheel.

"Sort of." Her lips are now tightly clenched shut.

"Did it happen to you, is that why you sound so compelled?"

"My parents got ripped off by a scumbag like him. There's no need to have people like him steal from others. He needs to be put away."

"Be careful. Don't let your personal emotions get in the way of doing something foolish. We don't want him to be freed based on a technicality or any other mishandling. It's not worth it."

"Nothing to worry about, I'm in control." Her eyes stay widened as before.

"You don't sound it and you don't look it. Pull out of it, now!" Her voice rises to a louder more ominous sound. "Do you hear me?"

Sarah nods her head without saying anything in return.

Le Boeuf swerves off to the side of the road.

Sarah looks her way, "What are you doing?"

Le Boeuf grabs her by the arm. "Listen to me! You've got to keep in check your feelings, rein them in, whatever it takes! Do you understand?"

"I'm OK, really, I'm OK."

"Let me make it very clear. If I suspect that you can't keep your emotions under control, I'll get you removed from this case and have you evaluated by the Bureau's shrink. I'm very close to doing that now. So help me I'll do it. I don't need a reason, only a suspicion, which is what I'm close to having now."

Sarah's head nods like that of a bobble doll. "I'm OK now." She looks away, eyes still glazed over a bit, but becoming more alert with time.

"I'm going to trust you because that's what partners do, but don't let me down."

"I won't, I promise."

Le Boeuf turns to the steering wheel and swings onto the road. Silence masks the still felt tension.

Twenty minutes later, Le Boeuf stops the car in the driveway. "I don't see any vehicles around. I wonder if he's still inside."

"There's only one way to say for sure." Sarah opens the car door to step onto the ground.

"You take the front, and I'll circle to the back to cut off the other possible escape route."

Sarah rings the door bell and without delay knocks on the door. "Jim Ranger, come out with your hands up. We know you're in there."

She listens for movement inside. It is quiet, so she repeats the dual announcement with the same order. Again, there is silence. She places her hand on the door handle and then lowers the metal device. The door easily opens. She pulls out her revolver and then gently shoves the front door wide open. She walks inside, moving her head to the left, middle, and right to get sight of any evidence Ranger is still inside. She reverses the head movement with the same result. She sees Le Boeuf spot her through the back glass sliding door. She nods her head to the side, and then moves to open the back door. "I don't think he's here."

"I'll go upstairs. You keep sight of any movement down here." Le Boeuf approaches the stairs leading to the second floor. A few minutes later she yells, "All clear. The upstairs is empty."

Sarah grimaces, not happy to hear the news. "Shit."

"He's gone." Le Boeuf shakes her head, disliking the truth.

"What do we do now?" Sarah feels her insides tighten. Her chest expands in and out as she tries to cope with what's happened. "Shit," she repeats.

Le Boeuf, while more in control of her emotions than her partner, is still angry as hell. She feels her teeth grind against the other. She looks around one more time to see if she's missed anything. Then the door's edge gets her attention. She frowns and juts her head forward. In silence she walks towards the opened door.

"What are you looking at?" Sarah follows close behind.

"I hope it is what I think it is." Le Boeuf crouches to take a closer look see.

"What do you have there?"

"Looks like blood splatter. It's impossible to tell for sure, but I'm hoping it belongs to Ranger."

"If that's so then we know for certain he was here."

"And we can assume he didn't leave on his own. He was forced."

"Who do you think took him?"

"His life is full of near disasters, but he's always been able to escape. Maybe someone was after him for something? I don't know."

"We should get it sent down to the lab."

"And who is the one we should call?" Le Boeuf grins at Sarah.

"The Deputy County M. E.?"

"That's who I'd call, but she's County. We should tell Law what we've found. Let him make the decision. Why don't you call it in to him now to give him an update."

"I'll do it, but then I better get back to the office. I'm been gone too long. They might start suspecting something."

CHAPTER 14

A thin man, bald, late twenties drives a dark blue Pilot Honda. He keeps quiet for now. His eyes are fastened to the highway.

Sitting next to him is a portly man, same age as the driver who looks out the passenger door window. He too is silent.

Sitting in the back seat is a no nonsense type of guy, mid thirties, who prefers to work alone, but in this instance is doing what Xia asks. He is mostly grouchy.

Ranger is curled up in a ball alongside the grouchy man. His hands are tied together as are his ankles. There is a rag stuffed in his mouth to keep him quiet. He squirms and says something that is incomprehensible. The blood on his forehead has coagulated enough to stop the bleeding he sustained during the struggle inside Madeline's house.

"Stop moving around or I'll end it right here and now!" The grouchy man pulls out a six inch blade knife to point at Ranger. "I swear I'll do it."

The driver looks in the rear view mirror. "We've got to take a picture of him first to show Mr. Xia that he was alive and then another one to show what happened."

"I know, I know! He's just pissing me off!"

The portly man continues to look through the window, expressionless as if he is unconcerned about the goings on.

The driver continues, "We're almost there. Just a few more miles and we'll be there."

The grouchy man sneers at Ranger, "Did you hear that, you're almost dead?"

Ranger wiggles again with another grunt to no avail.

The portly man keeps staring outside. "I've been thinking about what I'll do with my share."

The driver gives him a glance, "What?"

"I think I'll get some good, I mean really good clothes. That's what I think I'll do."

The grouchy man says, "To cover up your fat?"

"Shut the fuck up."

"Just stop eating."

"I said shut the fuck up."

The driver continues to drive without getting into the conversation.

The talk ends for a short time without anyone caring about much of anything else to say.

The driver speaks. "I think I'll take a vacation on a cruise. I've never been on one." He smiles of the thought.

The grouchy man says, "Stay away from cruises. People die on cruises."

The portly man sides with the man in the back seat. "Oh, yeah, people die on cruises. I'd stay away from them."

The driver asks, "What are going to do with your share?" He looks in the rear view mirror again.

The grouchy man thinks for a short time. "Get some crack and have a good time."

"You're crazy, you know that?" The portly man twists his head to face the man in the back seat. "You are fucking crazy."

There is another round of silence for a short time.

Ranger's face is drained of color. He finds it hard to breath and his energy is almost gone.

"There it is." The driver pulls the Pilot into a stone pebbled driveway in need of repair. A sign is positioned atop a twenty foot pole, **Syd's Motel - Vacancy**. "Who's going inside to rent the room?"

The portly man straightens his body, "Me."

The driver stops the Pilot in front of a sign, **Office**, above a door. "Just one night, that's all we need."

The portly man opens the passenger door. "Not even that," he momentary looks at Ranger.

Ranger lets out a muffled noise.

As the portly man walks inside to rent the motel room, the driver moves the vehicle away from the **Office** door.

Within fifteen minutes, the portly man returns. "Room seven. Only forty bucks."

"Let's get this over with." The grouchy man is eager to end Ranger's life.

The driver sarcastically asks, "Got a date?"

With returned mockery, he says, "Yeah, with your squeeze!"

Now inside room seven, the portly man interrupts the quarrel. "OK, give it up. Where do I put his bag?"

The driver says, "Put it over there." He points to the top of the bed. "It's got to be seen in the picture after he's dead."

«« »»

Sarah walks into the office, still a bit keyed up from working with Le Boeuf only a half hour ago. She looks around to catch a glimpse of Dick and Karen at their workstations.

Both are on the phones talking with potential investors, still unaware of the scam they are perpetuating.

Sarah keeps calm as she makes her way to her workstation.

She stares at the pile of cards neatly stacked near the desktop phone. She reaches for the top one to take a look at it. She reads the personal information and then returns the card to the top of the heap. She stretches her hand to tear off two pieces of scotch tape from a nearby dispenser and then she gets hold of the phone's handset. She hears a dial tone. Quickly she applies the tape over the top of the phone's cradle, depressing the two hook switch buttons to prevent a connection. The dial tone disappears. She reaches for the top card again and then pushes the appropriate numbered buttons to fake making a call. She hesitates a few seconds as if she is waiting for someone to pick up. Then she continues with the phony call by speaking aloud. "Hello, is this Mr. Ed Demister?" She continues simulating a real call for a few minutes, and then pretends to have settled a deal with a raise of one hand high in the air. She repeats the same process for another hour.

She takes a breather to think about her next move, but her thoughts are suddenly interrupted.

"Looks as if you're having a good day."

The unexpected appearance startles her for a brief second. Her body jerks backwards. She turns to see Dick standing by her side. "You took me by surprise."

"Sorry, I didn't mean to." He smiles. "Seems as if you're in a groove, I hate to interrupt."

"Actually I'm thankful you came along when you did. This takes a lot out of you."

He keeps quiet.

"How have you been?" She feels her heart's beat slow down.

"I'm getting bored. I thought I wouldn't but I am."

No longer startled by Dick's appearance, she asks, "Why?"

"It's so repetitive."

Her short lived anxiety is no longer a threat to her composure. "Do you want to talk about it sometime?"

"Karen feels the same way. We're thinking of quitting."

"Oh, really?"

"We're planning to have drinks after work. Betty, you remember Betty?"

"Sure I do. What's with Betty?"

"She's going to join us."

"Oh."

"You're invited if you want to come, the more ideas the better."

Sarah hesitates.

"But if you've got other plans or don't want to, that's fine as well. But you are invited."

"No, no, I want to. What time?"

"Right after work."

"OK, don't leave without me."

"The bosses are gone for the day, so we might even sneak out earlier." He grins.

"Count me in all the way."

««»»

"I could have stopped by in person to see you, but I decided to call instead."

Madeline knits her brow. "What's it about?"

One word is sufficient from Law, "Ranger."

"Oh, did you find him?" She feels her mouth start to go dry.

"Not exactly."

"What's that supposed to mean?"

"He wasn't at your place. He's gone."

"Gone?"

"That's right. There was nothing to show that he had been living with you, no clothes, nothing."

"No evidence?"

"Well there might be something that belongs to him. We're not sure."

"Tell me, maybe I can identify it. What was it?"

"We think it's his blood."

"Blood?"

"That's right. We found what appears to be blood splatter on the edge of the front door. I'm having my people check it out further to determine if there's a match to Ranger. If so, then it appears he was taken from your house against his will."

"Oh, I see."

"I'd go further to say that he was already packed to leave you regardless."

"You're only saying that because it didn't work out between us."

"I may be insensitive, but I'm not cruel. I'm giving you my best guess."

"And that's all it is, a guess."

"Madeline, I don't want to argue with you anymore. I've had enough of that in my life. Let it be."

Madeline slams the phone's handset on it cradle. She stares at the desktop phone, "Bastard!"

««»»

Betty is the last to arrive at **Oscar's**. In spite of it being a weekday, the place is packed with single men and women in their twenties and thirties. Current music beats through loudspeakers overhead.

Betty shouts out, "Why are you here?"

Sarah meets the volume of Betty's pitch, "They invited me. I knew you'd be here too. I thought it was a good idea."

"I'm happy to see you."

Dick summons a roving server, "Four PBRs." He points to the three women and himself.

Sarah interrupts, "No, make mine a diet soft drink." She looks around at the others to see frowns on their faces. "I'm not good with alcohol so I stay away from it."

Dick nods his head, "Make it three PBRs and one soft drink."

Karen starts out. "I'm bored silly and don't see any job progression. It's the same old same old."

Dick agrees, "That's what I was saying to Sarah. I'm tired of it."

"I wish I had gotten to that point." Betty grins as she points to herself. "They fired me too soon." She lets out a laugh.

"Maybe it was the best thing they could have done," Karen says.

"Yeah, maybe you were the lucky one," Dick agrees.

Betty looks at Sarah, "How's it going with you?"

"I'm on probation, sort of. I mean Matt is supposed to coach me but he's disappeared. We were all told he'd be away for a few days but he hasn't returned. I'm actually being left alone. I'm OK with it, it suits me fine."

"Give it time," Karen says.

The server yells out, "Three PBRs and one soft drink." She hands one to each person.

Matt pulls out money to pay. "Keep the change. Thanks."

The server looks at the twenty dollar bill, and then at Matt, "Thank you." She smiles and hurries away to other thirsty customers.

Matt lifts the beer bottle in one hand towards the three women, "To friendship."

Betty leads it off followed by Sarah and Karen in unison, "To friendship."

Sarah finishes one sip and then asks Betty a question, "What's your take on all of this? You're far enough away to be more objective than us."

She moistens her lips with a quick swipe from her tongue. "I'd say the place is corrupt."

"You've got to be kidding?" Karen's eyes widen.

"No, but I wish I was."

Dick encourages her to continue, "Go on. We're listening."

"I've got good instincts about people. They're only gut feelings." She shrugs her shoulders. "I told Sarah that I didn't trust Matt and now he's disappeared. I've never felt comfortable with Jim Ranger. In fact, it wouldn't surprise me if they're somehow related to each other."

"Get out," Dick interrupts.

"It's only a sixth sense."

Sarah keeps secret what she knows.

Karen asks, "Who else?"

"Vince Allen is the only one I really liked, but he's gone. I don't know what else to say."

Sarah asks, "So it seems to me that I'm hearing you say we all should leave the place, is that what you're saying?"

"I'm not saying anything like that. I'm just saying I think the place is corrupt and I don't trust those people whom I've just mentioned. You've got to figure out yourself what to do."

"If I had another job lined up, I'd quit. But the job pickings are slim to none, so financially I've got to stay put." Dick takes another sip of beer.

"Same with me," Karen looks at the others. "If I had something else lined up I'd bolt out."

All eyes turn towards Sarah.

"I think I've caught a wave. Today for the first time I'm in a groove. I'm going to hang in there."

"It sounds as if nobody is leaving." Betty raises her beer bottle towards the others. "Good luck." She takes a swallow of beer.

««»»

Two days later, Chief of Police Max Monaco, makes a call to Area Director Jackson Law's office. "I'm about to help advance your career."

Law recognizes the voice, "Go on, I'm all ears."

"Early this morning during a routine sweep of known drug trafficking locations two of my men found a man's dead body in a bathroom. Do you know Syd's Motel?"

"Doesn't every law enforcement agent know about it?"

"The man's body was pronounced dead by the paramedics when they arrived this morning, but it seems the body has been dead for at least three days. There was a rope around his neck and a piece of the same material wrapped around the shower's rail above him. The death is consistent with hanging."

"I know you're not telling me all this because you have nothing better to do. Who is the man?"

"We think he's Jim Ranger."

"Go on, you've got my full attention."

"There was no suicide note, but according to my guys, and you'd probably agree, involvement from others can't be ruled out."

"I agree. The idea that he'd take his own life is ludicrous. What else?"

"Did he have any powerful enemies?"

"Probably too numerous to count."

"Anybody you might know?"

"Who are you thinking about?"

"No one in particular. I'm just wondering if you know anyone in particular. That's all."

"He's had several murder attempts, and I suspect he had money problems recently."

"What about women problems?"

Law hesitates before answering, wondering if he knows anything about Ranger and Madeline. "We've all got women problems, including yours truly."

"That's not what I'm asking."

"You mean anyone who'd be jealous enough for revenge, is that what you mean?"

"For starters, yes. Do you?"

"I'd heard he was a real ladies man. He had the ability to charm them to do whatever he wanted. A real gift, that's what I say."

"People die all the time, some under common conditions and others in suspicious ways that may sound like a good crime novel."

"I haven't been reading much lately."

"Oh, one more thing."

Law smiles understanding the last comment is often the most important one.

"There was a small black suitcase on top of the bed inside the room where he died. The contents seem to be his. He was either coming from someplace or going to meet up with someone. There wasn't much inside the suitcase, only a few clothes and personal items. Isn't that strange?"

"Could be."

"Do you want to take a look at the body to confirm that he's your guy?"

"Sure, what's a good time?"

"You should call our Deputy County Medical Examiner, Madeline Courier. It's probably going to be her last case."

"Oh, why, has she been promoted?"

"Smart answer, but no, she's resigned. I guess you didn't know that."

"No I didn't. I guess when I see the body I'll wish her good luck wherever she's headed."

"That's it. I hope this helps with your case."

"You're a good friend. Thanks."

««»»

As soon as Law hangs up the phone, he calls in his assistant.

"Contact all available Agents immediately for an urgent meeting in one hour. We're going to close down an operation today. The chase is over."

He then calls Sarah on her cell. "Stay put, don't go anyplace. We're closing the place down this afternoon."

"You've got enough evidence?"

"I'm not sure, but it's all we're going to get. Ranger is dead, but I'll brief you later on that."

"Dead, what happened?"

"Like I said, I'll brief you later. Are the executives in today?"

"Right now they're in their offices. I've already given you the layout so you know where to find them."

"Don't tell anyone about this. Am I clear?"

"What do you mean? Why would I want to tell anyone about what's going down."

"I'm just making sure there isn't anyone working today that for whatever reason you do not want present during the raid?"

"Except for the executives, I'd tell everyone to leave."

"That's exactly what I mean."

"There are more than the victims who've had money taken from them who are innocent bystanders."

"There always is, but we can't let anyone know right now."

She spends too long of a time thinking about something.

Law emphasizes his order. "Don't say a word to anyone. When this comes down you need to act as surprised as the rest. Can you do that?"

"There's no choice, yes I will."

"That's correct, you don't have a choice. Close to two this afternoon is when Le Boeuf and others will arrive."

"I wish I could be on their side."

"You already are. It will be over with shortly."

"I understand."

"I know you do. You don't want to jeopardize the mission. Stay in character."

"I understand."

"I've got to brief the Agents. We'll debrief this soon."

««»»

CHASE

Right around two in the afternoon the same day four F. B. I. Agents burst into the office where employees busily work, unsuspecting of what is about to come. Three other Agents are positioned on the ground floor at all exits while three more Agents remain in the fifth floor hallway outside the office to prevent anyone from escaping.

Agent Le Boeuf shouts, "Hang up those phones and move away from your desks! We are the F. B. I."

At the same time, Agent Larson runs to Reggie Ward's office, Agent Castillo moves to Marshall Crum's office and Agent Crawford rushes to David Shea's office.

In less than a minute all personnel stand with hands up, bunched together.

"What's this about?" Shea manages to keep control of his emotions, although inside he knows it's all over.

"We haven't done anything wrong." Ward echoes.

Crum knows it's come to an end, so he keeps silent.

Karen, Dick, Sarah and all other personnel keep quiet. Except for Sarah, no one else is sure what it means.

Karen begins to cry.

CHAPTER 15

One month later, Law drives to the County Morgue.

The receptionist recognizes him. "Sir, Ms. Courier is waiting for you. I guess you know your way to her office."

"Yes, thanks."

In less than a minute he is face to face with Madeline. She looks aloof and sounds remote.

"Why have you come?"

He decides to confess a few things with her. "I came with mixed feelings."

She interrupts with more sarcasm than intended, "Oh, really. Now you have feelings."

"Please, let me finish."

She waves one hand to acknowledge him.

"On one hand I was anxious to see you. I might not ever see you again. Today is your last day of work."

He clears his throat as he puts his hand to cover his mouth. "But, on the other hand I was not pleased with having to come face to face with you after all we've been through. I don't know if I was protecting myself from further pain, or just didn't want to say good-bye again."

She suddenly feels a sudden lump in her throat. She coughs a bit to relieve the irritation. Yet, she decides not to say anything.

"I know you're angry at me, and probably will stay that way for quite a while, maybe forever."

He curls his shoulders inward. "I'm lost at what to do next about you, except to let you go your way, do whatever you need to do. But there is something I want you to remember, to never forget. I love you and always will."

He feels pain throughout his body as if he is being tormented with the truth. "My father passed away two days after we argued for the last time. He told me to get out of his life and I showed him the same hot-tempered and irate behavior. He never told me he loved me and I never said it to him. I was very close to telling him the last time we were together that I loved him, but as usual, our conversations quickly turned to arguments and shouting matches. In a weird way, I miss him and I love him. I only wish I had said it to him the last time we were together."

He turns his back to walk away. After taking one step he says, "I'll be here if you should ever need me."

He leaves the Morgue.

Madeline's eyes swell with tears, unable to say anything for a while. She feels her body begin to shake, so she steadies herself by sitting in a nearby chair. Softly, just loud enough for only her to hear, she says, "I wish I knew what love is."

««»»

Sarah pulls into an empty space in front of *McHale's* alongside the same late model white Ford Galaxy she saw the last time. The place looks the same as before. She turns to Andrea, "This is it."

Andrea twists her face, "You weren't exactly complete with the description you gave me."

"What do you mean?"

"It looks worse than how you described it."

"That's good, isn't it?"

"In what way?"

"You've always liked challenges. Here is one."

"Right. Let's go see your friend. I'm eager to meet him."

As Sarah and Andrea enter **McHale's** the door's bell rings.

Andrea looks up to see a tiny metal bell just above the door. "That's the first thing to go."

A voice from inside the kitchen is heard. "Be right there."

Sarah turns to her sister, "That's him. I recognize his voice."

He slowly walks towards the two women, head down as he rubs his hands with a towel. When he looks up he stops. His mouth opens wide. "I don't believe this. It's the student." He smiles.

"Hi. I bet you thought you'd never see me again." Sarah returns his smile with one of her own. She walks towards him with arms stretched out to hug him.

"My, my, this is a big surprise." He extends his arms to greet her.

She stays held tightly in his bear hug for a short time, enjoying the embrace. Then she pulls away.

As big as Sarah's grin is, it is no match to the enthusiastic sound of his voice. "Want something to eat, maybe another frittata?"

"In a bit." She nods towards Andrea. "I want to introduce you to someone." She grabs Andrea's arm to bring her toward him.

"She's your sister."

"How can you tell?" Sarah shakes her head in surprise.

"This old man still has pretty good instincts, and you look alike." He steps forward. "Glad to make your acquaintance." He reaches out to shake hands with Andrea.

"Yes, me too." It's about all she can think of at the moment.

Something dawns on Sarah. "I don't even know your name."

"McHale, that's really my name, Eddie McHale." He pauses. "And you never told me your real name. You said it was Lela, but that didn't fool me."

"I'm Sarah and this is Andrea."

"And what do you really do? I know you weren't a student when you first came here."

"I'm not working."

"What did you do?"

"I was in law enforcement, an F. B. I. Agent."

"Really, what happened, disability?"

"Something like that."

"What specifically, why did you leave, get kicked out?"

"I realized that sometimes good people who want to do good have to do bad things. I didn't want to become someone like that. So, I quit."

"I see."

"Maybe you do, maybe you don't, but that's not important. What's important is that my sister can help you promote this place, to get swarms of customers in here. That's only, of course, if you want it."

McHale turns towards the kitchen. "Hey Josh, get out here. You've got to hear this."

Everyone faces the kitchen.

A male, late twenties, six feet with a slender built slowly walks their way. Underneath a cook's hat, the ruddiness of his face is evident. His smile is captivating. His deep brown eyes carry a lot of warmth.

"This is my nephew, Josh. Say hello to the girls."

Sarah and Andrea are captivated by his appearance. They remain still.

"Hello." The one word is sufficient for the time being.

McHale continues. "Josh just graduated from culinary school in Napa, California. He needs a first job to experiment and fine tune his cooking skills. I could use the company. He's family."

Andrea is the first one to pull out of the daze. "Hi." She nods and then nudges Sarah.

Sarah returns to consciousness. "Hi." She tries to cover a swallow but is unsuccessful. She feels her face blush.

McHale resumes. "The girls say they can help us promote this place. What do you think about that?"

Josh turns to his uncle. "Like I've said to you before, nobody knows this place exits, and those who drive by are probably blasé about coming in. Let's be honest, the exterior isn't a welcoming look." He turns to Sarah and Andrea. "I'm game to try out any new ideas."

McHale reminds everyone. "I don't have a whole lot of money."

Andrea gets back into the conversation. "I'll do it for free. Once your customer base increases to a certain level that all of us are comfortable with, I'll only charge you based on the increase in gross revenues beyond that benchmark level. If you don't see any increase, then you don't owe me anything."

Josh looks at Andrea. "You're gambling on an increase in customers."

"It's not a gamble. I'm convinced I can do it." Andrea looks at Sarah. "We both are positive about this."

McHale turns to Sarah. "What's your part in all of this?"

She clears her throat. "I've always wanted to try my hand at cooking. Put me in the kitchen and I'll help out anyway you need."

McHale rolls his eyes and then directs them at Josh. "Do you think you can work with her?"

Sarah's face suddenly gets serious looking. Her eyes widen. She sets her sights on Josh.

Josh puckers his lips, shrugs his shoulders a wee bit, and then smiles. "I'm willing to give it a try if she's willing."

McHale finalizes it all. "Then it's all settled. When do we start?"

Sarah jumps in quickly. "Now, right now."

- The End -

ABOUT THE AUTHOR AND HIS WORKS

Antonio F. Vianna is a prime example of someone who has re-careered himself. In fact, you might say he wrote the book on it with "Career Management and Employee Portfolio Tool Kit, 3rd edition." He holds a M.M. from Northwestern University's Kellogg Graduate School of Management and a B.S. from Union College. He has been able to re-brand himself from a former U.S. Air Force officer and Human Resources executive to an author and educator. His 21 books and 6 screenplays since 2003, and three popular workshops, "Re-Careering at Any Age," "How to Write a Book and Get Published," and "How to Write a Screenplay" enjoy much success. Vianna is frequently a guest on television and radio discussing strategies for re-careering at any age. He is a member of Publishers &Writers of San Diego and Read Local San Diego. He lives in Carlsbad, CA. His books are available in paperback and electronically wherever books are sold. For more information about Antonio F. Vianna and what else he's been up to, go to his website at www.viannabooks4u.com.

Non-Fiction

***Career Management and Employee Portfolio Tool Kit
Workbook***, 3rd edition (2010) posits that your career is a
dynamic process that requires constant reevaluation and
fine-tuning as experience dictates. With practical exercises
focusing on his model, *Five Sigma of Success*, this *Workbook*
helps the first-time job seeker, those reentering the workforce
or changing jobs/careers, and those currently employed who
seek advancement evaluate who they are, what they want to
be, and how to get there. (ISBN: 978-1-4107-1100-7).

In ***Leader Champions: Secrets of Success*** (2004) Vianna
and Dr. Mark B. Silber create a dynamic text about your
choices for leader champion actions. Their goal focuses on
what it means to be a leader in the 21st Century and what
some practical techniques used by those who have made it
to that exclusive suite. This is a no-nonsense text to stimulate
your leadership, human relations, and personal growth
competencies. (ISBN: 1-4184-3684-4).

Fiction

A Tale from a Ghost Dance (2003) is Vianna's first novel.
The story centers on the title's reference to the ancient
Native American ceremonial dance where the spirits of
the ancestors are called upon for their wisdom and advice.
But, in this tale, it is an Anglo woman executive who has
unwanted visionary powers. The protagonist, Victoria, is a
high-powered marketing executive who does not accept her
gift until she encounters a Native American elder, Joseph.
However, some tribal members resent Victoria. These ensure

intra-tribal conflicts as well as mysterious circumstances involving one of her clients that place her life and others in peril. (ISBN: 1-4107-1384-9).

In *The In-ter-view* (2003) Vianna employs some of his professional human resources experiences to turn something as ordinary as a job interview into a life and death drama. While Laura Simmons interviews with Fred Wheeler and Associates, a disgruntled former employee bursts in and takes her and seven others hostage. As the action plays out, each character reveals their true self and demonstrates how each individual reacts under duress. It soon becomes evident if they want to survive the ordeal, this disparate group must become a cohesive force. (ISBN: 1-4107-0876-4). (This story has been adapted to a screenplay.)

The backdrop of *Talking Rain* (2004) is a twenty-year-old murder case that sent a man to death row. One evening, however, alone, with no one left to talk with, Lucy Lodine unexpectedly walks into Precinct 21 to break her silence. She confesses to the murder, but unsuccessful in convincing the authorities that her husband on death row is innocent of the crime. When people who had been involved in the crime start to die, she gets the authorities' attention, specifically Detective Jack Bogle. Mix in academic rivalry, problem gambling, an alleged affair, and a callow policewoman with her on-again off-again boyfriend reporter, and you have an incredible topsy-turvy ride. (ISBN: 1-4140-6648-1).

Uncovered Secrets (2005) takes place in a local movie theater. What would you do if your darkest secret was about to be uncovered? Blend in a ghost, the theater's sexy and manipulative employee, the theater's film projectionist, a callous cop, the theater's manager who shows signs of being in a profession too long, a brash young female executive, and an emotionally needy woman. The final secrets are revealed on North County Airport Road. (ISBN: 1-4208-1795-7).

In *Midnight Blue* (2005) after two bodies are exhumed, the police begin to suspect foul play and question their original findings. Were lies purposely told and the real suspects purposely not questioned? Throw into the mix a love affair between a cop and the daughter of the prime suspect, and you have a story you will want to read straight through. (ISBN: 1-4208-6397-5).

Veil of Ignorance (2006) is a suspense novel about Tommy Hogan, an outstanding University educator, whose loneliness and search for happiness gets him embroiled in life and death situations. As his vulnerabilities surface, he easily becomes a target by those seeking revenge, greed, and status at the expense of others. It takes Tommy a while to realize he is being conned, and when he does, he understands that his misguided affection is actually towards the very person who seeks his demise. The face-off at the end helps him remove the veil that shrouds his ignorance. (ISBN: 1-4259-1695-3).

In *Yellow Moon* (2006) one year after the conviction of Jimmy Lupo, a man accused of robbing a bank, Bella Lupo, the daughter of the convicted man reaches out to Ned Francis, a private investigator to dig up evidence that her father had taken a fall and been wrongly imprisoned for the crime. Although the hard-nosed detective is initially skeptical, he eventually believes that her father was in fact a patsy. Although he slams into one dead end after another, the detective never gives up the search for justice. However, he begins to fall in love with the prisoner's daughter, and it seems he is captivated by the daughter's good looks and seductive ways. Is he really convinced of her father's innocence, or is he too much in love to see the real truth? As strange obsessions and lust for power grow, a climactic standoff will shock you. (ISBN: 1-4259-5112-0).

Hidden Dangers (2007) follows a journey into hidden dangers of espionage, revenge, greed, love, and hope. It all starts one night with a strange telephone call to Connie Marz, a Specialty Leasing Manager with a local shopping mall. Drop into the mixture a mysterious mall walker's disappearance, cozy American and Russian government agents spying on one another, an unlikely love relationship, and one person with the courage to put it all to an end. Characters agonize over their self-doubts and pleasure at their misplaced sense of superiorities. It all sounds crazy, and to someone it is. (ISBN: 978-1-4259-9710-6).

In *Haunted Memories* (2007) thirteen-year-old Dave Stagetto goes missing, even though his best boyhood friend, Billy, keeps something a secret. While the small town of Hadley grieves for a short time, Dave's mother falls deeper into depression to the very core of her soul. She suspects something just does not make sense, but is not sure what. Worse of all, the haunted memories, thought to be discarded with time, emerge twenty years later to everyone's surprise. Childhood relationships change as people grow older, often times in strange and surprising ways. The search for the truth shifts between San Diego, California and Lisbon, Portugal until the terrible secret is unveiled. (ISBN: 978-1-4343-2852-6).

In **Bound and Determined** (2008) Susanne Attrice likes being in control. However, when she unexpectedly becomes pregnant, not sure the identity of the biological father, her life turns upside down. Then, suddenly, her infant child is abducted. She suspects who the child snatcher might be, so she now is bound and determined to be reunited with her baby. It proves tougher than she ever imagined. As she begins putting pieces of the puzzle together, she shoves aside those who are willing and able to help her the most. Does she have enough inner strength to go it alone or will she reach out for help? (ISBN: 978-1-4343-7450-9). (This story has been adapted to a screenplay.)

Stranger On A Train (2009) is Book 1 of a vampire trilogy. Are there bounds of human behavior that you will not cross, or aren't there? What someone may believe in and subsequently do as acceptable, another may find despicable. Paul Autore, an aspiring novelist, meets Marcus Varro on a train. Later Paul receives two unusual letters from Marcus inviting him to Sanibel Island, Florida, to tutor Anne, Marcus's beautiful daughter. Even before he arrives at the spacious white mansion, Paul suspects something else is up; and when he and Marcus almost die from an automobile accident on their way to the Varro residence, tensions rise even further. Simmering family hatreds heat up and put Paul in the middle. Caught up in things shockingly different than what he has ever written about or experienced, he might have to cross a boundary he never thought he would. Is Paul prepared to go to extreme lengths to protect him? (ISBN: 978-1-4389-1490-9).

The Hiding (2009) is Book 2 of a vampire trilogy. There are places, deep below the earth's surface where vampires exist, unknown to mortals. It is their Hiding place. No one knows for certain their origins, although myths and legends abound. Yet, one thing is for certain. They battle each other to maintain some sort of balance of power among them. This all changes, however, as Anne Marcus, a beautiful young woman begins a mysterious transformation to become a hybrid, part human and part vampire. A bitter feud erupts as two clans of vampires fight to claim her as their own. (ISBN: 978-1-4389-6206-1).

The Vampire Who Loved (2009) is Book 3 of a vampire trilogy. As this novel opens, Anne is awakened from a horrifying nightmare. She wonders if the dream is a predictor of events to come. All the while, her enemies, some old and some new, are intent to have their own way . . . vampires who set in motion seemingly irreversible measures to do away with her. Paul has become the X-factor . . . his predictability is uncertain. She calls upon Vincent Blackfoot, now her closest friend and ally, to help figure out a plan. As the story rushes to a surprising climax, a sudden twist appears. (ISBN: 978-1-4490-2488-8).

Second Son (2010). What if a child's birth order determines the degree of love he receives from his parents? Robert struggles to find love by becoming a Catholic Priest. His moral fiber is turned upside down when his older brother asks for a favor that would violate his sacred vows and cause him to commit an act filled with deceit and lies. (ISBN: 978-1-4490-7473-9). (This story has been adapted to a screenplay.)

Unintentional Consequences (2010). Rand Bauge never thought he was simply working for wages when he was employed by the U. S. Government, although there were enough situations that would contradict that notion. He got things done any way he could; usually it was his way. No one seemed to care about the means he used. Questions were rarely asked. Only the results mattered. He and his boss saw eye to eye on their relationship because it worked well for a good long time. Things are now different. He's on his own, retirement urged upon him against his wishes. The panic call he got from his second wife threw him for a loop . . . something bad had gone wrong at home. He's got to get there fast before it is too late. However, along the way, unintended surprises block his advancement. Who's really out to get him? This might be the biggest test ever. (ISBN: 978-1-4520-6901-2).

Time and Money (2011). He was a bad-tempered young man at 18 and got even surlier as he aged. Then, his life got more complicated. The old man took advantage of others for most of his life. In fact he enjoyed reaping the benefits from the pain of others. He figured it was just the way it was, as the Sun rose in the East and set in the West. Then, late in his years, he meets Riley Sullivan, a good natured fellow, someone who perfectly fits into his scheme to put the last touches on his existence. However, all his ill deeds and future schemes meet up with unexpected guilt as he tries to make amends. (ISBN: 978-1-4634-3945-3).

Unordinary Love. (2012). When Carl joins the Whitaker family as an adopted boy, he is shunned by his older stepbrother Paul and younger stepsister Kay. However, over a short time, Kay's affection toward Carl grows while Paul's animosity with his stepbrother quickly deepens with jealousy. Kay and Carl become locked in a relationship so unrelenting that they become the center of each other's worlds, and are prepared to cross a boundary they never thought they would. As their teen years turn to young adulthood, unexpected changes occur that put more than just the two of them in life threatening conditions. Who will live on and who will perish is not necessarily a matter of choice, but rather a matter of chance. Their almost unconscious acts seem to turn into their lives' fulfillment. (ISBN: 978-1-4685-4677-4). (This story has been adapted to a screenplay.)

Scarlet Rose (2013). What if two former college lovers, Cass Westfield and Mike Aviara, rekindle their relationship at a college class reunion? While she thinks it is understood to be a simple one- time fling, he refuses to allow it to end, resulting in emotional blackmail, stalking, and ensuing obsession on his part. Cass must distance herself from Mike to remain loyal to her family. However, when Mike finds out that her daughter, Scarlet Rose, was conceived by he and Cass during their senior year in college, he threatens to expose her long-held secret unless she leave her husband and take Scarlet Rose to live with him. (ISBN: 978-1-4817-0577-6). (This story has been adapted to a screenplay.)

- end -